International Library of Psychology
Philosophy and Scientific Method

The
Social Basis of Consciousness

International Library of Psychology Philosophy and Scientific Method

GENERAL EDITOR . C. K. OGDEN, M.A. (*Magdalen College, Cambridge*)

PHILOSOPHICAL STUDIES	by G. E. MOORE, Litt.D.
THE MISUSE OF MIND	by KARIN STEPHEN
CONFLICT AND DREAM	by W. H. R. RIVERS, F.R.S.
PSYCHOLOGY AND POLITICS	by W. H. R. RIVERS, F.R.S.
MEDICINE, MAGIC AND RELIGION	by W. H. R. RIVERS, F.R.S.
PSYCHOLOGY AND ETHNOLOGY	by W. H. R. RIVERS, F.R.S.
TRACTATUS LOGICO-PHILOSOPHICUS	by L. WITTGENSTEIN
THE MEASUREMENT OF EMOTION	by W. WHATELY SMITH
PSYCHOLOGICAL TYPES	by C. G. JUNG, M.D., LL.D.
SCIENTIFIC METHOD	by A. D. RITCHIE
SCIENTIFIC THOUGHT	by C. D. BROAD, Litt D.
MIND AND ITS PLACE IN NATURE	by C. D. BROAD, Litt.D.
THE MEANING OF MEANING	by C K. OGDEN and I. A. RICHARDS
CHARACTER AND THE UNCONSCIOUS	by J. H. VAN DER HOOP
INDIVIDUAL PSYCHOLOGY	by ALFRED ADLER
CHANCE, LOVE AND LOGIC	by C. S. PEIRCE
SPECULATIONS (*Preface by Jacob Epstein*)	by T E. HULME
THE PSYCHOLOGY OF REASONING	by EUGENIO RIGNANO
BIOLOGICAL MEMORY	by EUGENIO RIGNANO
THE PHILOSOPHY OF MUSIC	by W. POLE, F R S.
THE PHILOSOPHY OF 'AS IF'	by H. VAIHINGER
THE NATURE OF LAUGHTER	by J. C. GREGORY
THE NATURE OF INTELLIGENCE	by L. L. THURSTONE
TELEPATHY AND CLAIRVOYANCE	by R. TISCHNER
THE GROWTH OF THE MIND	by K. KOFFKA
THE MENTALITY OF APES	by W. KÖHLER
PSYCHOLOGY OF RELIGIOUS MYSTICISM	by J. H. LEUBA
THE PSYCHOLOGY OF A MUSICAL PRODIGY	by G. REVESZ
PRINCIPLES OF LITERARY CRITICISM	by I. A. RICHARDS
METAPHYSICAL FOUNDATIONS OF SCIENCE	by E. A. BURTT, Ph D.
COLOUR-BLINDNESS	by M. COLLINS, Ph.D.
PHYSIQUE AND CHARACTER	by ERNST KRETSCHMER
PSYCHOLOGY OF EMOTION	by J. T. MACCURDY, M.D.
PROBLEMS OF PERSONALITY:	in honour of MORTON PRINCE
PSYCHE	by E ROHDE
PSYCHOLOGY OF TIME	by M. STURT
THE HISTORY OF MATERIALISM	by F. A. LANGE
EMOTION AND INSANITY	by S. THALBITZER
PERSONALITY	by R. G. GORDON, M.D.
EDUCATIONAL PSYCHOLOGY	by CHARLES FOX
LANGUAGE AND THOUGHT OF THE CHILD	by J. PIAGET
COMPARATIVE PHILOSOPHY	by P. MASSON-OURSEL
CRIME AND CUSTOM IN SAVAGE SOCIETY	by B. MALINOWSKI, D.Sc.
THEORETICAL BIOLOGY	by J. VON UEXKÜLL
THOUGHT AND THE BRAIN	by H. PIÉRON.
THE PSYCHOLOGY OF CHARACTER	by A. A. ROBACK
SOCIAL LIFE IN THE ANIMAL WORLD	by F. ALVERDES
THE ANALYSIS OF MATTER	by BERTRAND RUSSELL, F.R.S.
THE EFFECTS OF MUSIC	edited by MAX SCHOEN
SOCIAL BASIS OF CONSCIOUSNESS	by TRIGANT BURROW, M D., Ph D.

IN PREPARATION

SEX AND REPRESSION IN SAVAGE SOCIETY	by B. MALINOWSKI, D Sc.
RELIGIOUS CONVERSION	by S. DE SANCTIS
POLITICAL PLURALISM	by KUNG-CHUAN HSIAO
DIALECTIC	by M. J. ADLER
POSSIBILITY	by SCOTT BUCHANAN
NEUROTIC PERSONALITY	by R. G. GORDON, M.D.
PROBLEMS IN PSYCHOPATHOLOGY	by T. W. MITCHELL, M.D.
THE LAWS OF FEELING	by F. PAULHAN
STATISTICAL METHOD IN ECONOMICS	by P. SARGANT FLORENCE
COLOUR-HARMONY	by JAMES WOOD
THE INTEGRATIVE ACTION OF THE MIND	by E. MILLER
INSECT SOCIETIES	by W. M. WHEELER, Ph.D.
PSYCHOLOGY OF INSECTS	by J. G. MYERS
PLATO'S THEORY OF KNOWLEDGE	by F. M. CORNFORD
THEORY OF MEDICAL DIAGNOSIS	by F. G. CROOKSHANK, M.D.

The Social Basis of Consciousness

A Study in Organic Psychology
Based upon a Synthetic and Societal
Concept of the Neuroses

BY

TRIGANT BURROW
M.D., Ph.D.

LONDON
KEGAN PAUL, TRENCH, TRUBNER & CO. LTD.
NEW YORK: HARCOURT, BRACE & COMPANY, INC.
1927

THE SOCIAL BASIS OF CONSCIOUSNESS

Chapter I, Part I, was first published in *The Journal of Nervous and Mental Disease*, and Chapter II, Part I, in *The Psychoanalytic Review*. Acknowledgment is made to the Editors for permission to include these papers in the present volume.

> *I am that which began;*
> *Out of me the years roll;*
> *Out of me God and man;*
> *I am equal and whole;*
> *God changes, and man, and the form of them bodily;*
> *I am the soul.*
>
> "Hertha."—SWINBURNE.

CONTENTS

	PAGE
PREFACE	XV
INTRODUCTION	1

Significance of Freud's basic conception—Misconceptions in psychoanalysis due to present personalistic basis—Psychoanalysis entails the element of personal differentiation and sponsorship presented in other therapeutic systems—Need for abrogation of personal equation—Societal concept an outgrowth of essential objective findings of Freud—This thesis an initial presentation of an organismic interpretation of human consciousness.

PART I

THE PHILOSOPHY OF THE NEUROSES

CHAPTER I 9

PSYCHOANALYSIS IN THEORY AND IN LIFE

Theory of psychoanalysis rests upon conception that nervous disorders are substitutive manifestation of repressed sexual life—Sexuality itself, however, as now existing, symptomatic of repression and quite preclusive of the organic instinct of sex—Popular analytic view places a premium upon the reaction embodied in normality but substitution and repression in this collective reaction identical with the unconscious of neurotic individuals—Substitution of self-image for reality, present in reactions of normal, is not as yet recognized by psychoanalysis—Psychoanalysis remains in so far a theory only—In truth, the neurotic personality is index of the urge toward an essential organic mode of consciousness —Continuity with organic processes registered as subjective feeling cannot be approached by objective methods—The insanity of the individual not to be cured as long as there is the insanity of the social mind about him.

CHAPTER II 32

A RELATIVE CONCEPT OF CONSCIOUSNESS: AN ANALYSIS OF CONSCIOUSNESS IN ITS ETHNIC ORIGIN

The Newtonian system assumes an unqualified absolute and fails to take account of factors operating within the larger system in which it is itself an element—In the sphere of psychic phenomena a similar system of absolutism dominates our presumably conscious world—Analysis of our judgments reveals the assumption that the position intrinsic to the observer is all-inclusive and authentic—But our world of impressions is artificial and reflects the artificial systematization that fails to include our own organisms—This autocratic interpretation of life is based on a bidimensional or image system which in its arbitrary and personal evaluation distorts the universe of reality—Normality is consensus comprising the personal absolute vested in the unconscious of the collective mind—Need to replace pictorial mode by organic coalescence in common affectivity—Personal systems of men, single and collective, are but relative with respect to an organic societal consciousness—Concept of relativity of consciousness abrogates absolute standard and embraces dimensional element of the system, individual and social, of which we ourselves are a component part—Transition from bidimensional (contemplation of aspect) to tridimensional (participation in function) affords basis for measuring deflections of personality, socially as well as individually.

CHAPTER III 50

THE ORIGIN OF OUR INDIVIDUAL UNCONSCIOUS

Organic societal consciousness can be comprehended only through subjective identification with it—Discussion of the tridimensional reality of human consciousness with its three determinants—Present phase of consciousness admits only the bidimensional image—The position of the bidimensional elements " right and wrong " as incorporated in the life of the child—Advantage of the parent the real motive underlying this moral bidimension—Long-continued experiments with personal mood reactions as substantiation of view that induced image of right and wrong is at the root of human psychopathology—Non-inclusiveness of others is meaning of unconsciousness, individual and social—Present social adaptation is merely collective response, not societal extension of consciousness—Substitution of the absolute of personal interest for inclusive participation as relative elements affords no basis for inclusion of larger whole in which the individual is a contributing element.

CHAPTER IV 63

THE UNCONSCIOUS FACTOR WITHIN THE SOCIAL SYSTEM

Daily reactions betray state of anxiety in the social mind—These anxieties, sponsored in earlier times by medical and religious fetish, still substantiated by the systems of medicine and religion—Organic analysis of the element of social authority—The systems of psychoanalysis and the Roman Church as paradigms—Factor of resistance in psychoanalysis analogous to factor of doubt in religion—The systematization comprising the social corporation of individuals as much an aspect of the unconscious autocracy of the personal absolute as the systematization of the individual—In the conflict between these two mutually opposed absolutes (socially systematized authority and the resistance of the individual) there is an organic impasse.

CONTENTS

CHAPTER V 78

SOCIOLOGICAL IMPLICATIONS OF UNCONSCIOUSNESS FROM A VIEWPOINT OF RELATIVITY

The established system demands conformity to its prescribed norm—The limitation of life to a bidimensional alternative of one's own pleasure or one's own pain results in division of personality and in compulsion neurosis involving the entire social consciousness—Bidimensional replacements in social system found in art, science, education, marriage, etc —The mood alternations of the individual are but obverse aspects of the same bidimensional portrait of personal advantage—This element of unconscious alternation bars unbiased observation of the personal absolute—In the field of preventive medicine the personal cure of the individual subordinated to safeguarding of community health—But within the subjective sphere there is resistance to an approach that would consider the individual's position as part of a societal unity because such an approach would menace the illusion of personal prerogative — Psychopathologists equally involved unconsciously in the social neurosis—In an objective study of the neurosis the psychopathologist escapes the subjective acknowledgment of its presence within himself—Possibility of fundamental readjustment for dissociated personality lies only in surrender socially of bidimensional or pictorial illusion in favour of tridimensional actuality.

PART II

THE PSYCHOLOGY OF THE NEUROSES

CHAPTER I 107

ANALYSIS OF FREUD'S DYNAMIC AND INDIVIDUALISTIC CONCEPTION OF THE NEUROSES

Freud's theory assumes breach in integrity of consciousness due to effort of delimited area to establish itself as a separate self-governing unit—Distinction of Freud's work lies in conception of central totality of consciousness ; limitation of Freud's work consists in assigning totality of consciousness to single individual—Conception of totality of personality tenable only from point of view of inclusive societal consciousness.

CHAPTER II 114

FORMULATION OF AN ORGANIC OR SOCIETAL BASIS OF INTERPRETATION

The mental life of the infant organism is wholly subjective and is one with the organism's inherent feeling—With entrance of the ulterior motive appearing in the command and prohibition of the parent there is the issue of personal gain or loss (suggestion and repression)—Appearance of self-consciousness and self-interest forces interruption of the organism's societal life and a separation from its basic continuum—Maintenance of separativeness of individual destroys organic integrity—There is need to stand apart from self and view it as element within the larger organism of mankind—Instinct of tribal preservation and not self-preservation is the dominant urge among us.

CHAPTER III 134

THE ORGANIC SIGNIFICANCE OF THE UNCONSCIOUS

Development of the idea of the parallel between individual and phyletic trends in unconscious manifestations—Unconscious worship of self-image source of suggestion and repression—Because of this self-image what man assumes to be cerebration is fictitious brain-state withdrawn from continuity with organic life—Where there is individual lesion, separation among elements is followed by pain and recourse to remedial aids, i.e. the organism as a whole demands relief—In the organic societal whole the individual as separated element is source of lesion but seeks to escape through symbolic disguise the pain of his societal separation—Conflict is between part and whole wherein individual is embodiment of both.

CHAPTER IV 154

ORGANIC ANALYSIS OF REPRESSION AND OF THE FACTOR OF RESISTANCE FROM THE SOCIETAL VIEWPOINT

The resolution of repression or resistance is regarded by Freud as the essential problem of psychoanalysis—Neurosis, according to Freud, is life's repression of sexuality—According to an organismic attitude repression and sexuality are concomitant and are equally the results in the individual of organic disunity and interruption of function—The biology of resistance is found in the breach in individual's continuity with life as confluent, organic whole—Health or disease, psychologically or physiologically, depends upon whether the cell functions integrally or separatively, congruently or resistantly—In social fabric each element is against each—In our unconsciousness we deny the reality of this biological phylum embodied in our organic consciousness and underlying the processes of our individual mentation—Sexuality, currently confused with sex, is egoistic, infantile expression and antithesis of organic expression of sex — Only continuity of the confluent subjective sphere can make possible an analysis that will synthesize the scattered elements of personality.

CHAPTER V 165

ORGANIC ANALYSIS OF REPRESSION AND OF THE FACTOR OF RESISTANCE FROM THE INDIVIDUAL VIEWPOINT

Transference is an unconscious condition which involves as much the analyst as the analysand—Resistance and repression are the factors in this mutual situation—Under

CONTENTS

present personalistic procedure in psychoanalysis the analyst deals objectively with an inherently subjective situation—He regards only the disparity of the patient and so preserves the apparent differentiation which is the underlying cause of the patient's disorder—There is a confusion in psychoanalysis due to the failure to discriminate between the mother-image and the mother-organism—The analyst, being socially dissociated, seeks to reinstate the comfort of his own childhood through an unconscious self-interested response (pleasure or displeasure) to the analysand—The transference which is thus introduced by the unconscious attitude of the analyst cannot be analyzed because of the analyst's own involvement—This is the impasse of the individualistic analysis—From a societal viewpoint the analyst can be interested only in the patient's delusion of separateness and will direct his endeavour to an understanding of the social repression which dissociates them both from the common, generic consciousness.

CHAPTER VI 177

THE DREAM AND ITS ANALYSIS IN AN ORGANISMIC INTERPRETATION OF THE NEUROSES

To analyze the dream from a basis that is equally separative and repressed is to exchange the symbols of the individual's repression for analogous symbols of the social repression—The night's reaction, being individual, and the day's reaction, being social, both represent an endeavour to adjust vicariously man's societal disunity—The affective or subjective life cannot be adjusted through the study of the objective mechanisms that merely reflect it but only through the subjective (conscious) reabsorption within us of the affects to whose suggestion the dream is the mirrored reaction—The drama and the dream are identical in mechanism—An organic mode of consciousness can regard with equally objective clarity the vicarious processes of the day and of the night.

CHAPTER VII 187

THE BIOLOGICAL SUBSTRATE OF THE NEUROTIC CONFLICT IN ITS ORGANIC SIGNIFICANCE

Two types of reaction : the *autocentric* who withdraws *in toto* and has completely negative attitude toward his congeners, and the *allocentric* who makes effort at social compromise or adaptation (" sublimation ")—Both reactions equally self-centered : autocentric (precoid, psychasthenic) showing adaptation through individual dream ; allocentric (hysteric, hypomanic) through social dream—Biological substrate of these reactions lies in lack of balance between cerebro-spinal and sympathetic systems—In the preconscious form preserved among animals no break between the two systems ; there is maintained rhythmic and harmonious co-ordination of response—Period of Greek thought essentially allocentric ; Christianity essentially autocentric.

CONTENTS

CHAPTER VIII 197

THE DISTINCTION BETWEEN SEXUALITY AND SEX IN RELATION TO UNIFICATION AND ORGANIC MATING

Psychoanalysis, unconsciously influenced by a division based on the bias of its own arbitrary alternatives, has assumed contrasts of behaviour not warrantable from an organismic conception—Such alternatives are "homosexuality" and "heterosexuality"—The organic instinct of mating has become distorted by the image system of "good" (conceding social consensus) and "bad" (repudiating social consensus)—Both types are response to social consensus and are ego-sexual—Sexuality is effort of conjunction of peripheral and visceral spheres while sex is effortless and non-personal conjugation of organismic poles comprising male and female—Union is of personality as realized in man and woman through identification with life, the one embodying the peripheral, allocentric component, the other the internal, autocentric component—Organically, man is not opposite woman but each is complement of other—Concept of intermediate sex is misnomer for composite sex—Social demand of oppositeness necessitates repression in male of female component and in female of male component—In present stage of society's development marriage is mutual adjustment of ego-sexual claims, a pooling of the private unconscious of each where each withdraws from an organic place as a societal element—Biological significance of unity of personality is conception of *principle of primary identification*—Autocentric types as Buddha, Plato, Christ, and allocentric personalities of Socrates, Napoleon and Nietzsche equally manifest this urge of the inherent organism of man—In organic integrity of personality is societal instinct that is the composite life of the race.

CHAPTER IX 221

ULTIMATE RESOLUTION OF THE SOCIETAL NEUROSIS IN ITS SOCIAL IMPLICATION

Back of the pretence of the social mind lies a basis of social fear and mistrust—The mutual accommodations of external agreement used to cloak the introversion of the individual—The development of group analysis permits study of the resistance of the social consensus with respect to the individual as well as the resistance of the individual with respect to the social consensus—Group analysis, like individual analysis, presents an unconscious and bidimensional situation involving reaction clusters which constitute a pooling of the unconscious of the several members—This group situation offers opportunity to secure relative and societal background against which the individual may view in impersonal perspective his habitual arbitrary and personal evaluations—According to the group or relative conception the causative element of the neurosis is societal or phyletic and correction must proceed upon a societal or phyletic basis.

CONTENTS xiii

PAGE

CHAPTER X 238

ULTIMATE RESOLUTION OF THE SOCIETAL
NEUROSIS IN ITS PERSONAL IMPLICATION

Demand for wider concept of organized consciousness of man in order to replace disintegrating structures of present social system—Need to dispel illusion of mental oppositeness and the restraints of an alternative system of morality which aims merely to establish temporary balance between its opposites — Experimental basis for group conception here formulated in practical experience of a few students—As the societal and the individual are organically one in mode, the unification of the individual is a step toward the unification of the societal consciousness—Organismic (societal) group differentiated from collective (social) cluster—The period of man's substitutive image-production first interrupted by Darwin's theory of evolution and further threatened by Freud's theory of the evolutionary processes of the unconscious—The social basis of consciousness, however inadequately formulated, invites an analytic approach to social or mass reactions, exemplified in our national, political, industrial and religious life.

INDEX 253

PREFACE

I DO not know whether I can make clear in what manner the conception embodied in the following pages first arose. Conceptions derived from data of reason and observation necessarily proceed from a mental basis. Scientific and philosophical treatises are the outcome primarily of scientific or philosophical ideas. With both inductive and deductive methods of reasoning the conclusions that flow from the assumptions are our accepted basis of procedure. With the method of the present study, however, we are upon other ground, for the inception of this work was in no such wise; and yet to say that it is based upon no conceptual premise would, of course, not be true. The difference is that what follows here has been the outgrowth of events that were prior to and independent of any conceptual formulation of them. Biological necessity preceded and argument followed after. My meaning may for the moment be best understood when it is considered that these events are the processes of personal experience inseparable from the sequences here embodied. While this is not the place for detailing personal history, the presentation of a thesis as intimate as this would not be complete without some concrete account of its origin.

Having years ago been " analyzed " in preparation for my work in psychopathology, I had been for years duly " analyzing " others. It unexpectedly happened one day, however, that while I was interpreting a dream of a student-assistant, he made bold to challenge the honesty of my analytic position, insisting that, as far as he was concerned, the test of my sincerity would be met only when I should myself be willing to accept from him the same analytic exactions I was now imposing upon others. As may be readily judged, such a proposition seemed to me nothing short of absurd. Had I not been " analyzed "? Needless to say I had heard this proposal from patients many times before, but while my reaction to the suggestion in the present instance was chiefly one of amusement, my pride was not a little piqued at the intimation it conveyed. So with the thought that in the interest of experiment it could at least do no harm to humour for a time the waywardness of inexperience, I conceded the arrangement.

Not many weeks after I had taken the patient's chair and yielded him mine I realized that a situation to which I had agreed with more or less levity had assumed an aspect of the profoundest seriousness. My " resistances " to my self-appointed analyst, far from being negligible, were plainly insuperable, but there was now no turning back. The analysis proceeded on its course from day to day and with it my resistances took tighter hold upon me. The agreement to which I had voluntarily lent myself was becoming painful beyond words. Whatever empirical interest the situation may have held for me at the outset was now wholly subordinated to the indignation and pain of the position to which I had been brought.

It is possible to indicate only in their broadest lines the progressive events of these trying months. I need hardly record the growing sense of self-limitation and defeat that went hand in hand with this daily advancing personal challenge, nor the corresponding efforts of concealment in unconscious symbolizations and distortions on my part. What calls for more vital emphasis, however, is the fact that along with the deepening, if reluctant, realization of my intolerance of self-defeat, there came gradually to me the realization that my analyst, in changing places with me, had merely shifted to the authoritarian vantage-ground I had myself relinquished and that the situation had remained essentially unaltered still.

This was significant. It marked at once the opening of

PREFACE

wholly new vistas of experience. In the light of its discovery I began to sense for the first time what had all along underlain my own analysis and what, as I now see it, really underlies every analysis. I began to see that the student before me, notwithstanding his undoubted sincerity of purpose, presented a no less personal and proprietary attitude toward me than I had held toward him and that all that had been needed was the authoritarian background to bring this attitude to expression. With the consciousness of this condition I saw what has been for me the crucial revelation of the many years of my analytic work—that, in its individualistic application, the attitude of the psychoanalyst and the attitude of the authoritarian are inseparable.

As from day to day this realization came more closely home to me, and with it the growing acceptance of the limitation and one-sidedness of the personalistic critique in psychoanalysis, my personal self-vindication and resistances began in the same measure to abate. At the same time the analyst too, Mr. Clarence Shields, came at last into a position to sense the personalism and resistance that had unconsciously all along actuated his own reaction. From now forward the direction of the inquiry was completely altered. The analysis henceforth consisted in the reciprocal effort of each of us to recognize within himself his attitude of authoritarianism and autocracy toward the other. With this automatic relinquishment of the personalistic or private basis and its replacement by a more inclusive attitude toward the problems of human consciousness, there has been not alone for myself but also for students and patients a gradual clearing of our entire analytic horizon.

It will later become clearer how this newer formulation of psychoanalysis on the wider basis of its more inclusive impersonal meaning has occurred entirely apart from the commonly predicable processes of logic. Only the accidental circumstance of a student's protest against my own personal bias, and my subsequent observation of an identical personalism in himself, as empirically disclosed upon our interchanging places, are answerable for the altered insight into psychoanalysis that the recent years have afforded me—an insight which the investigations of the small group of students working along analytic lines identical with my own have more and more substantiated. It was due, then, entirely to this unexpected turn of the tables, which placed me in the rôle of the patient and the patient in the analytic rôle, that I was fortuitously launched into six years of social experimentation upon the discrepancies of an individualistic analysis. If the outcome of the process has been the retraction of my earlier analytic outlook, it has not been the expression of any personal acumen or distinctive asset on my part.

The chance eventuality I have mentioned is alone responsible for enforcing the relinquishment of my habitual personalistic basis in psychoanalysis and bringing me to feel the need of a more comprehensive interpretation of the unconscious. Coming to sense, through a wider recognition of the unconscious, the correspondingly larger meaning of the consciousness of man, I have come to feel the need of its more adequate interpretation in such an organismic view as I have here attempted to outline under the theme of " The Social Basis of Consciousness."

I cannot consistently cite authoritative reference in support of this work. There is none. It is sponsored alone in the spirit of common endeavour actuating the group of students who have united in its common realization. But if I am loath to shift to others the responsibility for my own venturesomeness, I need not forgo the pleasure of acknowledging—as I do with whole-heartedness—the impetus that was given me in the beginning of my psychoanalytic work through the sympathy and encouragement of Dr. Adolf Meyer.

TRIGANT BURROW.

THE TUSCANY,
BALTIMORE, MARYLAND.

THE SOCIAL BASIS OF CONSCIOUSNESS

INTRODUCTION

AFTER sixteen years devoted to psychoanalytic work based on the principles of Freud, I have come to a position which differs so essentially from the followers of Freud as well as from his dissenters, that I am impelled to set down some account of the development through which my conceptions have passed, and to state as clearly as I can the position to which they have led.

The conceptions which Freud has brought to the study of abnormal and individual psychology have been of incalculable significance in aiding us to understand the causes and mechanisms underlying mental disharmonies. The personalistic basis, however, on which psychoanalysis rests has not in my experience proved sufficiently broad to meet the demands of a more inclusive societal psychology in its application to the needs of human life. While, in reconstructing the mechanics of the unconscious, psychoanalysis has given the impetus to a truer comprehension of the many distorted expressions of individual mentation, it has not as yet really uncovered the essential meaning of our human problems as they touch the consciousness of man in its organic reality.

To speak, however, of the organic reality of life is to enter upon a new universe of consciousness. It is to acquire a wholly altered concept of the inherent consciousness of man. This concept is not one that is interpretable upon our accustomed individualistic basis. As its envisagement is societal, its realization must necessarily be societal also.

To-day it is not possible to contemplate the significance of psychoanalysis without realizing the arbitrarily constricted point of view that has come to characterize the popularizations of psychoanalysis in their various phases. Psychoanalysis possesses as yet no specific definition. Personalistic in conception, it is personalistically interpreted, and its variations are to-day as whimsical as they are many. By one process of handling, psychoanalysis has become closely allied with Mysticism and New Thought, by another with propagandist measures for scientific birth-control, by a third with an authenticated programme of sexual licence, and with all it is but a new form of application of the old programme of palliative medication.

If, however, the essential truth of Freudian psychology, like all vital scientific movements, has been attended by personalistic misconception and even by the cruder aims of individual exploitation, it has been equally attended by a genuine scientific concurrence of spirit such as alone animates the disinterested conscience of the laboratory investigator. In the midst of the cheap and shifting divagations of a day, there have remained the sounder interpretations of at least a few outstanding investigators. While neither Freudian nor anti-Freudian, there are those to whom I, as well as others, owe the inspiration of those more thoughtful evaluations that are based upon a steadfast fidelity to the inclusive spirit of an evolutionary interpretation of human pathology, sociological as well as biological. It is these few students who, I feel, will welcome an interpretation of our human processes that offers a more inclusive, organic comprehension of our mental life.

But before undertaking the study of the organic psychology of man, it will be necessary first to establish a position

INTRODUCTION 3

that is based upon an organismic [1] or societal viewpoint as contrasted with a position based upon a viewpoint that is systematized and personal. Many years of psychoanalytic practice have led me to the conviction that the basis of Freud's psychology is inadequate to render completely conscious those disorders of the personality the essential meaning of which is their unconsciousness. The following essay, therefore, is an attempt to offer a more adequate concept of the essential consciousness of man than I feel has been attained through the interpretations of the unconscious patterns embodied in the present system of psychoanalysis. I have come to feel that what we have called analysis in the sense of our present personalistic systems is just another application of the method of suggestion, and that with us analysts, as with others, the method involves a situation in which we are as truly the unconscious dupes of the suggestive process we employ as are the unconscious subjects upon whom we employ it.

After all, it is the fallacy of personalism and of differentiation in our human relations which is the essential element in our unconscious agencies of suggestion, and I cannot doubt that this same fallacy underlies no less the constructions upon which we rest our analytic procedure. In the work of psychoanalysis as in our human endeavours everywhere, there enters unavoidably the personal bias that is inseparable from the position of observation concomitant to the observer. It is to abrogate this prejudice of personal partisanship and differentiation besetting the intrinsic system of psychoanalysis as well as of our private dogmatizations elsewhere, that I have undertaken the investigations of which this study is in part the outcome.

[1] The word "organismic" refers to the feelings and reactions common to the social body regarded as a coherent, integral organism. The term organismic, as I use it in its social application, is identical with the term organic in its individual application. The difference is that the term organismic is employed in a more generic sense. But in general the usages, organic and organismic, are interchangeable.

With the growth of my experience in psychoanalysis, the factor that has exerted the deepest influence in altering my outlook upon the problems of the neuroses as upon the processes of life generally has been the gradual, if reluctant, elimination of the personal equation in relation to those problems. By the personal equation I mean the unconscious and arbitrary tendency within us all to adopt *a personally systematized mental attitude* toward life in substitution for the physiological reality of life itself. The technical procedure of Freud necessarily rests upon this extrinsic mental attitude, whereas in the work of my students and myself during the past several years our position has tended increasingly toward the more inclusive fulfilment of the personality as a whole. Only in an inclusive analysis are our affects experienced upon a basis that is common and organic. Accidental diversity cannot issue out of organic unity. When the elements of consciousness will be truly unified, an association of conscious personalities will be unified also. The reason why there are to-day as many systems of psychoanalysis as there are psychoanalysts, is that our assumed principle of conscious unity is in reality but a personal principle of differentiation and unconsciousness.

Let me say at once, however, to anyone who may have lacked the opportunity or the candour to verify within himself the essential objective findings of Freud, and who is disposed to read into this thesis a vindication of his personal reaction against Freud's formulations, that he will find this study in nowise adapted to assuage his sense of outrage to injured sensibilities. Whatever may be the value of this work, in the spirit of its presentation it is in no sense a personal discrimination against the teaching of Freud but rather it is the acknowledged outgrowth of that teaching. If in our widened outlook we have outgrown the personal interpretations of psychoanalysis, there is due our full acknowledgment that it is to those interpretations that our position owes its rise. Far, then, from representing an antagonistic exclusion of

INTRODUCTION 5

Freud's theory of the unconscious, our position embodies the wider inclusion of it in what I feel is its more comprehensive interpretation on the basis of a societal concept of consciousness.

In psychoanalysis as in the social systems amid which, unconsciously, we are continually moving, we tend to gravitate toward an assumed static centre or toward a so-called personal cause that is coincident with our assumption of an absolute universe of consciousness. This gravitation toward a personal centre of consciousness embodies, in reality, a system that represents but the unconscious projection of our own ego. We substitute this delusion of an artificial world of causality for the reality of a universe of spontaneous sequence, not realizing that we ourselves are the subjective expression of the same organic sequence which we observe objectively in the world about us. When we have learned to accept inherent sequence as organically necessary, we shall no longer enforce unconscious causality as presumably inevitable.

It is this very general fallacy of personal sponsorship which constitutes the intricate disguise of our social unconscious and which in our personalistic outlook we have not yet begun to grasp. Ourselves unwitting participants in this illusion of personal determinism, we have not yet begun to compass the *system of unconsciousness* that lurks beneath its gratuitous assumption of personal agency.

With a view to the analysis and replacement of this absolute or self-determined attitude among us I have here offered what I conceive to be the more universal and encompassing interpretation of the common and organic consciousness of man. As, however, the field of Organic Psychology has yet to take a recognized place among us, and as it is a conception that is circumscribed only by the limits of life itself, naturally this initial step toward its establishment offers but a tentative view as to its real scope and meaning. Representing scarcely more than a preliminary outline, this work will be seen to embody but the merest syllabus in relation to further works based upon an organismic theory of consciousness, that doubtless will gradually be contributed to the increase of our understanding of life, both individual and social. In its present form the thesis here developed was first outlined in 1923.

PART I
THE PHILOSOPHY OF THE NEUROSES

CHAPTER I

PSYCHOANALYSIS IN THEORY AND IN LIFE

Now that the excitement following the inundation of psychoanalysis has died down and the clinical territories most affected have been once more built up and restocked, it is interesting to witness the changes wrought in different quarters as a result of the general havoc to habitual prepossessions. As we stand amid the debris of past conceptions there is no question but that the sudden descent upon us of Freud's postulates has destroyed many old landmarks that shall not be restored and that it has brought in a wealth of new material that has altered no little the configuration of the old.

As I happen to have been of those who were carried in upon the current of the general onsweep of new interpretations ushered in by Freud, my experience forms the record of a reaction to that movement that is internal because it is from the vantage-ground of a participant in it. Many of these interpretations are of epoch-making significance in their approach to mental disharmonies, but many, being immature and unsound, only obstruct the passage that psychoanalysis has contributed so splendidly to open. And so my position may be of interest to others who, like myself, have earnestly tried to bring order and a permanent coherence out of the large mass of conceptions that cluster about Freud's dynamic idea.

The theory of psychoanalysis rests on the conception that nervous disorders are the substitutive manifestation of a repressed sexual life; its basic position is that this substitutive factor is responsible for neurotic processes and that it is the sexual impulse for which recourse is sought in the process of substitution. This position of psychoanalysis is, in its essential significance, now generally accepted—the position; namely, which affirms the factor of replacement as the essential account of nervous manifestations and assumes the urge of the sexual instinct as the element replaced.

While, with other psychoanalysts, I am in full accord with this thesis, my finding in regard to the relation of these two propositions to one another is so entirely at variance with the prevailing psychoanalytic view, and alters so fundamentally for me the ultimate interpretation of psychoanalysis in its bearing upon the problems of consciousness, that I shall make clearer the ideas expressed in this work if, at the outset, I may state briefly in what manner my interpretation of this relation differs from the accepted conception.

The difference lies in the fact that I do not regard this replacement as *primarily* a replacement for sexuality as we now know it. On the contrary, sexuality, as manifested to-day amid the sophistications of civilization, is itself a replacement for the organic unity of personality arising naturally from the harmony of function that pertains biologically to the primary infant psyche. This original mode I have referred to in a previous work as the preconscious, and this preconscious mode [1] I regard as the matrix of the mental life. The spontaneous process of the organism's unhindered growth through the gradual development of experience or awareness from this unitary mode as a basis is, in my interpretation, the meaning of consciousness. The whole meaning of sexuality on the other hand is substitution, compensation, repression. In a word, sexuality, as it has come to exist socially to-day, is identical with the unconscious, while a unification of personality is alone to be found through eliminating the recourses of substitution and sexuality and thus reuniting the elements of the conscious and organic modes now

---

[1] "The Preconscious or the Nest Instinct," a thesis presented in outline at the Seventh Annual Meeting of the American Psychoanalytic Association, Boston, Mass., May 25, 1917.

kept asunder through the interposition of the unconscious.

Hence the modern substitutions existing under the name of sexuality, whether repressed or indulged, are but a symptom of this denial of man's organic affective life. Sexuality, as it now exists, is not only utterly unrelated to sex but it is intrinsically exclusive of sex. Sex is life. It is life in its deepest significance. Sex is the spontaneous expression of a natural hunger. In the instinct of sex there is felt a yearning from the depths of man's organism for mating and reproduction, while sexuality is the personal coveting of momentary satisfaction in mere superficial sensation. By sexuality, then, I mean something very different from sex. I mean the restless, obsessive, over-stimulated quest for temporary self-gratification that everywhere masquerades as sex and is everywhere substituted for the strong, simple, quiet flow of feeling that unites the organic and the conscious life in a single stream and is the expression of personality in its native inherency.

With this altered conception other modifications have followed which necessarily entail a distinct departure from certain accepted psychoanalytic formulations. The organic denial and the restless compensations and substitutions comprising the unconscious are, in essence, the psychology of the mental reaction-average known as normality. The popular analytic view places a premium upon this manifestation of the collective unconscious and assigns the criterion of normality as the desired goal of adaptation for the neurotically repressed personality.

I cannot accept this view. For an analysis of the social unconscious shows that the collective reaction embodied in the adaptations commonly accepted as normal betrays a tendency to repression and replacement that is no less an indication of disease-process than is the reaction presented in the individual neurosis. Indeed, from the point of view of constructive consciousness and health, our so-called normality is, of the two, the less progressive type of reaction. In truth, normality, in evading the issues of the unconscious, envisages less the processes of growth and a larger consciousness than the neurotic type of reaction, which, however blind its motivation, at least comes to grips with the actualities of the unconscious.

It is the hall-mark of normality that, suspecting nothing, it takes itself completely for granted. In the spirit of true conformity, it accepts its expressions of the vicarious at their face value and assumes the burden of its self-inflicted compensations with entire complacency. The neurotic, on the other hand, at least senses the inherent discrepancy in his life. He at least demurs in so far as to withhold assent from the mass-compromise embodied in the substitutions and connivances of the social unconscious. In a word, it is the distinction of the neurotic personality that he is at least consciously and confessedly "nervous."

This, as far as I can see, is the chief distinction between the condition represented in normal adaptations and that represented in the neurosis. The distinction lies merely in the greater weight of numbers. Normality, in its numerical strength, concedes acceptance to the average-reaction and so yields it right of way. In normality the unconscious carries the day, while in the neurosis it is pushed to the wall. The distinction psychologically lies in the successful compromise of the one as contrasted with the enforced doubt and self-questioning of the other. On the one hand there is the compact security of the social polity; on the other, there is the more sensitive isolation and uncertainty of the individual unit.

From the point of view of life, therefore, many of our normal reactions are psychologically as truly a manifestation of the distorted and substitutive as are those more isolated manifestations we commonly stigmatize as neurotic disharmonies. I cannot see but that the element of the repressed and substitutive on which is based Freud's theory of the neuroses is an element that underlies the expression of consciousness in all phases of its manifestation and that hence underlies also the phase represented in normality. In brief, normality too is nervous. Normality too, since it is actuated no less from motives of the ulterior and vicarious, even though it supposedly represents the criterion of adult consciousness, is no less an expression of the distorted and symbolic. This distortion is to be seen upon every hand in the restless greed and obsessive self-seeking that underlie the national, industrial, political, social and religious possessivism and competition which are the typical psychology of the normal mind, notwithstanding its plausible exterior of human progress and universal goodwill. Universality and goodwill are not there. These are but the manifest symptoms embodied by the social personality after it has undergone the distortion represented in the substitutive reactions characteristic of the social neurosis, that is, after it has been subjected to the mechanism of diplomatic repression and modification. What is there, in reality, is the will-to-self and the particular aim which best serves the narcistic advantages of the individuals comprising the social unit in question. The mechanism is identical with that which underlies the individual neurosis, namely, the covert aim toward the satisfactions of self which constitute unconsciousness.

Normality too, then, is neurotic. Normality too has its repressions and its substitutions, its secret symbols and equivocations. The difference is that as normality possesses the warrant of the institutionalized and current, it enjoys the protection of the consensus. And just as the neurotic fails to comprehend the meaning of this vicarious manifestation in its individual expression within himself and is a prey to the inscrutable symptoms in which his organism finds its compensations, so we, who are accounted normal, as little suspect the meaning of this same symptomatology existing in its social expression within ourselves. The neurotic resolutely defends his **unconscious duplicity behind an ingenious charade of** unconscious symbolism, and we no less resolutely defend ours through recourse to an identical device. But if we will look beyond the narrower confine of the clinic and face squarely the logical issue of Freud's thesis, we cannot avoid the conclusion that it is an indictment of man's consciousness in its entirety. Hence normality too must make answer for its complicity in the unconscious ruse of substitution and evasion which we observe in its more intense reaction as the introversions of personality presented in the obviously arrested expression we call neurotic.

If anyone is disposed to question this view, let him consider but one symptomatic reaction recently manifested throughout the social organism. Could there be anywhere imagined an unconscious reaction more wasteful and destructive or one of wider scope or severer intensity than the symptom-reaction represented by the war that has recently convulsed the world? Or consider the equally unconscious expression presented in the tendency to religious emotionalism that has followed in the wake of this world-war, with the corresponding effort towards compensation and self-propitiation through recourse to the sentimental and spiritualistic. Yet all the while the existence and the significance of the unconscious motives that are latent in the two extremes of emotional reaction underlying these manifest expressions have not yet begun to be suspected and reckoned with on any clear, conscious, analytic basis.

What, then, is the meaning of this tendency to substitution as shown in the reaction of the social as well as of the individual organism? If sexuality is the element substituted for, what is the psychology of this factor called sexuality? What is its meaning? In analyzing the unconscious of the neurotic personality it has become gradually clearer to me that the factor underlying and actuating the conflict Freud describes as repressed sexuality is nothing else than the personal desire of ascendancy or the lust of acquisition *concomitant with the organism's unconscious reversion upon its own image.*[1]

Sexuality, then, is but a larger word for self. Sexuality is the effort to limit life to the ends of personal aggrandizement. It is the greed of the self-limited personality to compass the whole, as contrasted with the societal personality that is encompassed by the whole. But, since the unconscious is the same under all forms, self or sexuality, with its pride of possession, its lust of gain, is no less the unconscious element underlying the psychology of the normal reaction-average. And precisely as in the individual reaction these unconscious wishes are manifested only in the disguised symbols and substitutive equivalents portrayed in neurotic symptoms, so too in the social organism these egocentric interests antagonistic to consciousness and growth venture to express themselves only in the corresponding substitutions of the mass unconscious.

Thus the unconscious represented in the social reaction we call normality is no whit different from the unconscious represented in the individual reaction observable as the neurosis. We are habitually deceived by the give-and-take policy of normal adaptation with its secret covenant of good manners and outward forms. But the apparent difference between the social and the individual neurosis consists merely in the fact that the poignancy of the conflict underlying the symptomatology of the social personality is largely mitigated and condoned by reason of the wider numerical distribution of the social organism and the consequent freer dissemination of the elements involved.

But, though of wider distribution, there underlies the expressions of normality no less of conflict and repression than exists in the acuter expression seen in the individual neurosis. In the personality of the more sensitive or feeling type we think of as neurotic, this tendency to self-

[1] "Social Images versus Reality," *The Journal of Abnormal Psychology and Social Psychology*, Vol. XIX, No. 3, Oct.-Dec., 1924.

acquisitiveness or sexuality and its organic incompatibility with the physiological inherency of life become, as it were, stalled and impacted within him; while in the social organism the discrepancy of personality, occasioned by its sexuality or pride of ascendancy, apparently entails no such organic blocking as that occurring in the individual. But the pain and impaction are present nevertheless, and are betrayed no less in the recourse to the substitutive and symbolic manifestations, characteristic of our prevalent social hysterias, not to mention the more violent disorders that crash upon the world in the reactions of political and industrial dissension and in the fiercer paroxysms of war.

Such is the meaning of our so-called normality. To a degree that is quite unsuspected by us its psychology is unconsciousness, and the psychology of unconsciousness is the psychology of the self-image secretly worshipped under the habitual guises of symbolism and replacement. It is time we should recognize that this recourse to the vicarious image is the psychology of many of the reactions of the normal as well as of the neurotic, that in ourselves, no less than in the neurotic, there is the putting forward of that which *stands for*—the exploitation, under countless different aspects, of that which may be adroitly put *instead of* rather than the simple acceptance of that which *is*.

Part of the purpose of the present study, however, is to try to bring into clearer light a substitutive reaction that is much nearer home. As psychoanalysts we need to take into account a distortive process that has a much closer bearing upon ourselves and our responsibility toward the problems of our common social consciousness. For, of all the forms of substitution to which normality has recourse, the form that seems to me of deepest significance for us and that presents the most vital need of analysis and understanding within ourselves, is the vicarious expression growing out of the tendency to an extrinsic approach to the problems of consciousness that has come to be embodied in the formulated *system* of psychoanalysis.

In the whole symptomatology of normality with its social expression of the vicarious there is no symptom-complex that is of greater significance than that embodied in the attempt to apply to the reality of human life the *system* of human life offered in psychoanalysis as it is to-day interpreted and applied. For a system of psychoanalysis is itself but a substitution for life, a theory of life in place of life itself. The theory of psychoanalysis sets out with a premise ; life does not. Psychoanalysis offers a solution ; life is its own solution.

It is not theory as theory at which I demur ; it is theory as application to the needs of human growth. From the point of view of the theory of psychoanalysis this therapeutic recourse in the treatment of nervous disorders seems to me completely adequate and true ; but from the point of view of life I have come to regard the application of the system or theory of psychoanalysis to the problems of individual needs as an utterly futile procedure. I have come to feel that what is here of value in the text-book is utterly worthless in our daily relation to human personality.

I would not, of course, be understood as repudiating theory as such. Seen clearly as the extrinsic expression it is, theory undoubtedly has its place, but its place is not in the earnest relationship of one human being to another such as obtains in the confidence and communication offered in the actuality of psychoanalysis. It has not yet been recognized, however, that we who are psychoanalysts are ourselves theorists, that we also are very largely misled by an unconscious that is social, that we too are neurotic, in so far as every expression but that of life in its native simplicity is neurotic. Our disharmony, however, is a phase of that widely diffused neurosis that exists under the prevailing social consensus represented in the normal adaptation.[1]

[1] " Our Social Evasion," *Medical Journal and Record*, Vol. CXXIII, No. 12, June 16, 1926.

And so, as I now see it, there is no more subtle form of substitution or one that is more successful in its capacity to evade the censor of consciousness and obtain the stamp of genuineness than the symptom represented in the *theory* of the reactions of human beings as a replacement for the reality of these reactions in life itself. Personal experience compels me to concede that it is such a symptom that is comprised in the theory of psychoanalysis as it is widely operative in the consultation rooms of psychoanalysts to-day.

We have assumed that, in envisaging the unconscious, psychoanalysis presupposes a more inclusive position than is generally characteristic of the theoretical or systematized clinician. But it is a far-reaching commentary upon the analyst's capacity of discrimination that he still presumes to analyze another on the basis of a system or theory, as though a neurosis which is an essentially subjective condition were of the nature of an objective bodily lesion. A dissociation within the personality may find its analogy in a bodily lesion but never its understanding. In the field of objective phenomena, theory is entirely commensurate with its application. After all, the theory of a mechanism is but the description of the principle of its operation. In the objective world such an objective description presents no discrepancy. It is the application of the objective method to an objective principle. The theory of the hydraulic press is perfectly consistent with its application. Between theory and application there is here complete conjunction. No disparate element intervenes to mar the transition from the descriptive to the practical.

So too with the theory of psychoanalysis as long as it pertains to the objective viewpoint of the text-book. But in the subjective sphere a totally different situation is presented. In dealing with life in its actuality, we are not dealing with the descriptive and objective. Human life is subjective. It is something experienced, something felt. Life is not theoretical; it is actual. It is not descriptive; it is dynamic. Human life *is;* it is not a *theory* of what is. Life, as it is felt, is our ultimate subjective actuality. Subjectivity or intrinsic feeling is the very basis of life. As such, feeling is life's reality and no theory of feeling is an adequate substitute for this reality. And so the objective theory of psychoanalysis or the objective theory of the motives of human life is wholly inapplicable to the subjective experience or to the actuality of human life as it is felt in individual personality.

We have not begun to reckon in the least understandingly with the nature of the subjective as contrasted with the objective sphere of life. We are, in fact, quite naïve in our attitude toward the whole subjective field, preferring to adopt toward it either a mood of beatific reverence and mysticism, in which we conjure unwarranted images of "psychic phenomena" that are allied with man's pseudo-religious vagaries, or we adopt a pseudo-scientific attitude which repudiates as non-existent or regards as unworthy of serious thought any phenomena that do not lend themselves to objective observation. Neither position seems to me tenable. We may dismiss at once the attitude of the occultists, for mysticism entertains no argument. But there is the need to consider very seriously the subjective field of scientific reasoning and to keep clearly before us the distinctive and impassable interval between the subjective and objective domains of scientific inquiry.

It is most true that objective observation is the sole method whereby we may obtain knowledge concerning the phenomenal world. This is true whether the knowledge concern substances themselves or the manner of their interaction. But we forget that knowledge thus gained is always knowledge *concerning*. If I consider any object—a book, a flower, or a stone—all that my knowledge will ever yield me is restricted to the attributes that pertain to the substance in hand. I observe that the stone is smooth, hard, ovoid. Submitting it to certain physical and chemical tests I learn still further about its qualities, and so, little by little, bring myself into ever closer touch with the object in question. But always my data furnish only *closer touch with*. The essential matter informing the substance we recognize as stone remains as inaccessible at the conclusion of an ultimate analysis as in the beginning. It is still knowledge *concerning* and my facts, however widely accumulated, are but attributive. Thus the *essential* nature of the objects about us is not to be approached by a method that is *unessential* or attributive.

The same circumstance confronts us in dealing with the phenomenal world of our own experience. Here too we proceed upon the method of objective inquiry—a perfectly legitimate field of "observation." We posit and collate all manner of phenomena and note no end of "reactions." But always we are restricted to a knowledge *concerning*, to data *in regard to*. In brief, we remain apart from—are ever outside of the reaction observed. Not that we may hold the attitude of the philosophers and assume the "existence" of a "metaphysical essence" that is inaccessible to us. We need rather to recognize that the alleged essence is merely that organic condition of matter with which our conscious processes are not organically continuous. There are, however, organic conditions or processes with which our consciousness is continuous—namely, the organic processes occurring within our own bodies and registering themselves within us as feeling. It is this continuity registered within us as feeling that is an essentially subjective state of mind and that must not be confused with the objective state of mind that merely registers impressions of the observable action or outer condition of such feeling processes. This subjective continuity is organic and inherent. True, it is possible through a shunting of interest or attention (repression or misplaced affect) to divert the course of our organic processes from their natural perception in consciousness. But this artificial situation through which we divert organic process from conscious participation and acknowledgment is the condition of unconsciousness.

My whole contention is precisely this : we are constantly attempting to deal objectively or attributively with experiences that are subjective and essential. We fail to understand that our knowledge *about* our feelings is but attributive, that it brings us no nearer the feelings themselves ; that our feelings are essential, physiological and that we may no more know our essential feelings through *observation* of their *attributes* than we may reach the essence of any object about us through a knowledge of *its* attributes.

The basis of this essay is precisely the recognition of this impossible breach between the condition of consciousness produced through a knowledge *about* feeling and the condition of consciousness that is the feeling itself, between the state of mind that is *commentative* and the state of mind that is *functioning*. The former is objective, the latter is subjective. The failure of our psychological methods to recognize this intrinsic distinction is to my mind the failure of our entire approach to the problems of mental and social disharmony. It is this unwitting substitution of the *theory* of human feelings for the unannotated experience of the feelings themselves as recorded in our interactive functioning as human beings that is the impossibility of our present " method " of psychoanalysis.

This position is for me an all-important one. Upon the acceptance or rejection of it, I believe, depends the growth or the decline of psychoanalysis as an agency of release for the intrinsic needs of the neurotic personality. To-day, under the impetus of psychoanalysis in its theoretical or vicarious form, we are carrying theory to the point of absurdity. There is now, for example, the psychoanalytic theory of the nursery. Anxious young mothers are running about looking for texts which will serve them as guides in the love of their children. They are diligently searching upon every hand for the latest approved theory of maternal love. And in response to the demand the popular literature is supplying them with full details. But there are no librettos of the nursery. Baedekers to motherhood are not to be had. The motherhood that is true is a subjective relationship, and it is only subjectively that it can be felt and understood.

I shall not forget the experience told me by a patient whose mother, actuated by the theory of motherhood in its highest " scientific " interpretation, undertook to enlighten her upon the significance of sex. The incident left the most painful impression upon her. The mother, having gathered courage for the performance of her maternal duty, delivered her errand with a punctiliousness which from the point of view of technique was irreproachable. She spoke out of the strictest regard for the theory of motherhood. But unfortunately her theory left out of account an item that needs to be reckoned with, namely, the native simplicity of the consciousness of childhood. The woman spoke out of the theory of a truth, but her child listened with the organic susceptibility of truth itself. The mother had not accepted within herself the actual significance of life, and so, in accordance with the formality of a theory, was vicariously imposing its acceptance upon her child. But childish perception pierces the veil of pedagogic finesse. The rigid demeanour of her instructor readily disclosed the discrepancy between the verbal recital and the utter lack of conscious acceptance within herself. For the child, now a middle-aged woman, the moment was an unforgettable one. She had witnessed in her mother an outrage to organic truth, and the shock of that experience caused a psychic disunity between mother and child from which there resulted an introversion of personality that covered half a lifetime. And so, while the theory of the nursery is from the point of view of theory wholly irreproachable, it is from the point of view of the nursery wholly absurd.

A lesson which parents have yet to learn is that the child is closer to the heart of things than the grown-up—that the consciousness of childhood stands in a far more truthful relationship to the actuality of life, as it is, than the consciousness of the conventionalized and sophisticated adult. For years it has been my feeling that beneath the conflict of the neurotic personality there is reiterated an urge toward the expression of this primal inherency of consciousness. To-day, it is more than ever my view that in the neurotic reaction there is expressed an inherent plea for the native simplicity and truth of this organic consciousness. It becomes more and more clear to me that the pain of these personalities is due solely to the organic discrepancy of an unconsciousness and indirection within themselves, and that essentially their urge is to bring themselves again into harmony with the law of their personality by reuniting the needs of their consciousness with the needs of their organic life.

As Nietzsche says: " May there not be—a question for alienists—neuroses of health ? "[1] This question for alienists is indeed a vital one but it is one which, as far as I am aware, has not as yet even dimly occurred to us. There is nowhere, it may be noted, a clearer argument for Nietzsche's hypothesis than Nietzsche's own neurosis. Unfortunately, however, alienists are still as little interested in the positive processes that bespeak the organism's conscious health, as physicians in general are interested in the positive processes that insure the organism's physical health. But, as long as the collective social mind remains the collective unconscious mind, it is not to be expected that we shall approach the unconscious of the individual, in either its psychic or in its somatic aspect, from the basis of an inclusive consciousness and health. The question is often asked whether insanity will ever become curable. The answer can only be that

---

[1] " Giebt es vielleicht—eine Frage für Irrenärzte—Neurosen der Gesundheit ? "—Nietzsche's *Werke*. Erste Abt., Band I. *Die Geburt der Tragödie*. Leipzig, 1903.

the insanity of the individual cannot be curable as long as there exists the insanity of the social mind about him. It is not humanly possible for the psychiatrist to remedy conditions of mental disorganization as long as he himself is part of a disorganized social mind.

If the psychoanalyst, in applying to the lives of his patients a theory of life, is himself unconsciously resorting to the self-protection of the substitutive and symbolic ; if the blocked personality of our patients meets with a blocking in ourselves, with a compromise, a theory, a something which stands as a *sign for* rather than that which *is*—a situation which offers a compromise mechanism identical with that for which they have sought aid from us—then clearly the way is not yet open for the release of the conflict within these personalities. For a patient may be untrammelled only in so far as the analyst is himself untrammelled.

In taking this attitude I do not make any personal claim for myself. This position is not one to which I have come through the success of my work but rather through its failure. For in the measure in which I have adhered to the dictates of a preconceived normality, in just that measure has my work defeated itself. Though I have for some time theoretically disavowed the mental status represented in the normal reaction, I have tended unconsciously all the while to ally myself with this standardized brand of unconsciousness and thus, in my own work, have inclined to hold to a theory of life rather than to its actuality. Not, then, with the neurotic alone, but with us all, it would seem that consciousness is mainly employed in efforts of self-protection and evasion. Truly, consciousness makes cowards of us all. But this is not consciousness in the sense of life and growth ; it is consciousness in the sense of retention and self. It is not a free consciousness ; it is consciousness with a reservation. It is not true consciousness ; it is unconsciousness.

In accordance with such a mode of consciousness each

of us is elbowing for a place for himself. Each is seeking more territory for his own expansion. Each of us is an unconscious overlord striving to secure the supremacy of his own " personality." Universal and normal as this reaction is, its tendency is obsessive and ill. I do not believe that life is aggressive and that growth is concerned for itself. Personality is impersonality. What is needed is the quiet acceptance of life in its actuality. In this and this alone lies the opportunity for freedom and growth.

We hear much to-day of the technique of psychoanalysis. In truth there is no such thing. It is just another defence mechanism, just another resistance to the actualities of life. As in all instances of therapeutic specialization, the technique of psychoanalysis has become a fetish with us. It has become a veritable complex, a disorder from which I find patients actually suffering. The situation is quite ridiculous. The more I think of it, the more I am convinced that the so-called technique of psychoanalysis is but another hobgoblin wherewith the unconscious tendency of professionalism with its egoistic striving for preferment contrives to preserve its own separateness and distinction. I confess that, in my own unconsciousness, I have more than once laid stress upon the importance of the analytic technique. But let us not be misled by what is called the technique of psychoanalysis. It is but another subterfuge for the reality of life. A technique of psychoanalysis is no more possible than a technique of love or of friendship or of motherhood. There is a technique and a very difficult technique of the *theory* of psychoanalysis. But that is quite a different thing. Psychoanalysis itself or, as its name implies, the loosening or freeing of consciousness is nothing else than the conscious acceptance of life. As such, it is the exact contrary of the objective and technical. Life is not a technique. It does not express itself in terms of technique. Technique is an objective instrument. Life is a subjective experience. It is a joy or a sorrow, a disappointment or an aspiration, and it can no more be handled from the point of view of technique than it can be handled with the scalpel of the anatomist.[1]

From these and similar reflections I have come to regard the formality of applying a system of psychoanalysis to the life of an individual as an actual hindrance rather than as an aid to the true expression of his personality. It is but an added repression, blocking the very way it attempts to open. For to meet the unconscious of a patient with unconsciousness within oneself, is only to answer symbolic substitution and indirection with the same substitution and indirection in an altered, more subtle, socially plausible form.

The whole meaning, therefore, of an analysis that is actual and not theoretical is the realization and acceptance on the part of the analyst of the utmost unconscious symbolization and distortion within himself. The analysis of a patient is the analysis of oneself. It cannot be otherwise. And when I say analysis, I do not mean an analysis that is a mere unconscious concession to normality—a giving vent to the egoistic erotism of the individual by diffusing it among the widely distributed elements of the social personality in the manifold distortions of sexuality. I mean an analysis of personality in its widest expression—an analysis through which the individual comes into the conscious acceptance not only of the repression or distortion that is personal and that is comprised within the individual introversion we know as the neurosis, but of the distortion or substitution of personality that is social and that constitutes the confederacy of unconsciousness popularly endorsed as normality.

The prime requisite for clear, free, untrammelled work in the analysis of human personality is the unqualified

---

[1] An instance of this inversion of natural expression is seen in the system of technique that is the obsession *par excellence* of singers. In the art of singing, as correspondingly in any art of life, technique is applicable only to the theory of vocalization but not to the actuality of spontaneous musical expression.

rejection of the unconscious compromise embodied in the social reaction of normality. The analyst who is not himself capitulating to the concession of the social unconscious will repudiate the attitude of the psychotherapist whose criterion is the restoration of his patient to a 'condition of normality, and will take his stand against any recourse that is based upon a programme of compromise and habituation. He will see that normality is merely unconsciousness on a co-operative basis and he will not be deceived by its insidious offers. It is only through such an attitude of complete freedom within oneself that it is possible to offer the opportunity of freedom to the personality of the neurotic patient, the very heart of whose disharmony lies in an inner repugnance, however bewildered and confused, to the untruth of the social unconscious comprising his milieu. Viewed analytically, normality is but the self-flattery through which we pretend we are not unconscious. By so pretending, however, we are only furthering our tendency to deeper unconsciousness.

As long as there is self-protection, there is self-limitation ; as long as there is self-limitation, we are necessarily setting a limitation to the possibility of growth and consciousness in others. Only through rejecting such protection may we come to accept the testimony of the unconscious within ourselves. Otherwise, we ourselves become the inhibitors rather than the liberators of consciousness ; we who are psychoanalysts become mere guardians of disease-processes instead of the willing repositories of these unconscious factors, as they exist in others, through our understanding and acceptance of these processes as they exist within ourselves. For consciousness grows upon the medium of consciousness. It cannot be nourished upon an extraneous soil. Theories of consciousness are extraneous. In the presence of the actuality of life, theories of life become mere intellectual snobbery. Being wise, sophisticated and remote, they are inadequate to meet life in its native simplicity.

Bearing the testimonials of authority, the credentials of office, they do not come low enough. These insignia of rank only tend to intimidate personality in its natural simplicity. What is needed for the release of the neurotic individual is the personality who imposes nothing of his own and thus allows the completest opportunity for the unfolding of the repressed and introverted personality of others. As psychoanalysis develops and our understanding deepens, it will be seen that it is not scientific equipment alone but also directness of outlook that make the psychoanalyst. It will be seen that the personalities who are adapted to an understanding of the needs of human life will not necessarily occupy places of importance amid the distractions of affairs, but that their place may be an unobtrusive one in which understanding for understanding's sake will be their sole concern. The various rules laid down by medical or other syndicates with a view to determining what are the literal qualifications for a psychoanalyst are wholly beside the point.[1] The qualifications for understanding are not literal. Although we may formulate the most meticulous of programmes setting forth the requirements of tuition, it will be found that personality will, in the final count, override them all. Besides, I cannot think that it is due entirely to the

[1] I realize that a patient should have the protection of the medical expert's knowledge. This means that the analyst, if not himself a physician, should be directly associated with the office of a physician. We know, of course, that charlatanry exists no less within the medical profession than elsewhere ; yet while a medical degree is in no sense a certificate of personal sincerity, it is a social surety of professional responsibility. On the other hand, I have yet to hear the suggestion offered that a physician who is not himself a psychoanalyst should be closely associated with the office of a psychoanalyst. It seems odd, as one thinks of it, that this provision should not have been offered by those who have been conscientious enough to recognize the reverse need. As a matter of fact, the number of instances in which mental disorders are mistaken for somatic conditions is incomparably greater than those in which there is failure to recognize the existence of the somatic component. If it is important that the analyst should be competent to trace the source of structural diseases, the internist should be equally competent to trace the source of mental disharmonies.

accidents of chance that the spokesman for the adoption of this or that recipe as a prerequisite to " sound training " in psychoanalysis should unfailingly submit a menu that tallies in detail with his own catalogue of merits. After all, psychoanalysis is a very large name for a very simple thing. I well know that this statement offers a delectable morsel to any who are disposed to misinterpret my meaning. It will be readily regarded as recklessly casting aside as valueless all the years of my own medical and psychological training. But the responsibility for such a misinterpretation rests upon those who are unable to distinguish between the culture that is applied academically and the academy that is applied culturally. All that I mean is that whosoever follows the calling of psychoanalysis is merely one who seeks to understand and accept life as it is without intruding himself or imposing his view or exerting his authority. Indeed psychoanalysis is essentially the abrogation of authority. For the psychoanalyst is not content but receptacle. Lacking method or design he offers nothing, but is the recipient of all there is of human experience as subjectively substantiated within himself.

But there enters here a consideration of vital importance and one that has not yet been adequately reckoned with and understood. If the psychoanalyst is to be the recipient, there must be those who stand to him as recipient also. If he is to understand, he must be understood. If the life of the analyst is to be a reality and not a system, he himself must in reality participate in the life in which he invites others to participate. If it is his thesis that human life cannot subsist alone, that communication is life, that it is the very meaning of consciousness, neither can he subsist without communication.

And so there need to be in the life of the analyst the personalities with whom he may share, with whom he may communicate, who accept him and are accepted by him in turn. For to analyze is to be analyzed, to understand is to be understood. Needless to say these are conclusions to which I have not come alone. I could not have. They are the outcome of my own opportunity of participation and expression, as the need of communication has come to unfold itself in my own experience.

Clearly, then, we who stand as the promoters of a new and untrammelled consciousness must look carefully into our own lives to discover whether we ourselves, as part of the social consciousness, are not theorists rather than unified personalities actuated solely by the law of understanding and of growth within ourselves. Clearly, we ourselves must realize the completely vicarious and repressed element underlying the expression of unconsciousness embodied in the social unrest of normality, and, fearlessly repudiating this collective reaction of substitution and evasion, break completely with the popular policies of compromise and untruth underlying it. In this course we shall take our stand for the freedom and clarity of a mode of consciousness that aims solely toward the growth of self-understanding and communication. For life is not a system, it is not a technique. Life is simple, and its course is one of quiet flow. In so far as psychoanalysis is technical, it is not life. In so far as its aim is normality, it is not free.

The choice is an unequivocal one. It is a choice between expediency and truth, between fixity and growth. For the habitual or normal mind whose criterion is expedience the choice is already determined; but for the personality that is sensitive to the values of life, the choice of growth is no less inevitable. It is organically so. Hence it is for each of us to make his choice on which side he will take his stand—whether, adhering to a theory of life, he will blindly protect himself against the recognition and acknowledgment of the vicarious element of normality and compromise within his own unconscious, or whether he will stand for a mode of consciousness that flings away every habitual protection and accepts only the conditions of life as they unfold themselves in the development of his own personality as well as in that of others.

The outlook is really not ambiguous. The question is whether life will be a theory or system corroborated by the technical outfit of the consultation room or whether it will be the deeply fulfilled experience that comprises consciousness in its organic reality.

The definite biological theory on which this thesis rests implies an organic or societal continuum as the essential basis of consciousness. To understand this theory we shall be helped if, in the beginning, we will seek to replace the more or less arbitrary divergences of personal outlook with a conception that attempts to stand far enough removed from this personal mode to contemplate within its more ample formulation the personal outlook as well. For this purpose we must discover, as far as possible, our tendency to personalistic delimitation—a tendency due to the unconscious systematization of the restricted individual unit—and in this way approach consciousness anew from the more inclusive basis of its societal meaning.

CHAPTER II

A RELATIVE CONCEPT OF CONSCIOUSNESS—AN ANALYSIS OF CONSCIOUSNESS IN ITS ETHNIC ORIGIN

IN presenting a psychological discussion that presupposes the altered basis of the relativists, I am under no illusion as to the wide disparity between the mathematical conception of the relativists in regard to the universe and the clinical preoccupations of a psychopathologist. It is now conceded, however, that the theory of relativity is not without its revolutionary influence upon our scientific thought processes generally. And so, although I am not competent to an appreciation of the theory of relativity in the objective sense of the physicists, I hope I shall not seem presumptuous in attempting a discussion of consciousness that demands as its basis a viewpoint that is analogous to theirs.[1]

As I understand it, the inadequacy of the Newtonian system of astronomy is its autogenous exclusion of data requisite to a principle which presupposes a basis of universal applicability. Assuming an unqualified absolute to reside within the limits of its own circumscribed area, it posits a principle which fails to take account of factors

[1] " To free our thought from the fetters of space and time is an aspiration of the poet and the mystic, viewed somewhat coldly by the scientist who has too good reason to fear the confusion of loose ideas likely to ensue. If others have had a suspicion of the end to be desired, it has been left to Einstein to show the way to rid ourselves of these ' terrestrial adhesions to thought.' And in removing our fetters he leaves us, not (as might have been feared) vague generalities for the ecstatic contemplation of the mystic, but a precise scheme of world-structure to engage the mathematical physicist."—A. S. Eddington, F.R.S., " The Theory of Relativity and its Influence on Scientific Thought," *The Scientific Monthly*, Vol. XVI, No. 1, Jan. 1923.

ETHNIC ORIGIN OF CONSCIOUSNESS 33

operating within the larger constellation wherein its own system is but a contributory element. So that, in estimating the components requisite to a more inclusive scale of computation, the Newtonian postulate omits to reckon with the principle of the time-space element that is constitutive of the extension intrinsic to itself and that is, therefore, mathematically indispensable in an encompassment of the universal and all-inclusive astronomical purview with respect to which its own system becomes but relative and extrinsic.

Little by little the necessities of a widening outlook have demanded a gradual broadening of conceptual principles generally. Of late I have been led to views that appear to warrant the conclusion that, in the sphere of psychic phenomena no less than in the realm of physics, a system of absolutism, preclusive of data existing outside its own autogenously circumscribed principle, wholly dominates our presumably conscious world. Accordingly, if we are to reckon with consciousness upon a true and inclusive basis, it is required that the system of absolutism thus embodied shall give way to a conception of relativity in the conscious sphere comparable to the principle of relativity in the physical universe.[1]

I do not see why, in his mental and emotional reactions, man may not so far free himself from the traditional superstitions of imbued inference as to recognize at last that, even with respect to conceptions that are the basis of his own mental operations, there is a difference between the values that *seem* and the values that *are*. I do not see why he may not recognize that processes which he has

[1] It is, of course, not possible to trace through mathematical intricacies a detailed analogy between the cosmic theory of relativity, as it bears upon the objective data of an abstruse calculus, and the organic theory of relativity, as it bears upon the subjective data of the all-inclusive principle of psychology here regarded as the basis of a universally comprehensive scheme of consciousness. The comparison has significance for me merely in the aptness of its theoretical alignment with a conception of consciousness which includes data extrinsic to our habitual psychological system, i.e. the system intrinsic to ourselves and commonly accepted as the totality of consciousness.

C

hitherto regarded as habitually inevitable are not by any means organically necessary, but that the two may in fact be essentially contradictory one of the other. If in the objective world man may ungird himself of the accustomed limitations of a hitherto accepted Euclidean geometry, may he not within the sphere of his subjective consciousness also rid himself of prepossessions which, though they appear to us now as no less basic, may ultimately prove equally non-essential?

We have recently waged a world-war which, according to the *state of mind* of its participants prior to its occurrence, was the admittedly inevitable recourse, but which, in the opinion of thinking men subsequent to its enactment, is now equally admitted to have been a wholly unnecessary eventuality. How then, upon our present basis of mentation, may we conclude what is an adequate criterion by which we may determine a dependable process of thinking? If we may know our states of mind only after we have vented the emotions that first incited them, of what use is it to know them? If states of mind can produce calamities that gather their toll of human life by the millions and we can, by subsequently taking thought, come to regard them as unnecessary, what must be felt toward states of mind that have produced such calamities? Surely it is not the part of intelligence to feel regret of a disaster only after the disaster has befallen. If disaster need not befall, would it not be wiser to deplore it beforehand and so avert the disaster? This would seem the logical course, but the truth is that the logical course is not accessible to man in his present state of unconsciousness. Man may think logically but he cannot be warranted to act logically. For, in his present stage of development, his actions are predominantly under the guidance of his emotions and his thought can therefore only follow after.

Consciousness is the individual's acquiescence in sequences that are determined by the necessities of organic law. Unconsciousness is the individual's resistance to these organic processes. As consciousness is anterior to its own realization, so unconsciousness ever follows in the wake of its own event. We think to-day only in terms of what ought to have been yesterday, and the event of to-morrow embodies again the reaction to the issues of to-day. Thus our actions are always but the unconscious reflections of the day preceding, and in our unconsciousness it is only in the aftermath of the morrow that we interpret the omens of to-day.

If man's judgment is competent to apprehend the data of events subsequent to their occurrence, why may it not be equally possible, through our prior apperception of the mental states leading up to them, to envisage the same events with the same clarity anteriorly and thus forestall the useless mistakenness and destruction that now follow inevitably with their enactment? Surely it is clear that, in continuing to preserve unaltered this same state of mind whose world-wide consequences we have just witnessed, we may be, at the present moment, preparing a similar if not a yet greater catastrophe, the while we are at the same moment as completely oblivious of it. Indeed, from a position that is anterior to the emotional inducements to which our mental states are inevitably subject in our present absolute view, it will be seen that an unconscious and destructive disposition toward life is as inseparable from an absence of self-cognizance on the part of the social mind as the factors of disintegration and unconsciousness are inseparable within the life-sequences of the individual unit.

In its necessary limitation with respect to the relativity of consciousness in its universal compass, the constellated system of processes which at present comprises the sphere of the mental life will, in my view, ultimately appear analogous to the traditional system of Newton with respect to the universe of relativity in the encompassment of objective mathematics. As in the intrinsic principle of absolutism comprising the Newtonian system of gravitation, so in the self-determined principle of absolutism, comprising our present system of psychology, a dimensional factor has been left out of account, the inclusion of which completely shifts the basis of former calculations and so distorts our habitual reckonings as to demand the fundamental reconstruction of accepted values.

But while the principle of relativity comprehended by the objective formulæ of the physicists is mathematically beyond my reach, the conception of relativity within the subjective life appears to me not only compellingly clear, but organically necessary. Indeed, in the absence of this conception of the relativity of consciousness, it is no longer possible for me to reckon adequately with the processes of the mental life. For in default of a working basis broad enough to embrace the dimensional element of the system, individual and social, whereof we ourselves are a component part, there is lacking the scientific comprehensiveness requisite to a universal principle of evaluation.

It is worthy of note that between the objective or mathematical theory of relativity of Einstein and the subjective or organismic theory of relativity here considered there is to be traced, however inconclusively, a philosophical parallelism that is significant.[1] My feel-

[1] Newton observed the universe from the point of view of his fixed position upon the earth. Einstein observes the universe from the point of view of all possible positions within the universe. Likewise our present-day systems of psychology regard the conditions of life from the position of observation that is one's individual point of view toward them. In the conception here advanced these conditions, on the contrary, are regarded from points of view that are socially relative to and inclusive of all possible positions of observation.

The reader will recall that the conceptions of the physicists first led them to a theory of special relativity through their calculations of uniform motion, while their deductions came only later to embrace data pertaining to difform motion, or to motion that is not uniform, as contained under the conception of general relativity. With regard to the theory of relativity in the subjective sphere, it was upon noting the habitual deflections from a predictable organic constant, observable in the erratic reactions of the neurotic personality, that the conception of relativity in the sphere of consciousness first occurred to me. It was only subsequently that the relativity of consciousness as applied

ETHNIC ORIGIN OF CONSCIOUSNESS

ing is, though as yet it is little more than an intimation with me, that this cosmological parallel between the subjective and objective spheres of relativity marks a concomitance that is consistent throughout. I do not see how it could be otherwise since the subjective and the objective spheres of life, embodying the bipolar aspects of the phenomenal world, represent but obverse phases of one and the same universe. The analogy that interests me here, however, has to do with the feature that is equally the basis of the two modes of relativity, namely, the feature which entails the abrogation of absolute standards of evaluation and the recognition of the kinetic factor that is organic to both. In the objective interpretation of astronomy this factor comprises the mathematical space-time coefficient of the physicists' fourth dimension; and in a subjective interpretation of consciousness it comprises correspondingly the kinetic element that determines the functional coefficient of the organic life as a whole.

The thought represented in "the organic life as a whole" is, like the inclusive scheme of the physicists, to be understood only by exclusion, that is, by exclusion of a point of view that is *not* organic, or by exclusion of the absolute system, individual and social, comprising our

to the uniform reactions characteristic of the collective social mind came to shape itself into the organismic conception of relativity here outlined as the underlying principle of consciousness.

While representing in no sense a detailed correlation between them, there is nevertheless a certain analogy, not only in the manner of inception of the objective and subjective theories with respect to the observation first of difform or abnormal deviation, and later of discrepancies of normal or uniform reactions; but there is also this further concomitance between the two aspects of the principle. The Newtonian hypothesis takes account of motion or reaction in the planetary system only in the large, while the theory of Einstein is adequate in contemplating the motion of planets both in the large and in the small. Conversely, our present Freudian theory of the unconscious takes care of the reactions of the personality in the small or in an individual or particular sense, while the theory of the relativity of consciousness regards **personality not only individually or particularly (whether regarded singly or in its collective social expression) but also societally or in the sense of consciousness in its universal or organismic meaning.**

present static basis of consciousness. As this organismic conception of consciousness is relativity itself within the subjective sphere, its encompassment can no more be apprehended in our present scheme of psychological evaluation than the relativity of the physicists can be apprehended on a static Newtonian basis.

Einstein's theory of relativity is not intelligible on the absolute basis of the older system of astronomy, of which conception the newer mathematical theory is, by reason of its wider inclusiveness, the logical replacement. Likewise, the theory of subjective relativity or the organismic conception of consciousness cannot be understood on the basis of the absolute principle resident in the Freudian conception of the unconscious, of which principle the organismic conception is, by inclusion, the more encompassing formulation.

Hence this organismic conception of consciousness, subsumed under the postulate of relativity, will be understood only as we discard entirely the absolute conception represented in our present system of psychology. Because of our own absolutistic basis, we do not realize that the absolutism intrinsic to the dynamic system of our present individualistic conception of consciousness maintains a position that is relatively not less static than the older descriptive systems of consciousness in relation to the dynamic psychology of Freud. The Freudian system is dynamic in respect to the system it has superseded but static in respect to the principle by which it must now in turn, I believe, be superseded, precisely as our own Newtonian system is dynamic with respect to the older Ptolemaic system of astronomy it has transcended but static with respect to the mathematical principle of relativity which now in turn has transcended it.

Of course, the fact that the intrinsic limitation of our astronomical systematization has led us arbitrarily to regard time and space as absolute entities, rather than as the functional co-ordinates of matter, has no immediate bearing whatever beyond the need of adjusting a quite infinitesimal error in the astronomical reading of certain minimal deflections. It does not in the least alter the practical conduct of human affairs. For the grocer and the apothecary our standards remain undisturbed. So also in the more intimate adaptations of our human relatións, the absolute basis of mensuration that has actuated our reckonings with respect to the objective world about us has not for a moment touched our subjective mode or the affective sphere of our living. But when this artificial basis of self-determined absolutism operates within the organic sphere of man's affective life, wherein is the very centre of his being, there are recorded errors whose consequences reach to the core of life itself. It is here, in the absolute system of evaluations pertaining to the affective reactions of human conduct, that there is needed the correcture in reading the deflection, both individual and social, that comprises man's unconsciousness.

We have yet to learn that it is in the common affects of men that there resides the basis of their collective biology. Only in the affective reactions comprising the native, organic continuum of life may we trace the menstruum of our human consciousness. And so, in approaching the affective or organic implications entailed through the arbitrary systematization that is our own absolutism, we are entering upon the study of the distorted sensations and reactions in which is embodied, I believe, the essential pathology of consciousness represented in the neuroses.

In considering the conception of the relativity of consciousness we shall acquire a clearer insight into the more comprehensive scheme subsumed under it, if we will begin with an analysis of the rudimentary processes comprising our personal judgments and consider the elements into which our primary impressions may be resolved.

Our judgments are formed from the material of our impressions or, as we say, we reason from observation. This being so, what must be the substance of our observations and what the nature of the processes of reason thus derived ? To observe is to stand apart from and record the impressions reflected to us from the object observed. So that upon consideration our observations are seen to consist of the *reflected images* or mental *pictures* of the world of objects by which we are surrounded. That is to say, impressions of objects consist of the aspect or surface which is reflected to us from them and which is thus mirrored in the reflecting surface of our own perceptions.

But in this very process of observation an unwarranted assumption has already been posited in advance—the assumption, namely, that the position intrinsic to the observer is an all-inclusive and authentic one. Already it presumes a universe of which the onlooker's own self-limited position is the basis. It does not account for the integral component that is the observer's own organic dimension. In brief, the very point of view of the observer lays claim to the prerogative of an absolute cosmogony whereof he is himself the unconsciously static, self-determined centre. Whatever the point of view, it is invariably " the point of view " of the observer. So that in constituting ourselves perceptual foci from which, according to our self-appointed terms, we look out as from a background upon the phenomena of life, we have unconsciously become artificially detached spectators of a merely static *aspect* of life. This is what I mean by the autogenous exclusion of data extrinsic to the self-determined system of which we ourselves are only a part, but which, in the light of the relativity of consciousness as a whole, is revealed, on the contrary, as an arbitrary system determined by our own static absolutism. Regarded from the point of view of relativity, to adopt such a detached, observational outlook toward life is to view it in the merely flat, bidimensional plane of the image. It is not to experience life through participation in the extension of its full-dimensional actuality.

Upon analysis, then, our world of subjectively tabulated impressions becomes but an artificial world reflecting the artificial systematization that is our own detached observation of it. Our unconsciousness is our failure to realize that bidimensional reproductions of actuality are not actuality. Our own organisms as well as the surrounding objects of actuality are elements that are equally to be included in the organic continuum of our human experience. The mental pictures comprising our bidimensional *impressions* of objects, however adequate as pictures, are not adequate as expressions of actuality in the sense of the dynamic extension comprising our own organic inclusion.

Contrary, therefore, to the casual assumption current among us, we do not apprehend the objects about us as they exist in their cubic outline, but only in the bidimensional "foreshortening" that is our own mental or pictorial impression of them. Our so-called objective apperception of the world of actuality is in fact superficial and unreal. Our alleged world composed of impressions is pictorial rather than actual. It is static rather than kinetic. In consequence of the bidimensional visual plane in which our objective fields are reflected, it is inevitable that our environmental actuality should appear in the form of pictures before us. Looking out upon the world from a bidimensional basis, we can perceive it only in terms of the reflected image formed upon our own bidimensional mental background. It is due also, then, to this contributing factor of a flat or reflected visual image within ourselves that there is registered within ourselves a flat or reflected mental image of the world about us. For in virtue of the bidimensional picture in which our impressions are necessarily reflected, our mental perception of objects is likewise necessarily pictorial and bidimensional.[1]

Such is the probable ethnological account of this mis-

---

[1] This psychobiological misconception is doubtless also aided in large measure by the physiological conditions of our visual organs of perception and by the bidimensional surface upon which our impressions of objects are received. Because of the disposition of the nerve terminals

construction of actuality that underlies our mental world. The significance of such a pictorial and artificially foreshortened representation of the objective world and its mental influence in foreshortening the tridimensions of actuality in general cannot be overstressed. We need to realize the circumstance of our remote or bidimensional position of merely mental or impressionistic observers. From this position the mentally reflected and artificially pictorial outlook with which the world of solidarity is individually viewed by us represents but the portrait of life whereof the reality is the inclusiveness of life as experienced through our subjective continuity as functional elements in the organic whole. So that while it is most true that we reason from observation, yet if our observation is imbued with a bidimensional or superficial bias, then our reason is also influenced by this same bidimensionally imbued bias. If our observation is not subjectively inclusive of the objective world about us, in the same measure our judgments are not inclusive of it.

It is this non-inclusiveness of consciousness that constitutes our mental systematization. In this perceptual relationship to life, due to our detached basis of interpretation of it upon grounds of the apparent aspect

of the retina upon a flat or bidimensional area, our visual perception of objects is limited to impressions of a flat or bidimensional plane. If by means of binocular accommodation objects present to us the appearance of "depth," it is of course not to direct visual perception that we owe our sense of perspective but to stereoscopic inference, seconded by our stereognostic experience of tridimensional solidity. Hence, what is actually "perceived" upon looking at an object of three dimensions is a visual facet, as it were, due to our own mentally flattened "cross-section" of the solid object before us as determined by the particular aspect of it that is momentarily presented to view. I think it cannot be doubted that this mechanism of our visual perception is a contributing factor in influencing our tendency to "see" mentally. One says "I see" when he means "I understand." There is the same implication in saying that one "sees" the logic of such and such a statement. So, too, we speak of a "mental point of view" or of "intellectual vision." This illusory character of our mental percepts probably owes its explanation also in part to the fact that our visual sense is the sense that best permits a distant and detached observation *of* rather than a contact *with* the surrounding world.

ETHNIC ORIGIN OF CONSCIOUSNESS 43

rather than of its solid actuality, consists the arbitrary absolutism of our present system of consciousness. Due to this organic misconception of consciousness, we habitually prefer the picturesque semblance of the aspect to the pragmatic inclusiveness of the actual. This is why we tend to explain life rather than to live it. This is why the adduced hypothesis of life counts with us more than life itself. But an account of life that does not include the consciousness that is our own kinetic function and repudiate the static pictures of life arbitrarily projected by us does not compass life in the full orb of its rounded actuality. A principle of life that does not embrace the principle arising out of the bias of our own self-made systems of personal absolutism and unconsciousness is not adequate to encompass life in the rounded sum of its functional inclusiveness. It is needful to recognize that, in the unconscious absolute underlying the personal relatedness of each of us to every other, there is involved an organic *resistance* or a mutual repulsion among the elements of the societal personality that forms an impasse to its concerted function. On the contrary, in the mutual inclusiveness of our individual organisms as elements within the confluent sum we thus compose, there is embodied the organic continuum that underlies the societal organism of man as a whole. It is this homogeneous substrate of man's consciousness in its totality that is implied in the principle of the relativity of consciousness.

If, however, an ethnological account is adequate to explain the remote, pictorial relation in which we stand with respect to the world of objective actuality, such an account is not adequate to an understanding of the pictorial view we have unconsciously come to assume toward the world of subjective actuality or in relation to the organisms with which we constitute a common species and with which, being subjectively akin, we are organically identical. If phylogenetic theory accounts for the deflections from reality of the reactions of consciousness in the large, it does not account for the deflections of consciousness in the particular reactions of the personality that determine our relations to our individual fellows. Thus far we have considered this absolute system comprising our personal basis only in relation to the objective world or to the world of things; we have not yet considered it subjectively or in relation to the individuals with whom a common affectivity renders us organically identical. It is only within the subjective sphere of our affects, representing man's organic racial continuum, that this distortion of our outlook is manifested in its deepest poignancy.

It is, therefore, only in its ontogenetic mode that we may fully realize the organic deviations within the consciousness of man, due to his bidimensional and unreal apperception of his fellows, and to his consequently false inferences resultant upon an artificially remote and pictorial attitude toward them. It is here alone, I believe, that is to be traced the philosophy of the deflections observable in the above-mentioned reaction of personal resistance as it appears not only in the difform reaction characterizing the isolated personality of the neurotic individual, but also in the uniform reactions presented in the *relatively no less deflected group-expressions comprising the collective personality of the social consensus*. It has become more and more clear to me that it is this error of our mental refraction, due to the subjective deflection comprising the bidimensional judgment of each in assuming a pictorial rather than a real relationship to others, that is the essence of our resistances. In this surface reflection, that is the personal attitude of each toward every other and that embodies the psychology of our resistances, is represented man's traditional systematization, both individual and social. For, in judging or viewing life on the *absolute* basis of how it appears to *me*, I automatically render it beholden to my personal interpretation of it. In my autocratic attitude of onlooker I necessarily repudiate the inherency of the individual or object looked on. Thus, as the self-assumed centre of the universe, the individual is completely detached psychically from the organic actuality of everything within his observation, and, in his present mental attitude, whatever he thinks that he knows and feels is unconsciously constrained by the illusory supremacy of his personal wish. This is the insidious fallacy of the reflected aspect. This constitutes the personal absolute or systematization which, in dominating our present mode of consciousness, completely distorts the universe of reality. It is such a reflective attitude of personalism and unconsciousness that is our exclusion of data that lie outside the system intrinsic to ourselves and that may be included only in the fuller comprehension of an organic relativity.

This reflective attitude entails an autocratic interpretation of life on the basis of one's own personal evaluation, and its effect is to sever the natural bond between the elements of the societal body. As the inevitable concomitant of this habitually reflective attitude toward life there is mental dissociation rather than an assimilative participation such as may only be realized in the inclusiveness of consciousness as an organic whole. Only an organic coalescence in our common affectivity, as contrasted with our present attitude of detached, bidimensional perception of one another, will open the course to spontaneous development in yielding the natural way to the instinct of mating and reproduction wherein alone is the basis of a constructive societal life. For resistance is of the affective life. It is a phenomenon that is essentially organic in that it marks an obstruction within the societal personality of man in the relation *inter se* of the elements, individual and social, of which our societal personality is composed. In our blind inversion of the essential processes of life, we fail to recognize that there can be no healthful growth of the organism apart from the soil to which it is indigenous. If isolation and an artificial medium are death to the growth of vegetation, they are death no less to the societal instinct of our common consciousness in which is found the natural medium for the growth and activity of man. In the measure in which we allow ourselves to participate in and become intrinsic and contributory elements in the world of organic actuality about us, will our pictorial mode of envisagement yield place to the subjective experience of a dimensional inclusiveness that is complete in its actuality. To view the world of actuality in its merely static, cross-sectional appearance is to know only the photography of life. Its kinetic reality may be known only through the subjective inclusion of our organic participation in it.

We cannot return too often to original sources in repudiating conceptions whereof they are the basis. We experience reality only in the measure in which we disavow the symbols of unreality. In proportion as we apprehend subjective fallacy may we encompass the reality underlying it. It is where our conceptual constructions of life leave off that our constructive conceptions of life begin. We have seen that the mathematicians have come to regard as theoretically worthless those objective calculations whose standards of evaluation are not measured in accordance with the principle of an inclusive relativity. Likewise a formulation of values in the subjective sphere of consciousness lacks an adequate principle of evaluation if it does not rest upon the relative principle comprising the organic and inclusive conception of consciousness in its societal totality.

If, in the dissociation of the consciousness of man from his organic individuality, he is unconsciously assuming a personal absolute that is merely a reflection of the mass absolute assumed by the collective social unconscious about him, then what we call the consciousness of man with its presumable function of dependable evaluation is at all times but a system of images, and his vaunted prerogative of a personal absolute is only a dissociative reaction due to his own secondarily adaptive systematization. Upon this basis, what we call our opinions are, after all, not our opinions, and our so-called beliefs are not beliefs at all. For all our formulations and systematizations with respect to human consciousness are but rationalizations serving as convenient foils for the blind assertion of the personal absolutism that is but the autocratic prerogative of our own dissociation, both individual and social.

While theoretically, the objective findings of Freud are of unquestionable validity throughout, as has been fully corroborated through the repeated investigations of those of us who have studied the manifestations of the unconscious in ourselves and in others, my researches within the last years have convinced me that our objective finding is not the point—that what we have called the objective evidence has been all along but our personal or adaptive evidence and that, being unconsciously based upon habitual bidimensional inference, this basis has no relation whatever to life in its organic inclusiveness. The system of Freud is thus adequate only on the adaptive basis of normality. *By normality I mean the consensus comprising the personal absolute vested in the unconscious of the collective mind determining the social average.*

It is disconcerting, I know, now that we have but recently settled ourselves to enjoy in comfort the established principles of Freud's psychology, to think that we may be compelled through the requirements of wider accommodation to seek other ground. Nevertheless, if the position in which we have settled to study the complexes of men is itself just another complex of the social mind whereof the individual mind we would study is but a reproduction, it is clear that we have no choice but to recognize the autonomy of our absolutistic values of reckoning and to readjust our measures of consciousness in accordance.

Surely, if the whole meaning of our mental orientation is a disorientation, if our rationality is everywhere but irrationality, if with all of us alike the vicarious image comprising the reflection of our systematized selves takes precedence over the native reality of our primary organic individuality, there is no other course than that we wipe the board clean and approach the problem of consciousness completely anew. For, clearly, since our present process of mentation is not spontaneous or from within out, it is necessarily adaptive or from without in. Hence, as the reflection of the absolute principle that is the personal basis of each, it can never lead to a realization of the relativity of our conscious life nor to the acceptance of the organic individuality that is the all-embracing life of man in the inclusive principle wherein alone his consciousness truly resides.

It is the position of this thesis that, when we neglect to take account of the *organic mass consciousness of man* to which the personal systems of men, single and collective, are but relative, we fail to reckon with a significant dimension entering into the determination of the subjective life of man. On the basis of the time-space extension of the astronomers' fourth dimension it is possible to compute errors of deflection only through a conception of the universe which regards our own planetary system as a function of and hence relative to a more encompassing programme of planetary motion. Concomitantly, it is possible to evaluate accurately man's place in the subjective scheme of consciousness only through a conception which regards his present personal and social absolute as being itself relative to a more comprehensive background comprising the relativity of man's consciousness as a whole. There is the need to recognize that in the sphere of consciousness, as in the realm of physics, it is in the kinetic dimension comprising the organic participation and inclusiveness of life itself that consists the functional component which actuates the other three dimensions and which, in uniting all, embodies the relativity of consciousness as an organic reality.

In this transition from bidimensional picture to tridimensional actuality, from contemplation of aspect to participation of function, a gulf is spanned that bridges a most significant hiatus in the course of man's evolution. It is no less an interval than that which separates the mode of man's unconsciousness from the mode of his consciousness. For in this transition we are no longer dealing with the mere static dimension of the pictorially reflected *image* of actuality, but there enters the kinetic extension of an organic inclusiveness corresponding to the functional or space-time extension of the physicists' universe of relativity—a universe which, in the psychological no less than in the physical sphere, entails the abrogation of our prevailing system of absolutism and its replacement through the conception of the relativity of the conscious life as a whole.

With a view to measuring the deflections of personality, by and large, in the light of the relativity of consciousness, it is necessary that they be regarded first in the concrete expression of their individual and social forms, and that subsequently we study these aberrations of consciousness in the yet wider expression of their sociological implications generally.

CHAPTER III

THE ORIGIN OF OUR INDIVIDUAL UNCONSCIOUS

IN the preceding chapter I attempted to indicate the analogy between the principle of relativity as set forth by the physicists and what I described as the principle of relativity in the sphere of consciousness. If the bipolar concomitance there outlined in its phylogenetic aspect possesses sufficient warrant, a no less consistent parallelism should be traceable in an ontogenetic concurrence of the two theories as we come to consider the principle of the relativity of consciousness in its individual implications.

If it is true in an ethnic comparison of mental values that a basis of absolutism is no more tenable in computing aberrations occurring in the sphere of consciousness than in the sphere of physics, it must also be true that a basis of absolute evaluation is inadequate to account for deflections of consciousness in its individual application. It is admitted that in the physical universe a principle of absolutism requires to be abandoned and a revaluation of standards established in its stead because it fails to take account of data extrinsic to its own static dimensions. Likewise, it would seem that, in the concomitant sphere of consciousness, an absolute basis of determination would be equally inadequate to reckon with data exclusive of its own absolute principle of measure and that, accordingly, there is here too demanded a restatement of values in terms of a more comprehensive conception.

In such an outlook the requisite readjustment is of so wide a scope that I do not find it easy to contemplate, far less to actualize. It involves no less a task than that of placing the fulcrum of one's mental processes upon a basis that lies outside the habitual domain of one's individual consciousness. For this reason the conception of the organic inclusiveness of consciousness, here understood, is, from our present individualistic viewpoint, a most difficult and elusive one. It is a conception that is not possible of comprehension on the basis of the static and absolute principle of consciousness that is our present mode of evaluation. In this conception, the evolution of individual knowledge enters the organismic sphere of the relative and subjective. It is only relatively, therefore, or through our subjective identification with it that we may participate in its meaning. As this subjective experience is the flux of life itself, as it is this component that is consciousness in process—the organic tide whose stream we ourselves are, the while we are carried along upon it—this experience is an extension which is, of its essence, inaccessible to objective cognition. This is the veil which life in its subjective reality draws across its features, rendering their meaning for ever imperceptible to objective observation. Except through the faint intimations of analogy, I cannot, of course, claim to do more than merely indicate the existence of this subjective extension. So that I must ask the reader to concede me the fullest measure of his hospitality by following my trend with the utmost intuitive participation on his own part. It is, after all, only in common that we may sense our common part in respect to the relativity of consciousness as a whole.

The child that is born amid the cultural influences of civilization comes at an early age to learn the names of things. With these labels he acquires his objective identification with the world about him. In these symbols are the talismans that insure the safety of his future wayfaring. They are indispensable to his proper equipment and an early adeptness in their use is a wise and salutary provision. In this same school in which the child is taught the handy designations for the objects surrounding him, he learns also to recognize the nameless signs of a certain immanent category called "right and wrong "—signs which, through the accidental empiricism of spontaneous trial and error, he comes likewise to sense and gradually to incorporate into the code of his adaptation.

As with others, who have been inured to a curriculum of daily adaptation from the impressionable years of earliest childhood, so with ourselves, it is well-nigh impossible to study the virgin soil of consciousness from our present adaptive premise without vitiating our conclusions with the bias of our own adaptation. And yet it is clear that an analysis of the reactions of consciousness, which fails to include the primary elements of which it is composed, leaves out of reckoning the basic ingredients of a structure which we are supposedly analyzing in its elementary content.

For the past three years I have been occupied with the daily challenge of my own habitual processes of adaptation—an inventorial procedure, be it said, which proved of the utmost discomfort in the necessity it disclosed for the fundamental reduction of personal assessments. The outlook of these inquiries, even though they mark as yet but the merest beginnings, will at least denote a tendency that cannot, I think, be without interest nor, I hope, without incentive in the further approach of others toward an envisagement of consciousness in its ultimate, pre-adaptive composition.

The present study, then, forms part of the altered conceptual insight into consciousness that was gradually induced through the spontaneous sequence of a long continued and uninterrupted experiment in individual reaction. The experiment consisted in repeatedly testing the personal reflex under the hourly present conditions of mood-variation due to the accidental release of affective stimuli arising from circumstantial and unpredictable sources both internal and external to the ego. The un-

OUR INDIVIDUAL UNCONSCIOUS

prepossessing details of this brief excursion into the underworld of personal motivation must be reserved for some subsequent chapter. I am now concerned with the complete shift of basis which these experiments have forced me to take account of in my attempts to reckon with the recurring problems of consciousness as they are presented in the daily routine of my analytic work.

Within the scope of the present thesis we shall have to do solely with the mental reaction inculcated under the manifesto of our early induced presentiment of " right and wrong " or of " good and bad " with its concomitant incitement to *hope* or *fear* as reflected in the unconscious attitude of *praise* or *blame* surrounding the child. It is my conviction, based on the subjective test of personal experimentation, *that the deeply entrenched root of our human pathology is to be traced alone to the conflict incurred through this suggestively induced image of right and wrong and that it is profitless, therefore, to seek beyond the impasse of this unconscious alternative for the ultimate source of neurotic reactions.*[1]

Because of some element implicit in the behaviour determining the " right " or " wrong " adaptation of the individuals surrounding the child in the formative period of his early growth, something is imposed upon him that operates to check spontaneous impulse. The check I am speaking of does not consist in the interdiction itself. Our admonitory " do " or " don't " is in itself quite harmless. Indeed these positive and negative commands may serve an undoubtedly useful end. I have never known of untoward nervous manifestations occurring among animals because of the restraining warnings of maternal solicitude. On the contrary, such mediation commonly proves an effective safeguard against misadventure. Of the inhibiting influence itself, therefore, I am not speaking. What I have in mind is something

[1] " Our Mass Neurosis," *The Psychological Bulletin*, Vol. 23, No. 6, June, 1926.

far subtler than this. It will demand our most searching scrutiny if we are clearly to apprehend its meaning.

As I see this miscarriage of instinct incurred through our embargo of good and bad, it is the cunning *pretence* underlying the interdiction which induces the reaction that works mischief in the child's organism. It is the insidious intimation of benefit or of harm inherent in the tabooed act itself that is the pernicious instance. The destructive occasion lies in the implied premium or forfeit appertaining to the act as it recoils upon the child in automatic retaliation. I believe that it is due to this enforced superstition of an arbitrary " good and bad " that there have been wrought the spurious reactions of our human consciousness. I believe that the utterly specious system of behaviour, which surrounds us as social beings on every hand, is definitely due to this falsely imbued suggestion of retributive sequence which, as commonly inculcated in early childhood, has been prompted through the implied mediation of invisible moral agencies. I furthermore believe that it is this pretence, and its unconsciousness, that is the basis of our adaptation, both individual and social, as embodied in the artificial code of morality represented in the collective unconscious of our present-day civilization.

What the adult arbiter of the child really has up his sleeve is the child's conformity to *him* and *his* convenience. Accordingly, the parent or guardian lays down the proposition that a good little boy doesn't destroy costly bric-à-brac or that only a bad little girl would play in the mud with her nice clean rompers on. Both these postulates are utterly false as every sponsor for them knows. But that is not the point. The point is that such statements are incomparably adapted to the ends of adult commodity. The truer rendering of the proposition in either instance would be to the effect that the misdemeanour in question would occasion inconvenience or chagrin to the parent. But so sincere a statement on the part of the parent might alienate the

OUR INDIVIDUAL UNCONSCIOUS

child's jealously coveted affection, as we commonly term the infantile dependence we secretly tend to beget. Hence, the real motive of interdiction must be hidden from the child and a comprehensive edict cunningly invoked such as will place an effectual check upon him and yet amply safeguard the parental interest. It is this bogus morality which, by our unconscious social consent, the conscripted phantom called " good and bad " is unanimously commissioned to represent.

Because of this attitude of pretence in others whereby the child is tricked into complicity with the prevalent code about him, there is begotten this self-same reaction of pretence within him. This illusion that is in the air he learns to assimilate from others through imitative affinity, and from now forward the ruse becomes self-operative. What began as a social coup is continued as an individual policy. The silent intimation of a mysteriously pervasive immanence of " good and bad " having now been engendered, the child henceforth responds automatically, not alone to the signals of make-believe about him but to the signals of make-believe within him. For in unconsciously succumbing to the contagion of the autocratic system of " right and wrong " about him, this hobgoblin of arbitrary make-believe becomes equally systematized within his own consciousness. Accordingly, the pretence involved in interdictions of conduct (fear-blame reaction) is accompanied by the mental suggestion of " wrong " or " bad," and the pretence underlying the inducements of conduct (hope-praise reaction) is accompanied by the mental suggestion of " right " or " good "—*that is, of good or bad as it reverts upon the individual from the point of view of his personal advantage as reflected in the image of the parent.*

An analysis, however, does not reach elementary principles if it merely discovers motives prompted by suggestion and repression corresponding to the two opposed factors of inducement and interdiction actuating human behaviour. It is not enough to invoke in explanation the sweeping denominator "self-consciousness." Such an account is historic or psychological; it is not organic or biological. It is, I believe, only as we unearth the mental reaction *intrinsic* to the organism when it responds to the subjective inference of right or wrong in its personal inflection that we shall reach the basic element responsible for the organism's inhibited mental states.[1]

One would think, as we look about us to-day at the utterly destructive processes, social and political, that have been incited throughout entire nations of individuals " brought up " in this vicarious fashion, that the spectacle would give us pause. But we have had a too thorough bringing-up ourselves. Our own bringing-up has seen to it that we shall not look about us and learn what *is* but that we shall only respond to the suggestion about us and acquiesce in what *seems*. If we should really look about us and see unflinchingly into the meaning of things, our children would do so too, but that would be subversive of their proper up-bringing. This is the self-contradictory element in the adult's "education" of the child. In truth, it is not possible to " bring up " a child at all. One may let a child grow up, naturally, as a plant, tending only the soil about its roots, or one may hinder its growth. But to bring a child up by moulding its personality to one's own is organically contradictory. A child comes up, if at all, only of himself or in accordance with the law of his own growth.

If it is true, then, that this factor of pretence is the ultimate element in the dissociations of consciousness, what is the nature of this factor of pretence actuating our behaviour? As has been said, in order to secure a substratum adequate to build upon, it is requisite that we forgo at the outset our present conceptions based upon a system of valuations which presupposes an absolute principle of consciousness. It should be understood,

[1] "The Reabsorbed Affect and Its Elimination," *British Journal of Medical Psychology*, Vol. VI, Part 3.

therefore, that it is from the fundamentally altered premise of a relative basis of consciousness that the present thesis sets out.

In an objective view of the components of man's consciousness, it may be seen that there are three determinants of the affective life, namely, one's own self, the selves by whom one is surrounded, and the positive or negative reactions of the self in respect to other selves such as comprise our progressive or regressive interrelationships one to another. So that, to return to the analogy of the physical world, a diagram outlining man's affective life would represent a contour of three components. There is first the dimension consisting of oneself; second, the collateral dimension, with its extension backward to one's parents and forward to one's offspring and comprising in general one's social congeners, singly and collectively; and third, the societal extension representing the reactions that depend upon the co-ordination or non-co-ordination of individuals in the assimilative processes of their common activities. Thus our subjective or affective life, statically considered, is as truly tridimensional in its actuality as our cognitive or objective world, statically considered, is tridimensional in its actuality. Nevertheless, as was pointed out in the preceding chapter, our cognitive apprehension of the world of objects about us invariably presents an outline corresponding to the bidimensional or pictorial aspect that is our perceptual image of it. So in the subjective sphere, it may also be shown that our affective reactions invariably present a pictorial or bidimensional plane analogous to the bidimensional impressions comprising our objective perceptions, and that they are due in the subjective as in the objective sphere to the unconscious factor of the personal equation.

But, to adhere to the test of experiment, it has been my analytic experience growing out of the study of personal reaction that, owing to the distortion of affect within our actual daily life, we do not in fact participate in the tridimensional actuality that truly comprises our affective world. On the contrary, owing to the rebuff to spontaneous impulse incurred through the system of self-conscious diplomacy reflected in the social pretence of "right and wrong" as first voiced by the parent and seconded on all sides by the community about us, the real world of affects is unconsciously replaced by an artificial cosmogony whose outline is limited to only two components, namely, the self plus the immediate interest to the self as derived from the selves (collateral dimension) by whom the individual is surrounded (advantage or disadvantage, good or bad, praise or blame). Thus our affective reactions invariably present a merely pictorial or bidimensional area corresponding to the two extensions comprising the personal element of the self plus the element of advantage for the self from other selves. Because of this personal foreshortening of our affects to the artificial dimensions of self and self-interest, our subjective experience of tridimensional actuality is reported not in the reality of its three essential determinants but in the pictorial aspect of the two-dimensional plane that is our personal and autogenous reflection of it. It is, then, the substance of these pages that, just as the world of cubic actuality is mentally foreshortened into a bidimensional aspect of actuality determined by our static and autogenous perception of it, so our world of affects is correspondingly reduced to the bidimensional or pictorial aspect that is our socially reflected impression of it.

This brings us again to the question we were speaking of—the reaction of pretence into which the child is early inducted. It was to help clear away the difficulties surrounding this early adaptive reaction of our subjective life that I turned to the consideration of the dimensional components that comprise our affective world. We have seen that the essence of this element of pretence is its implication of retroactive gain or loss intrinsic to the social act itself and automatically returning upon its

OUR INDIVIDUAL UNCONSCIOUS   59

agent. Coming a little closer still, we see that this attitude of behaviour imposed upon the child upon grounds of its retributive sequence is induced in him through the cunningly conveyed intimation that such has been the personal experience of those about him—that they have learned from experience and so are qualified to give warning that " good " behaviour is requited in reward or pleasure to one's self and conversely " bad " behaviour is requited in penalty or pain to one's self.

My position is that an attitude toward the child which posits at the outset of life a world of affective actuality, comprised of his own *ego* plus his own egoistic advantage, arbitrarily contracts life to the unreal aspect of a mere two-dimensional image. It is to dispose the mind of the child in such a way that its entire universe of feeling is limited to a mere picture of life consisting of the flat and lifeless image of his personal or social adaptation in the light of his personal or social gain. It transforms the reality of life into a reflection of oneself in a world of self-reflections like one's own. In other words, in falsely premising the bidimensional plane of one's personal image as the basis of actuality, we substitute at the outset a primary condition of unreality for the inherent reality of life.

From the altered angle of a relative and inclusive attitude toward the problems of consciousness, I am led to think that this artificially contracted outlook is the real crux of the dilemma of the unconscious. I have come to think that these two factors—the factor of oneself and the factor of social advantage for oneself—are insufficient, that there is omitted a third factor essential to a completely rounded consciousness and that in the absence of it the other two present but a static and artificial image of life rather than life in the functional inclusiveness of its full-dimensional reality. I refer to the component of our societal co-ordination—to the factor of man's organic continuum in the functional extension of his interrelationship with others. I believe that it is the miscarriage of instinct with respect to this societal co-ordination that is answerable for the artificial recoil of self-interest represented in our fancied apparitions of good or bad as seen from the limited point of view of one's individual advantage. In the flat bidimensional plane which, in the absence of the inclusive societal factor, only reflects the pictorial aspect of actuality in the image of the self, there is lacking the rounded extension that is the full complement of life in its inclusive, societal meaning. To what degree we substitute this reflected aspect of life for the reality of an all-inclusive participation in life in its full-dimensional extension—if my own experience in this regard is any guide—has not as yet begun to be suspected by us.

This primary societal component of consciousness must not be confused with our secondary and adaptive social relationships. Our social adaptation is as self-reflective and unconscious as our individual adaptation. By the societal component I mean the organic continuity of consciousness that unites the individuals of the species into a confluent whole. In the social adaptation of its members, on the contrary, there is registered merely the collective response to the reaction of pretence that we have just seen in its individual expression as our personal foreshortening of life to the bidimensional image. In the reduction of life to the image of self in the light of one's self-advantage, whether individual or social, consists the adaptive system that is the personal pretence within and about us. In this inversion of life that is the mirrored impression of each, as reflected in the aspect of others, is the systematization that is man's unconsciousness. It is our non-inclusiveness of others that is the systematization of each. It is this perceptual interpretation of life on the basis of a reflected or bidimensional impression, limiting life to self and self's advantage that is, I repeat, the meaning of our unconsciousness, both individual and social.

In studying this reaction of pretence in the social mind

OUR INDIVIDUAL UNCONSCIOUS

as reflected in the reactions of the individual, we are met with the need of a fundamental reconstruction of values in our reckoning with human personality as in our measures of consciousness generally. For, in this artificial gauge of conduct measured by standards of personal advantage, we find established in the individual a criterion of life that rests upon an unwarranted assumption of personal supremacy. This private criterion has become the arbitrarily assumed prerogative of each of us with respect to every other. For, through this distortion of the universe of reality into the unreal, bidimensional cosmogony that is one's self-reflection of it, there is unconsciously built up within us a mental adaptation whose basis is an inflexible assumption of personal absolutism and autocracy.

In the ultimate reduction of analysis it may be seen that what we have, through Freud's teaching, come to recognize as the reaction of *resistance*, within the individual personality, resolves itself into nothing else than this private prerogative of the personal absolute. The assumption of this personal principle of absolutism in the subjective sphere embodying the psychology of resistance is analogous to the absolute principle of evaluation applied to the physical universe—a principle which the physicists have lately shown is not competent to meet the test of universal applicability, for the reason that, in the absolutism of its own premise, it fails to account for data extrinsic to the static absolutism it embodies. Correspondingly, in the sphere of consciousness the absolute principle of personal evaluation comprising the adaptive basis of the individual is inadequate to stand as the universal principle requisite to an organismic inclusion of consciousness in its societal totality.

As was pointed out in the last chapter, the social mind interprets its objects of perception in the bidimensional aspect of its own pictorial and flat reflection of them. Likewise, our individual mentation, in its adaptive response to the retributive implications of so-called " right and wrong " or " good and bad," recoils no less upon a two-dimensional plane in the affective reaction that is limited to the component of self plus the component of pleasure or pain for oneself. This flat, static impression of life, comprising the arbitrary systematization that is the personal absolute of each, is inadequate to stand as a universal principle whereby we may evaluate the phenomena of consciousness in the full round of its organic compass.

In substituting the judicial absolute of personal interest for our inclusive participation as relative elements in the full-dimensional reality of life as a whole, we have unconsciously adopted a basis which fails to reckon with our individual selves as contributory elements in the more encompassing unit which our individualistic basis now mistakenly presumes to include. Our present basis is, therefore, not an inclusive one. In so far as the individual rests his theory of consciousness upon an individualistic basis, his theory cannot include the larger whole wherein the individual is himself but a contributing element. The consciousness of the isolated individual cannot encompass consciousness in its societal inclusiveness. Only consciousness in its societal inclusiveness can encompass the consciousness of the individual.

In the measure in which we, as an organic group, come to adopt the conception of consciousness that accepts the intrinsic reality of our common societal life, we shall learn to repudiate the personal absolute that is our individual resistance and, correspondingly, to participate in an inclusiveness of consciousness with respect to which the individual is but a relative and adaptive component.

CHAPTER IV

THE UNCONSCIOUS FACTOR WITHIN THE SOCIAL SYSTEM

WHATEVER is true of the individual singly, is true of the individual collectively. Whatever is observable as neurotic process within the isolated personality of the hysteric or precoid, is equally observable as neurotic process in the collective personality of the social mind. The attitude of psychopathology, which ascribes to the social consensus, represented in the average-reaction commonly called "normality," a criterion of constructive consciousness and health, and which, accordingly, seeks to correct the deflections of the aberrant neurotic personality in accordance with this limited outlook, is itself an expression of the bidimensional limitation that bases its system of consciousness upon an absolute principle of evaluation. After all, normality, like gravitation, is a mental abstraction. Our consensual normality is but the systematized abstraction embodying the absolute of its own unconscious basis, and, in its personal absolutism, stands opposed to a principle of relativity in the mental sphere. It is only as we abrogate the absolute standards now vested in the prevailing social systems about us and measure their dimensions in terms of the principle of an organic relativity, that we shall be enabled to challenge the element of personal systematization within ourselves and so encompass life in the actuality of a universal and inclusive consciousness.

Personal survival has been, from the beginning of man's history, the chief concern of his self-interest. Inventing medicine with a view to his security here, fabricating religion with a view to his security hereafter, he has safeguarded his preservation for the moment through recourse to " cure," and for the future through recourse to " salvation." Even in the interchanges of our casual social relationships, there is still preserved within the folk-mind the vestiges of this dualistic self-interest. Upon our meeting, it is the accustomed reaction to make mutual inquiry into the condition of health of one another. " How are you ? " or " How-do-you-do ? " we ask. Similarly, in parting we commend each other to the clemencies of the future with the expression, " Good-bye," that is, " God be with you." In the obvious apprehensiveness underlying this unconscious attitude of the social mind there is in one instance the implicit conviction that we are wicked and in the other that we are sick ! Both these reactions, however, merely betray the state of anxiety reflected in the fundamental condition of mind that is our ethnic self-consciousness.

In earlier times these two anxiety trends of the folk unconscious were duly sponsored through the common rites of medical and religious fetish under the combined auspices of a single functionary or guardian who, as priest or soothsayer, dispensed the benefits accruing from both. The fact is, I suppose, that the tribal medicine-man with his magic potion and amulet is psychologically, as well as ethnologically, our true progenitor. For to-day we observe the preservation of this concomitance of function between the two systems, represented by the science of medicine on the one hand and by the philosophy of religion on the other, in the current social phenomenon of our widely flourishing " sciences of mental healing " with their unescapable unconsciousness in metaphysical and theosophical implications. Aside, however, from historical analogies, the stupendous influence upon the societal mind of ecclesiastical and therapeutic canon cannot be denied.

Because of this preservation in our midst of such ancient repositories of human thought and conduct as are represented in the affiliated principles contained in the dogmas of church and psychotherapeutic system, a consideration of the psychology common to both these forms of our social adaptation cannot fail to help us understand the basic elements that enter into the making of our social personality. As illustration, let us consider on the one hand the Roman Church and on the other the system of psychoanalysis. The Roman Church represents at one and the same time both traditionally the longest established and politically the most compact organization of the many religious sects existing throughout our Western civilization. The system of psychoanalysis, representing as it does the most modern conception of medical psychology, possesses such scientific authority as only the ablest students of philosophy and medicine are qualified to bring to the substantiation of its principles. An analysis, therefore, of the social psychology that equally underlies and actuates the position of both these systems will not, I think, be without profit in the present study.

Due to the sophistication that was early begotten among the members of our human species through the limitation of man's consciousness to the bidimensional alternative of a consensual " good and bad," it is natural that we should find this same tendency to personal systematization expanded into the collective or social form we observe in the group reaction that is embodied in state or sect. Thus, from an organismic viewpoint, we should expect to discover the same resistances within the social as within the individual organism. Nor need we be surprised if, upon analysis, it should be disclosed that this social resistance represents likewise the bidimensional impasse comprised of our personal self-reflection.

Throughout the unconscious period of man's bidimensional arrest commonly called ancient times, a period belonging chronologically to the past but pertaining psychologically to the present as well as to the future for probably an indefinite term, the attitude of the Church toward incipient doubt or heresy was, is and for ever shall be to apply the remedy of prayer and, failing this recourse, to apply the penalty of excommunication.

From the vantage point of the psychoanalyst's disinterested and extrinsic angle of vision, such a policy appears manifestly unsound and without warrant. From his position of detached observer, it seems to him arbitrary and presumptive. And yet it must be conceded that, from the intrinsic viewpoint of a socially consolidated organization compact with the autogenous authority of infallibility, such a position is by no means inconsistent. A supremacy that is self-originated is self-operative. Autocratic prerogative and unimpeachable authority are here conterminous. Indeed the solidarity of the Church is unassailable precisely in that its premise and its conclusion are mutually inclusive. For inasmuch as both premise and conclusion are equally based upon the assumption of the personal absolute or the private prerogative of the system they embody, all access to it is summarily barred. If the Church precludes all question, dismisses all opposition, it is wholly within its self-determined rights. For by these same tokens all question, all argument, being of its nature extrinsic to its autogenic system, savours *de facto* of the aforesaid heresy of doubt and, as such, is automatically driven out of court as connoting *a priori* the presumptive fallacy of trespass. This relegation to itself of divine and hence unquestionable authority is the theological doctrine of self-actuative truth assumed by the Church to underlie its official pronunciamentos when it formally declares them to be *ex cathedra*.

I offer this preamble not without advisement. In its intimation of the heretical tendency of the present thesis, it will give to those to whom such tendency is unwelcome the opportunity to seal their ears against it. At the same time it will give to those of more pliant sympathies due notice of the undisguised aim of the present inquiry toward the adoption of a more comprehensive and open-minded outlook among us. For the trend of this thesis is in its intention confessedly subversive of the socially authorized version of truth now vested in the autogenous systematization that has come to underlie the principle of us psychoanalysts.

I do not know to what extent it is humanly possible, but, in so far as may be, let us adopt for the moment, at least mentally, a position of impersonal disinterestedness toward the social consensus in which we ourselves, as psychoanalysts, are also corporate elements. It will then become clear, I think, that the socially authenticated system, representative of us Freudians, embodies an unconscious attitude closely analogous to that of the social system embodied in the attitude of autogenous authority underlying the personal absolutism of the Roman Church.

To observe this element of social unconsciousness underlying the principle of Roman Catholicism has for us all a certain invigorating tang. With such a discovery there comes the refreshing release that is the spur to renewed investigation. It is the heartening response of the organism to its sense of conscious acumen. But, to observe the operation of the social unconscious within the autogenous systematization of principles which insures social coherence within our own consensus, entails a contemplation that is not pleasant. This contemplation disturbs the habitual repose of settled conviction that is our own security. It is to apply the acid test of self-analysis to our own socially systematized assumption of private prerogative and authority. Yet an attitude of impersonal disinterestedness presupposes that our inquiry shall proceed without regard to personal security. This attitude, indeed, is one which we ourselves have demanded of our patients as being an analytically basic one. It is, therefore, upon this understanding alone that an inquiry, which in its disregard of the personal equation is committed to a course equally unflattering to us all, may hope to be accorded an unbiased consideration. Surely in any other attitude the name of psychoanalyst can become only a term of opprobrium among us.

Let us, then, consider this factor of private prerogative or of the personal absolute, inseparable from the mental attitude expressed in the phenomenon of social systematization which we see in the Church's position of assumed infallibility toward its postulants, and seek to discover whether this same tendency to social systematization may not lurk within our own psychoanalytic ranks. Let us see whether we, too, are not actuated by an unconscious element of personal absolutism that obstructs the freer and more adult mode of consciousness such as it is our avowed aim to attain.

In mentioning the unconscious element of absolutism constituting the closed compartment within a socially organized system of principles, I have cited Catholicism merely as a convenient paradigm. Protestantism or Mohammedanism are, in their assumption of self-appointed prerogative, not less indefensible on the same ground, for the element of the personal absolute underlies no less the private assumption of each. By reason of its higher degree of organization, however, Catholicism more fittingly illustrates the absolutism of its social polity in relation to this phenomenon of doubt or defection occurring among its members. This is its aptness in affording a convenient position of comparison with our own socially organized system of psychoanalysis in respect to the phenomenon of defection as envisaged by us.

Within the body of precepts comprising our own organization, the accepted mark of defection is a *resistance*, and the remedy we apply is analysis. For, with ourselves, analysis is explicitly the only effective means of overcoming the intractable tendencies which, in the determination of our organized principles of adjudication, constitute the sole need of our patient. In the event that the patient should remain so far recalcitrant as not to embrace the opportunity we offer him to accept our socially systematized interpretation of truth as it touches his own particular needs, he is automatically excluded from participation in the agencies of regeneration such as it is our special delegation to dispense. Whence there follows our regrettable but none the less inevitable ultimatum of " inferior type of personality " and his coincident elimination from the pale.

It is, of course, clear that the actuality of the phenomenon of resistance in the patient can no more be denied than the actuality of the phenomenon of doubt in the penitent. Moreover, in accordance with the ruling of psychoanalysis, our specification of the condition when we posit a resistance is as indisputable as is the specification of the Church when it posits a doubt as the underlying disorder of the individual postulant. In either case there is the position that the individual is impervious to the benefits of the system whose principles he is, in the judgment of the system, in need of embracing. Indeed, it is precisely this factor of doubt in the one case, as it is the factor of resistance in the other, that is the whole occasion of the individual's quest of a means of adjusting this division within his personality whereof doubt or resistance is the idiopathic index.

The actual fact, then, of a resistance within the personality is beyond question. The fact is one that is equally admitted on the side of the individual as on the side of the organization, on the side of the defendant as on the side of the arraignment. But what is to be done about it does not as yet seem to me by far so clearly determined. I know, of course, that it is our attitude, based upon the repeated experience of us all, that any objection to psychoanalysis is invariably traceable to the resistance of the objector. This is a psychoanalytic corollary. It is accepted as universal among us all. So that a resistance to psychoanalysis is very justly, in the view of psychoanalysts, as self-convicting as is a doubt in the view of the Church. And from the point of view of psychoanalysis no less than of the Church the position of these two systems rests upon an undoubtedly sound basis, if we may be guided by the consensus of their several adherents as attested by the experience of each.

But the question which has of late come to engross my interest is *whether these points of view are sound as embodied in their respective systems*—whether, from a broader basis of envisagement, the intrinsic attitude of ourselves may not lend itself to an altered interpretation; whether there may not exist a criterion that transcends the scope of our present analytic outlook when we claim that the only possible motive for questioning our psychoanalytic position is found to lie in the resistance of the individual; whether, in brief, the socially entrenched systematization comprising the psychoanalytic affiliation possesses sufficient warrant for impugning the personally entrenched systematization comprising the individual. For, if the fallacy of the personal absolute underlies the systematization represented in the social consensus, in what way does the rigidity of the social prerogative differ from the systematized prerogative constituting the resistance of the individual ?[1]

For the purposes of our inquiry we shall be obliged to dismiss for the moment our habitual personalistic criteria of interpretation. We shall have to recognize, first of all, that what we call the individual is by no means the fresh and native expression of individuality pure and simple that we are accustomed to assume, but rather that he is an individuation resulting from the repressive forces acting upon him from the environmental social aggregate in which he is himself but an intrinsic and contributory element. For every individual arising amid the influences of the social system is but a special application of the social system about him. Whatever the code of the consensus, the individual is necessarily but an offprint of it—a new impression of the original by-laws.

---

[1] " Speaking of Resistances," address before the Sixteenth Annual Meeting of the American Psychoanalytic Association, New York City, June 10, 1926. *Psyche*, No. 27, January, 1927.

There is, therefore, the need to turn our attention not to the individuated excerpt of the system but to the original document wherein the system is primarily set forth. There is the need to discard the individual form and to occupy ourselves with the societal mould whereof the individual form is but the subsequent reproduction.

Assuming the broader outlook of this more encompassing sociological position, I think we shall come to see that the difference between the reaction of doubt, as interpreted by the Church, and the reaction of resistance, as interpreted by psychoanalysis, is, after all, only apparent—that the difference is by no means an inherent one, but that it is due merely to the altered circumstance of shade and light, so to speak, in which the two reactions are diversely reflected by reason of the contrasting sociological settings amid which the two phenomena have appeared among us.

As regards the sociological manifestation embodied in the Church, contrary to its age-old contention that doubt or question automatically indicated apostasy which reflexly discredited its adherent, it has long been shown experientially that such doubt or defection might be very logically and honourably entertained. Not only this, but it has been further made manifest that it is due precisely to the entertainment of such an attitude of debate toward the socially systematized consensus, represented in the Church, that there have arisen those far-reaching investigations of science out of which has sprung the splendid renaissance of modern thought with its accompanying incentive to human progress.

Hence the question that presents itself is this : May it not also be that, quite beyond the scope of envisagement of those of us who are intrinsic to the analytic consensus, there are motives inviting question of our position which do not fall within the category of resistance ? May it not be that, from a position of extrinsic or impersonal evaluation, we shall obtain so inclusive a survey of the phenomenon of resistance on the one side and of the social phenomenon of organized systematization representing the establishment on the other, that the two reactions may be included in an encompassment that is equally hospitable to both ? Surely it cannot be denied that, laying aside all consideration of personal involvement, the question of such a possibility is not without its vista of interest.

With a view to a fair appraisement of the contrast between the type of defection manifesting itself as doubt and the type of defection manifesting itself as resistance, there is first the need to take account of the widely dissimilar sociological aspect of the period in which doubt was originally viewed by the Church, as compared with the sociological countenance of the times in which resistance is viewed by ourselves, and, accordingly, to consider the difference between the two phenomena in the light of the contrasting sociological backgrounds surrounding each.

From this sociological angle the factor that immediately attracts our notice is the essentially negative, self-deprecatory character of the doubt-reaction in respect to the ancient dogmas of the Church. We note the sense of personal inadequacy that is its characteristic sign. We mark its habitually shamefaced, self-depreciative mien. For doubt, be it remembered, first arose as the self-accusing attitude of the subservient individual who lived under the social domination of monarchical forms of government in a period of man's history when, owing to his subjugation to the unconscious suzerainty of a fanciful father-complex, he meekly bowed in servile obedience to the socially systematized authority arbitrarily vested in Church and State, as personified in the office of Pope and King. Under the prevalent domination of this image of indisputable authority, men's social criterion resided in the apparent consensus of the *personal absolute*, social and individual, representing the particular individuation of a single man, rather than in the common supremacy of

THE SOCIAL SYSTEM 73

our impersonal relativity comprising the generic individuality of mankind.[1]

But the social mind has in the last few centuries undergone a significant metamorphosis. To-day we have to reckon with this. We have to take into account the tremendous expansion of the consciousness of man sociologically and, from the point of view of the historical record of man's rapid sociological ascent, mark the characterological difference in the temper of the individual's defection to-day as compared with his defection of yesterday. In the implication of the rights of individual freedom of thought implied in the defection of doubt, the predominant factor was the individual's acknowledgment of his personal remissness, of his unseemly presumptiveness toward the social constitution about him. Under the socially systematized autocracy of the Church's absolutism, the individuality of man dared not stand erect and maintain the freedom of his individual expression.

But in the present hour the consciousness of man proclaims itself a freer manifestation. Under the impetus of our sociological progress, man's individuality has more and more come into its own. And, though the socially organized prerogative has still the upper hand in respect to individuality, there are signs abroad to-day which are a significant advertisement of man's urge toward an expression of individuality that is an earnest of yet wider sociological horizons ahead. I think that it is due in no small measure to the advent of this factor of man's sociological rehabilitation that there is seen to-day the completely altered character of the individual's resistance as it recoils before the element of personal absolutism embodied in the systematized consensus of psychoanalysis.

Despite its undoubted unconsciousness and personal systematization, note the essentially ruddier countenance

[1] " The Heroic Rôle—An Historical Retrospect," *Psyche*, No. 25 July, 1926.

of resistance as compared with doubt. A resistance, unlike doubt, is no admission of ineptitude. Subsisting under the sponsorship of a new and freer sociological order, resistance is fashioned of sterner stuff. It is no personal deprecation ; it is a sociological affirmation. Far from being an abject confession of individual weakness, it is a proud assertion of individual strength. For although in the phenomenon of resistance there is to be seen the equally unconscious motive that is the protest of the individual absolute against the arbitrary domination of the socially systematized absolute comprising the popular consensus, there underlies this protest something that is more virile than this. There is here, I believe, a reaction that demands and that will ultimately have the consideration that is its due. Though the Church, while pre-eminent, might easily dispose of doubt, in our own democratic day it is doubt that has disposed of the Church. It seems to me that, unless we psychoanalysts recognize the group-form of unconsciousness underlying the social systematization embodied in the position of psychoanalysis when it pronounces the resistance of the individual as *de facto* anathema, without regard to the possible propriety of its remonstrance, we, like our less conscious analogue, the Church, shall ultimately find ourselves hoist with our own petard.

While the fact of resistance and of its unconscious motivation is admittedly true, yet to meet a patient's assertion of individual right with the mere assertion of the group-right, which is the unconscious protectorate of the organized system, is certainly not to answer the patient's need from the point of view of a larger and more encompassing mode of consciousness. If the assumption of arbitrary prerogative or of the personal absolute represented in the reaction of individual systematization is the meaning of resistance, then the private prerogative or the personal absolute underlying the systematization of the social consensus is no less a manifestation of resistance. For the attitude of systematization and of absolutism in the individual is necessarily but the reflection of a prior social systematization to which the individual's adaptation is but a secondary response.

Clearly it is not possible for the socially systematized consensus embodied in Church, State or psychotherapeutic system to afford the requisite condition of release from a resistance thus constituted, when its own systematization is itself the social or group embodiment of this self-same reaction of resistance. In the nip-and-tuck attitude between the resistance of the system comprising the single individual and the resistance of the system comprising the social corporation of individuals, there stands the organic impasse of two mutually opposed absolutes. In the autocratic position of each neither may yield, for in the absolutism of both each represents an identical state of unconscious impaction. As neither the individual nor the consensus, in its enfolded self-systematization, is as yet conscious of the process in which it is the blindly contributing element, both factors represent but altered aspects of the common delusion of the social adaptation of man, single and collective, namely, the delusion of the supremacy of the will-to-self or the unconscious autocracy of the personal absolute.

Naturally, I cannot speak of these inadequacies of consciousness from a remote or detached position. Needless to say, since I am at this moment a contributing part of this social maelstrom comprising the system about me, I am no less embroiled than others in its social fallacy. So that what is here very inadequately apprehended by me as a theory is, I confess, still less adequately accepted by me as a living, integral experience. Let it not be thought, then, for a moment that, in presenting the social basis of consciousness that is the substance of this thesis, I am under any illusion as to my own inaptness to embody in myself the personal expression of the conception whereof this essay offers the organismic interpretation.

It is, however, only in the measure in which this less

personal mode of approach becomes actual for me that my work with others grows in significance and in constructiveness of purpose. In this light I have come to feel more and more that it is only as we regard life from the point of view of man's generic individuality that we shall truly encompass the meaning of the neurosis; either individual or social, in its true organic assessment. In this more inclusive outlook we shall gradually come to realize, I think, that the neurosis, whether appearing in the arbitrary systematization of the individual or in that of the group consensus, consists essentially in the substitution of the personal absolute that is our secondary individuation for the impersonal relativity that is our primary individuality. In this outlook we shall come to see that it is only in the common inherency of life that is comprised the consciousness of man in the fullness of its meaning.

Resistance, then, is the personal systematization of men as contrasted with the unsponsored individuality of man. The individual unit like the social unit is but an arbitrary system, and in the resistance of each of us is to be seen the self-determined cosmogony that is the individual fallacy of us all. Whether this personal prerogative embodied in a resistance has its expression in the single individual or in the collection of individuals comprising the social aggregate, the factor of systematization holding its guarantee of inalienable rights under the syndicate of our common unconscious, is, I believe, the very kernel of the world-wide dissociation which we now diagnose as the neurosis of the individual.

Thus, through this systematization of each one, there is repudiated the individuality of each other. In the personal absolute of the private consciousness of each, there is denied the relativity of the common consciousness of all. It is this systematization that is the meaning of repression. It is this personal prerogative that is the essence of resistance. And so, in the *unconscious system* that is within and about us there is summed up, I believe, the entire philosophy of the neurosis. Being ourselves intrinsic to the system, both individual and social, it is no more possible to deal with it objectively in its social than in its individual phase. Our only approach is the subjective approach. Only subjectively is it possible for each of us to envisage completely the system of repression within him that is his individual reflection of the social system of repression outside him. In thus relinquishing the absolute principle that is merely the autocracy of our privately arbitrated system of personalism and unconsciousness, we are in a position to forgo the unconscious absolute comprising our own resistance and to accept in its stead the relative inclusiveness of our conscious life as a unified and organic whole.

CHAPTER V

SOCIOLOGICAL IMPLICATIONS OF UNCONSCIOUSNESS FROM A VIEWPOINT OF RELATIVITY

OSCAR WILDE says in one of his plays: "There are in the world two tragedies. One is not getting what one wants and the other is getting it." The epigram is peculiarly apt in telling us what appears, on the surface, to be true. But what appears on the surface to be true is not necessarily true inherently. Unquestionably there are these two fatal antitheses in life and in them undoubtedly is summed up whatever there is of tragedy in our human lot. But, in reducing life to these two issues of getting and of not getting what one wants, we fail to realize that these contrasting reactions are secondary to a condition of mind artificially induced in ourselves at the expense of a prior state of consciousness that is in its essence not antithetic but unitary.

Each of us is born in the midst of an established system whose password is conformity to its prescribed norm. Each of us becomes an automatic compartment within the systematized consensus that comprises its basis. The price of our initiation into this adaptive system is the forfeit of our primary individuality, and by the terms of its automatic statutes tuition is compulsory. Automatic obedience to traditional authority is the retroactive principle of its constitution. "Right" or "wrong" is the slogan of its guild. In the autogenous postulate of good or bad that is its absolute basis, our adaptive system stands rigidly opposed to a conception of truth such as comprises the relative and all-inclusive principle of consciousness in its organismic significance.

In the light of this ulterior motive of good or bad—of

SOCIOLOGICAL IMPLICATIONS 79

this adaptive response that is the secondary and reflected impression of each—is measured the conduct of us all. According as we see ourselves in this mirror of the systematized and prescribed norm is conditioned our happiness or unhappiness, our comfort or displeasure. But always the mirror of each that is the criterion of others stands as a solid wall confronting us. Reflected in the features of this one our bearing is quite pleasing; mirrored in the reaction of that one our countenance is not so prepossessing. And so it happens that, as we go on in life, we tend more and more to place ourselves in positions in which we may obtain the most flattering " likeness " of ourselves. Correspondingly, we tend to avoid those reflectors that distort our features to our own discomforting. In this way we come to " like " some people and to " dislike " others. So that, according to this account of our adaptation, what is called " ourselves " in the vernacular of the system about us is merely the reflection of ourselves as reproduced by the system itself.

In truth, because of the system of personal reflections amid which we move, our judgments are throughout undependable. We have no opinions, we merely reflect opinions. We have no perceptions, we have only pre-perceptions. We do not verify feeling through senses that are native to us, we imitate feeling by means of impressions that are extraneous to us. Thus there are great gaps within the sphere of our supposedly consistent experience—gaps involving wide intervals between our feeling and our reason, between processes that are organic and processes that are conscious. Our attempts to bridge these intervals have constantly led us astray and thus has come to pass the system of inconsistencies that is the unconscious. For, in this void of his reality man can only substitute the images that are his unreality, and no image may substitute for reality, no theory of life replace the organic consistency of life itself. Yet in our dissociative preferences we continually mistake the *image* of that which is for that which *really* is. Nor do we at all realize to what extent the actual masquerades as real. What is there, for example, more actual than illusion, yet what is there less real? An individual actually has a delusion but it is not on this account real. The voices he hears are actual to him (do they not call him by name?) but we who are outside his system know very well that they are not real.[1]

My position is that, in our response to the impressions arising from the social system about us, our inferences are no more dependable than those arising from the private systems of the insane. Our confusion, like theirs, is the unconscious breach between perceptions that are true and impressions that are inferred, between life that is function and life that is merely enactment. It is again the disparity between life as a system or theory, and life itself. All of us are familiar with the inconsistency of people who, in order that life may prove comfortable in theory, devote their entire energies to making it miserable in practice. It is the inconsistency of unconsciousness with its inevitable alternation between the opposed extensions of a bidimensional image of life in place of the all-inclusiveness of life in its functional reality. It is the personal absolute underlying the consensual social system within and about us.

If this absolute embodied in the system is, then, a standard that is but arbitrary and artificial, each of us, since he is a reflection of such a specious criterion, is himself but a personal representation of this same absolute. If the individual is but a reflection of the system of rules representing the collection of individuals comprising the social consensus about him, then the consciousness of man, in both its social and individual manifestations, represents an absolute that is throughout false and undependable. If, in brief, our standard of truth rests upon our own self-reflection in a social system that is

---

[1] Needless to say the distinction here made between "actual" and "real" is used very specifically.

SOCIOLOGICAL IMPLICATIONS

itself self-reflected, then the evaluation of the individual, as of the social organism about us, comprises throughout a merely fictitious image, and our criteria of verity are everywhere spurious and without support.

In the artificial pretence of " good and bad " or of " right. and wrong " that represents the arbitrarily reflected *aspect* of life based upon the personal absolute of each, life, as I have said, is henceforth contracted into the opposite alternatives determined by the two components that comprise one's own pleasure or one's own pain. This shifting choice imposed by the contrary issues inseparable from our bidimensional outlook confronts us on every hand, and it is this limitation of us all to the artificial bidimension of personal loss or gain that reduces life to the tragedy of getting or of not getting what one wants.

Such a division of personality as this personal bias unconsciously entails, amounts to nothing short of a compulsion neurosis, the scope of which involves our entire social consciousness. The symptomatology of this mental division within the social personality finds its projection in such familiar antitheses as heaven or hell, love or hate, peace or war, idealist or materialist, Stoic or Hedonist, Jew or Gentile, aristocrat or proletarian, and so on *ad infinitum*. For such are our ever-shifting alternatives of getting or not getting as they are reflected in the assumption of private advantage underlying the so-called " good " and " bad " that is the preliminary outfit of us all.

In this eternal whether-or-no that is our superstitious alternation between good and bad lies the meaning of the social division constituting the reaction unconsciously sponsored under the shifting incertitudes of our popular forms and moralities. In our trembling vacillations between the ever-pressing issues of personal advantage, as apprehended through our superinduced images of " good " or " bad," is the substance of the obsessive oscillations of will commonly saluted as man's conscience, a reaction, however, in whose irresolutions an eminent psychologist long ago discovered the element of hesitation that tends to make cowards of us all.

This perpetual reflection of the self in the mirror of self-interest so operates as to invert completely the natural processes of life. Due to this unconscious distortion of reality, our every experience is viewed in the light of the fanciful image that is our own self-projection. On the basis of the absolute premise of self, that is the result of our own recoil upon the image of our own self-interest, everything is subordinated to the bidimensional component comprising our own personal aspect. For example, this inverted image of self, determining the personal absolute of each, underlies the delusion commonly concealed under what is popularly known as our " right." After all, what is held most dear within each of us is this private reservation that is one's own " right." Indeed, it is no other factor than this alleged prerogative or " right " of the individual based upon his autogenous assumption of personal absolutism that, as already stated, is our unconscious " resistance " both individual and social. Taking our stand upon the inflexible basis that is the individual resistance or personal absolute of each, we approach life wholly from the position of this personal bias on the ground that it is our right. It is the preservation of this personal right that is the sole propriety of the law. But the laws of men as they appertain to personal claim and title are the direct antithesis of the law of man as it pertains to the organic unity of his life. In truth, what is called the rights of private ownership is shown upon analysis to be the ownership of private rights.

We do not see—being wholly won over to a policy of unconscious self-interest we will not see—that our so-called " right " is not a reality inherent in the conditions of life itself, but that it is an illusion secondarily derived from our personal reaction to the system of autocracy that is the unconscious self-interest of the social unconscious everywhere about us. Here we find the psychological concomitance between the reaction of resistance and the process of inversion, between the bidimensional aspect reflecting one's own image and the unconscious illusion of the personal absolute assumed to be the private "right"' of every individual. For, in the measure in which one's outlook upon reality is restricted to a bidimensional or pictorial aspect of reality, one's range of perception is necessarily confined to alternations of self-advantage or to the issues of good and bad such as are determined by the autocratic absolute of one's own personal right. From the fixed background of personal right we can look out upon the world about us only from the angle of our personal satisfaction. In this outlook the sole test of human experience narrows itself to the question as to whether an issue bodes good or ill *for me*. My personal right being my standard of measure, every value will be weighed by me in accordance with its reading. Here, you see, is the very essence of inversion. Here in this element of personal prerogative the introversions of unconsciousness are to be traced to their biological root. Thus, in this repercussion of consciousness embodied in our assumption of personal right, we come upon the very nucleus of the neurosis.

I believe that in this bidimensional alternation of our unconscious self-reflection existing within the societal personality lies the basis of our social mania of competition, as it is the basis of our tireless discussions and altercations within the various spheres of man's activity. It is again the obsessive shift of our compulsive self-interest, and our social alternations of competition merely reflect our own oppositeness. I believe that this delusion of self-interest is the sole validity of our vaunted " opinions " as of the endless wranglings and disputations and outstrivings that actuate our social interests generally. The claim that we go to war because our " right " is disputed is not true. We go to war because in the fallacy of our personal absolutism our assumed right is held by us to be indisputable. Far from possessing warrant for what is called our "right" to institute war, it is precisely because of the presumptive and illusory nature of our arrogated right that we are driven to this alternative of immeasurable wrong. The fact is not that we are right because we think such and such to be true, but that in our compulsive response to unavoidable alternative we think such and such to be true in vindication of our assumed right. In other words, our "rightness" is not the natural result of our logic but our logic is the enforced result of our "rightness." By reason of this secret reservation of personal prerogative within each of us, everything is made subservient to this autocratic absolute of our individual right. If it is true, then, that the self-assurance and inflexibility of the personal absolute within each presents the true account of the mental and social rigidity comprising our resistances, there is here a significant commentary upon our so-called adult social consciousness.[1]

This mechanism of unconscious autocracy underlies our sociological reactions in a degree that is beyond our suspecting, and it is to the social no less than to the individual consciousness that we must turn for a solution. If we disregard the individual implications of the social neurosis, it is not possible to envisage the social implications of the individual neurosis. Due to the subjective concomitance between the individual and the social aspects of consciousness, to attempt to deal with one and not with the other entails a contradiction that is organic. Just as in the individual personality there are alternations of will entailing contrarieties of mood that correspond to getting or not getting what one wants, so in the social personality there are these same alternations of will with their corresponding antitheses of mood depending upon our getting and not getting what we want.

The element of failure in Christianity is the element of

---

[1] "Insanity a Social Problem," *The American Journal of Sociology*, Vol. XXXII, No. I, Part I, July, 1926.

the bidimensional in Christianity. Christ repudiates the consensus and the consensus exacts his life in return. Judas betrays Christ and in expiation exacts his own life. In the real motto of Christianity " Do unto others as ye would have others do unto you " there is betrayed the familiar alternative of secret self-interest. It reveals at once the mark of arrangement, of bargain, of conduct-with-a-view-to that here, as always, is the private guarantee of personal advantage. In the note of reciprocity underlying the Lord's prayer, with its " Forgive *us*, as *we* forgive," the bidimensional is at a premium. Only this bidimensional basis is adequate to account for the constant dissensions—religious, national, political and economic—that exist throughout the world of Christianity under the name of " right."

The truth is that the consciousness of man is not secure within itself, and our right is the protection of our own insecurity. An insidious division underlies the personality of man. Beneath his outer show of amity and covenant there resides a restless self-doubt, an anxious fear, a divided will. At the heart of his consciousness there is a deep-seated uncertainty driving him to temporary appeasements which can find issue only in the alternations of getting or of not getting what he wants. It is everywhere the aspect of the personal advantage under a new and altered guise. It is everywhere the alternation of self-interest, with its bilateral illusion of advantage or disadvantage, due to our fear-ridden obsession of " good and bad."

The vacillations of this illusive alternative likewise explain the anxious fascination of the shifting incertitudes of " fate." Here in the uncertain eventualities of chance is the irresistible appeal of our endless speculations in enterprise and game. In the indispensable element of suspense that lends pith to the drama there is again echoed this artificial note of self-division. For that which constitutes dramatic suspense merely sustains the converse extension inseparable from a bidimensional situation, and the interest of the drama, as of all art-forms based upon the element of conflict or of periodic alternation, is its unconscious projection of the dual issues that reflect the shifting bidimensions of our social self-inversions.

With the descent of the curtain upon the bidimensional situation with which the accustomed drama invariably closes, there remains, in essence unaltered, the same situation upon which it first arose. This is why it is always necessary at the end to create an artificial situation such as will temporarily satisfy the demands of a *seeming* conclusion and bring the episode to a halt. But a conclusion in the sense of a resolution of elements is not possible. The drama that is built upon the dilemma of the bidimensional is inevitably committed to one or the other of its two horns. Thus the end can be designed only with reference to one of the two alternatives in accordance with the unconscious ambivalence of author as of onlooker. And so the question of termination rests always upon the issue as to whether the audience shall smile and be pleased with itself (comedy) or weep and feel sorry for itself (tragedy) according as it gets or does not get what it wants.

The art of the dramatist is, therefore, in the final accounting always constrained. It is this exigency that causes to be perpetrated in the name of dramatic precedent the unpardonable affronts to organic verity which we are constantly witnessing. In real life a girl, who has had a liaison with a man with whom her relationship has been wholly sexual or self-interested, does not confide the secret of her inadvertence to a subsequent suitor with whom she is now " in love " upon a no less self-interested basis. Such a course involves an organic contradiction. She knows in her heart that in the unconscious concealment of his equally secret self-interest in her it is as intolerable to him to have the secret of his illusion disturbed as it is intolerable to her to disturb her own. But in the drama the psychological verities are thrown to the winds, and the heroine, to the artificial delight of a bilater-

SOCIOLOGICAL IMPLICATIONS

ally disposed audience, tells everything that has been in the " past " exactly as she would not tell it, and to the one person who hears it exactly as he would not hear it. But with drama that is bidimensional we must put an ending somewhere !

Such· are the organic discrepancies with which our ablest writers, whether in the form of the drama, the novel or the screen, still continue to banter us. The reason is to be sought in the unconscious and compulsive bondage which they themselves are under with respect to the illusion of the alternative that is their own self-reflective basis.

It is this illusion of unconscious self-reflection that explains also the greater fascination of the bidimensional *picture* we see sketched upon the wall or presented in the pages of literature as contrasted with the inherent *experience* that is the tridimensional actuality of our daily life. It explains our greater pleasure in the surroundings which one's art may contemplate or portray than in the surroundings which one's life may by participation fill and render beautiful. For art as image is the portrayal of unreality ; art as life is the expression of reality. Art to-day is merely the distinction of the individual interpreter. It is unrelated to the conscious aims of days and dreams that may be shared in common among all people. The truth is that in our prepossession with the bidimensional and pictorial our interest is centred far more in the distractions of art as image than in the inclusiveness of art as life.

This illusion of the pictorial aspect with which we replace the world of tridimensional actuality finds nowhere a happier vehicle than in the mechanical bidimension afforded through the medium of illusion achieved by the motion-picture. There is no device better adapted to reproduce the flat, scenic aspect such as gives the real zest to our dreams. For through the device of the motion-picture there is reflected the social drama that comprises our day, just as through the device of the dream there is reflected the individual drama that comprises our night. It is in this illusory *bidimension* of the photo-play that we are so much at home. We like its facile reproduction of ourselves. This is why we can accept without remonstrance the childishly naïve sequences standing for plot as represented in the bidimension of the screen. The same narrative would appear too utterly obvious and banal to pass muster in the solid perspective of the spoken drama, but presented upon the screen it finds ready acceptance, because in the motion-picture there is reproduced the pictorial aspect that corresponds to the habitual aspect of self-reflection that is our own image. We like moving pictures because we are moving pictures.

This element of unconscious dramatization, prompting the activities of the normal mind, we need somehow to realize within us. We need somehow to realize that in the manifestations of the unconscious comprising the collective enactment of the social drama around us there is this same reduction of actuality to aspect. *For in the active motor images of the social mind with its manifold gestures of a self-reflective actuality there is inherently no less unreality than in the passive sensory images of the individual mind in the private theatre of its self-reflective phantasy-building.* Yet so involved are we now in our retroactive processes that in our purblind efforts toward their presumably conscious readjustment we still proceed retroactively. Such is the futility of our personalistic methods of dream-analysis, as it is the futility of our personalistic envisagement of the disorders of affect comprising the neuroses.

In view of this central defect of our mental vision, whereby it is contracted into the artificial bidimension of the self- or dream-image, our outlook is everywhere dis-torted. Being vitiated throughout with the prejudice of the circumscribed and personal, our affective response is not spontaneous and true. As our subjective feeling is self-reflective or self-interested, our perception is neces-sarily pictorial and unreal. So that in our presumable

SOCIOLOGICAL IMPLICATIONS

contemplation of the objective world of reality, the experience that reaches us is not reality. On the contrary, in the element of the wish or dream that is our bias toward actuality, the aspect perceived is merely a foreshortened projection of the fanciful image of self. It lacks the tridimensional depth and solidarity of an inclusive reality.

This habit of personal dogmatization and autocracy has induced in us an autocracy of the mental processes generally. Our representations of the aspect have become, throughout, the organic antithesis of our participation in the real. From a basis of unreal images we can only reproduce unreal images. Out of a mental system of false impressions we can only elaborate impressions that are false. It is precisely this flat unreality of the pictorial, whether fanciful or actual, that lends to all our so-called " art " its obsessive fascination. Not only is there a distortion of reality in the flat mental picture we form of it, but in the necessarily detached adaptation of the mere onlooker each of us becomes unconsciously an arbitrary centre of personal opinionativeness. Each one stands as a sort of solar centre within a planetary system comprising his own self-determined affects. He thus reflects the universe surrounding him, and it is thus by him defined. And there has come to be built up in each of us in respect also to the world of art a system of personalism or unconsciousness that is well-nigh logic-proof in its absolutism.

Thus every stimulus—every impression that reaches our self-conscious mental retina falls upon the flat, self-reflecting surface of the wish, the dream or the personal *right* of each. Of such is the supposedly cognitive reaction underlying our " beliefs," of such is the presumably affective reaction we express as " love." But belief and love trace their etymology to a common organic root that unhappily betrays the equally illusory origin of each. In the Anglo-Saxon *leof*, meaning lief or wish or bias, both reactions are reduced to a single motivation that is the tell-tale of their phantastic import. And as belief and love (inverse cognition and inverse affect) are the very tissue of our personalistic consciousness, we may begin to understand to what extent the wish or the preconception comprising the bidimensional self-image underlies our every perception !

And so, after all, our world of " actuality " is not more real than our world of phantasy, our day not less self-reflective and unconscious than our night, our waking not less apparitional than our sleep. For both alike are motivated by the arbitrary reflection that is the inverted process of the will-to-self. As yet we do not realize that the personal absolute embodying our so-called " right," motivated as it is by self-reflection and unconsciousness, is as truly the product of our day-dream as the wish, motivated by unconscious self-reflection, is the product of our night-dream. We do not as yet see that the wish or self-satisfaction comprising the sleeping dream of our individual unconscious is itself but a reproduction of the wish or self-satisfaction comprising the waking dream of our social unconscious. We have yet to recognize that here again in the oscillations of its unconscious *form* is to be traced the bidimensional alternation of our own self-reflection as determined by the " good " or " bad " aspect that is our social as well as our individual advantage.

Here, in the contrasting circumstances of its affiliation with the social unconscious on the one hand and of its personal isolation within the individual unconscious on the other, is doubtless the dynamic element determining the vacillation of form that comprises the periodic alternations of the sociological bidimension generally. After all, what is " good " for me is that which is socially approved, what is " bad " for me is that which brings me into disfavour with the social consensus composing my environment. If the social unconscious about me is willing to connive with my individual unconscious and applaud my egoistic self-strivings, all is well. If, on the contrary, it withholds acquiescence and repudiates my self-inverted interests, my state is a correspondingly

SOCIOLOGICAL IMPLICATIONS

unhappy one. This accounts for our artificial dependence upon the social give-and-take with which we hedge ourselves about and is the basis of the periodic alternations of mood that make up our day. Being unconscious, one is a prey to the unconscious about him. Being self-reflective, one reacts to the impressions of a self-reflective environment. This oscillation of mood, depending upon whether our adaptation toward the social consensus is assimilative or discordant, explains also the alternations of mood observable in the contrasting reactions characteristic of certain pathological states, as it is the basis of the daily variation of mood registered in the neurotic and in the normal constitution. It is here, too, that is found the basis of the pleasure-pain shift represented in our mood alternations of elation and depression, whether existing in the diurnal variations characterizing our normal mood alternations or in the more pronounced reactions characterizing the extremes of affective tone presented in manic-depressive insanity.

It cannot be too strongly urged that, however intrinsically opposite these extremes of mood may seem, they are in essence identical. For, in reality, these seeming antitheses represent but the obverse aspects of one and the same bidimensional portrait of personal advantage. As regards this intrinsic identity between such seemingly opposite mood-tones it is interesting to note the etymological concurrence in the Anglo-Saxon root *saed* (English sot, meaning filled), in which we find alike the source of such apparently unrelated derivatives of current usage as the words *sad* and *satisfied*. There is, indeed, an unescapable concomitance in the mental attitudes of joy and sorrow, of elation and depression, of satisfaction and sadness. This coincidence is but an altered form of the common alternative of good and bad, of praise and blame, of getting and of not getting, and, as always, its presence denotes the conflict involved in our inverted self-interest.

Doubtless to this bidimensional alternation are also traceable such sociological antitheses as one may witness in the contrary reactions expressed in our various economic and political factions. This one, failing to suspect the element of traditional self-reflection determining his so-called party affiliation, registers his personal allegiance under the socially augmented symbol or principle embodying the standard that is *his* private absolutism or right ; that one, no less oblivious of the part he is automatically enacting in his character of party promoter, assumes the symbolic rôle that tends to further the party principle representative of the absolute criterion that is *his* right. So, too, are to be explained the alternations of reaction represented in the social antitheses of prohibition and anti-prohibition. The anti-prohibitionists are by imputation the ultra-liberal, the prohibitionists are by imputation the ultra-conservative element, but both are in point of fact equally the dupes of the personal reaction that is their own self-reflection. For both, in their unconscious response to what is commonly called " early training," equally embody expressions of their original infantile reaction to the opposed issues involved in the social pretence of " good " and " bad."

Extending into every phase of our social life, it is this bilateral motive that is likewise the failure of the schools. With credit, praise or privilege and their opposites (depending upon whether the child " succeeds " or " fails " as judged by the bidimensional standard of good and bad, of praise or blame constituting the arbitrary *picture* of his personal conduct), it happens that, through an unconscious substitution of the image of the child's person for the function of the child's personality, the entire incentive of the schools becomes ulterior and artificial. The so-called liberal schools of to-day are in no better case. Despite their much ado about advanced methods that will give greater freedom to the child they afford mere imitations of freedom. But this is freedom in aspect, not in function. It is merely the ideal of freedom contemplating its own image. Thus it is futile to attempt to alter our situation through recourse to mere

SOCIOLOGICAL IMPLICATIONS

progressive methods of education. The elimination of formal standards of efficiency is likewise unavailing. For the ulterior is present still. We find it present in the bidimensional attitude that actuates the entire pedagogic system with its underlying idea of *preparation*. Apparently it is not realized that this element of the preparatory or ulterior is the criterion also of the teachers, being likewise the basis of their own promotion as it is the standard of promotion in the world at large. But whatever is preparatory is based upon the illusion of the personal image. It is commentative, premeditated, moralistic, and substitutes a mental impression of life in place of life itself. When we offer an image of life for which we seek to " prepare " the child, the very basis of our educational programme becomes pictorial and untrue. Life knows naught of images in the personal sense. Life is the functioning of interests in constructive activities. The rewards of such activities flow naturally out of them and consist in a common earning for daily needs in common daily pursuits. The child, if given the opportunity, will learn to construct useful and beautiful things and his only reward will be the natural reward accruing from the intrinsic value, social and æsthetic, of the work produced. When schools will have become the productive plants of natural childish industry, there will not any longer be the absurd invention by the schools of ulterior rewards such as now supply the artificial stimulus necessary to lend vitality to their essential dullness. It will not be necessary for teachers to stimulate the industry of their pupils through resort to extraneous " merits " in palliation for their own lack of joy in the natural creativeness of spontaneous childhood.

There is, perhaps, no more subtle expression of the bidimensional replacement than in the psychological counter-impaction of the marital neurosis. In this conjugal vis-à-vis unconscious self-reflection is at floodtide. This is why, in the opposite extensions of the conjugal conflict, there are presented concomitantly in husband and wife such familiar antitheses as are presented alternately in the single individual, as, for example, the opposed reactions of mania and depression, the psychasthenic and hysterical extremes, as well as the contrasts of homosexuality and paranoia. Where such reciprocal conditions exist, the opposite rôles are in every instance unconsciously assumed, of course, with entire consistency by the opposite parties in question. This explains also the anomaly presented in so seemingly contradictory a spectacle as that of a man of outwardly serious deportment enjoying vicariously, through the cosmetics and extravagances of self-adornment worn by a narcistically inverted wife, the satisfactions of an unconscious exhibitionism. It is the law of the marital neurosis, as of the balance-scale, that its termini are diametrically opposite and that their variation is inverse one to another.

The unconscious mechanism described by Freud under the term "psychic ambivalence" (Bleuler) is of all reactions perhaps the least understood, but, because of its invariable association with neurotic processes, it is as important biologically as any of the mechanisms that psychoanalysis has disclosed to us. Yet again, in this quality of contrast inherent in the manifestations of neurotic states, there are represented merely the two opposed extremes of reaction due to the division of impulse that is inseparable from the alternation of aspect we have traced to the illusion of the bidimensional self-image. This replacement, as we have seen, occurs normally as well as neurotically, socially as well as individually. It is again the to-and-fro of the pendulum of good and bad. It is again but the oscillation that is our obsessive reaction to the make-believe of the self-reflective and ulterior.

The truth is that we prefer our impressions of life to an understanding of life, and in the ambivalence of our response toward others, our reaction is friendly or antagonistic only in the degree in which they correspond or fail to correspond with our personally preconceived impressions. In the present ambivalent scheme of things, the ultimate poignancy of one's grief is the element of secret pleasure it affords to others. The daily newspapers, seeking unconsciously to make capital of our human frailty in this regard, are ever alert to publish under glaringly conspicuous head-lines the most startling crimes and calamities. Under captions giving notice of some inexpressible " Horror " (a term supposedly conveying a sense of repugnance) they attain in fact their most intriguing effects. The newspapers are wise. They have read us before giving themselves to us to read and so are canny to supply the grim details we love to hear of another's loss or hurt.[1] It is this isolation of sorrow that is its desolation and its bitterness. Yet it may be traced wholly to the unconscious tyranny of this bidimensional division within us that we find the pleasure we do find, however adroitly repressed, in the unhappiness or calamity of those about us. It is, of course, not another's calamity that is the real cause of our satisfaction, but in the ambivalence of our attitude as we contemplate his misfortune we feel, by contrast, or in a *comparative* count so much *more* fortunate than he. It is again but the pro-

[1] I recall an incident that occurred several years ago in the office of a prominent newspaper that well illustrates this point. A member of the staff was called to the phone to receive the details of a drowning, word of which had just been reported. One can picture the professional zeal with which he turned to the phone, alert with the eagerness of expectant acquisition. If a moment later he dropped the receiver and drew back with a sudden cry of horror, his whole face gradually altering to a look of dejection and pain, it was not because he had been disappointed in the expectation of a thrilling item of news. Not at all. The item was as tragic in its details as one could wish. The disappointment lay only in the fact that, on inquiring the name of the boy who had been drowned, he learned that it was his own son. It was only this circumstance, then, that explained why his countenance suddenly changed from satisfaction to pain. A matter of information which was to have been sold to his readers as a delectable item of news concerning the drowning of another man's son became a poignant sorrow when the self-same news related to his own son. And so, upon examination, it may be seen that what really happened was an unexpected shift of affect due to the sudden alternation of the personal motive through the reversal of the bidimensional vantage.

jection of the bidimensional division within each of us individually as a reflection of the division within all of us socially. In this comparison of ourselves with others there is again reflected the bidimensional alternative that is the fanciful self-advantage of the personal image.

Turn where we will, this same phenomenon of mental alternation based on the bidimensional image looms ineffaceably before us. Opposed to the *mental image* " male " we project the *mental image* " female," in contrast to the *concept* " religion " we place the *concept* " science," against the *psychological attitude* of the artist stands the *psychological reaction* of the critic. Because of this mentally pictorial outlook among us, we fail to realize that in the unconsciously objective approach of the artist there is embodied an attitude that is as truly a criticism or evaluation of life as is the objective attitude of the critic toward the expression of the artist. We do not realize that in our unconscious personal alternation an element of criticism or evaluation everywhere substitutes the fallacy of a mental state toward life for the conscious reality of a state of life itself. Our bidimensional self-reflection is thus equally the impediment of art as of life. The insidious element of personal self-reflection is the fatal decoy no less of portrayer than of participant.

On the other hand, in the spirit of the more subjective artist what we sense is his insistent sway toward a self-realization that is impersonal. We feel that in the measure in which he yields it submission his expression becomes less and less a reproduction of life and more and more an actualization of life itself. This is because in the thought or feeling expressed through the art-forms of such a personality, he is himself not so much the causative or self-conscious agent reflecting a state of mind *in relation to* life as it seems, but rather the conscious link in a sequence that *identifies* him with a condition of life as it is. Thus again the truer the artist, the more he tends to round the orbit of his personality in a conscious universe of rela-

SOCIOLOGICAL IMPLICATIONS 97

tivity; the more imitative the artist, the more he tends to oscillate uncertainly between the alternate phases that merely reflect the assumed absolute of his own ego.

So it is with our alternations, social and individual, pathological and normal, as they exist on every hand. There is the precoid and the hysteric, the homosexual and the paranoiac, the religionist and the sceptic, the moralist and the voluptuary. It is the world-old tragedy of getting and not getting what one wants, and in the self-satisfaction of the one as in the self-abnegation of the other the element of self-consequence is equal and identical. It is the ineptitude of virtue that it is but the bidimensional reverse of vice. Generosity, like humility, contains its ambivalent element of pride. Though from time to time we may dispense no slight favours, yet always we demand to hold the reins of power within our own hands. Let our protégés presume for a moment to assert their own individuality and straightway we rein them in. Indeed, if we will look into this, we shall realize that it is precisely the person toward whom we are most lavish of beneficence that is the one of whose native and unsponsored expression we are most jealously critical. The fact is that our virtues are really too good to be true and that our amenities, after all, reflect only our own self-advantage. Thus, from the point of view of good and bad, our lusts and our repressions are but interchangeable adaptations of the central theme of self, and in the alternations entailed in the popularly conceded distinctions assumed as morality and immorality there is preserved under merely reversed aspects this identical fetish of one's own self-image.

Even in the sphere of psychology itself there is this same division inseparable from the personal absolute or the private arrogation that underlies the assumed right of each individual as reflected in our social contrasts of good and bad. For example, the propriety of studying the " merely motor expressions " of the behaviourists is regarded with grave question by the introspectionists,

G

while the behaviourists as ardently doubt whether introspective studies are the legitimate matter of psychology at all. The futility of dissension is again its two-sidedness. What we omit to reckon with when we consider the vying of these two schools with one another is the element of the personal prerogative within them that unconsciously goads each to an intolerance of the other. For all " rights " being mutually opposed to and exclusive of one another, the " right," or opinion, underlying any system except the system that is one's own is, of its nature, inadmissible. In the irreconcilable assertions of the multifarious opinions of men, whether occurring in group or in single expression, there is always to be traced this underlying motive of personal right corresponding to the private prerogative of each. By rights I do not mean the natural rights that are universal and common, but the personal rights that are autocratic and pre-emptive. But whether our divisions be national, political, religious, economic, professional or familial, their underlying meaning is the same. So that, in this antithetical " response " characterizing the periodic alternations of our bidimensional self-reflection, there is registered a reaction of the organism that invariably escapes the attention of either disputant—the reaction, namely, of the will-to-self or of the private privilege coincident with an absolute basis of adjudication. As long as there remains this element of unconscious alternation due to the self-reflective interest that now actuates human motives, students of science, also, are as powerless to bring to their problems an attitude of disinterestedness as are our national delegates when they attempt to consider the problems involving all the subtle self-interest of a peace conference.

The really classic division of opinion in the world—the division that is of major importance even amid academic fields of thought—is the conflict between Science and Religion. That the religionists, in claiming the undoubted authenticity of sources confirmatory of the

SOCIOLOGICAL IMPLICATIONS 99

truth of revealed religion, have offered indisputable "proof" of the validity of their position, cannot be denied. That the scientists' assertion of the doctrine of spontaneous evolution as opposed to the revealed truths of Theism rests equally upon the evidence of incontrovertible "proof" leaves likewise no room for doubt. In both instances, however, the proofs of each are acceptable only to the advocates of their own particular view and not to the advocates of the view that is opposite their own. But of what avail are the proofs of a position which are valid only in the minds which have anteriorly set out to prove it? What dependence is to be placed in the intellectual verifications of truth which are acceptable only to intellects which demonstrate them but which, in the view of those of an opposite trend, remain for ever inaccessible? These are reflections which necessarily force us to question very seriously our objective intellectualizations. If, in so wide and vital a division as that between Religion and Science, the "logic" on which is based the claim of each is so completely without meaning, beyond its facility to flatter established prepossessions, it is time that our "reasoning" upon all issues be summoned to account on suspicion that our position is, in every instance, merely the unconscious alternation due to the bidimensional image of gain or loss that is one's personal self-reflection.

This blindness of the personal restriction within our subjective life is the more interesting when one considers the far more impersonal outlook that often characterizes man's consciousness within the sphere of his objective interests. With the growing expanse of man's consciousness there has arisen the widely inclusive and impersonal field of preventive medicine with its essential preoccupation with the communal weal. Through this wider sociological approach we have come gradually to realize the incomparably greater significance of activities directed toward safeguarding the health of the community or of the group-life as contrasted with interests directed to the personal cure of the individual as a single element within the social group. We have begun to recognize that where, through recourse to measures of public hygiene, it is possible to control the general sources of disease, conditions are rendered such that there may be no need to treat disease-process within the single individual. In Panama, for example, where, through a far-reaching programme of civic hygiene, the malaria-breeding organism has been almost wholly exterminated, the medical and sociological functions of the community have become so completely merged that with the appearance of the disease-bearing Anopheles it is no longer the physician but the civic authorities who are consulted.

Such are the signs of the broadening communal spirit that is coming to influence more and more the various measures of improvement amid the objective conditions of life about us. But, within the subjective sphere of man's activities, his outlook is no whit more encompassing to-day than in the moment of his earliest quickenings of consciousness. The reason is not far to seek. Man's subjective life is throughout overlaid and oppressed by his inverted obsession of personal acquisition. Viewing everything in the light of the reflection cast by his own image, a broad communal programme of life is for him as yet subjectively impossible. An outlook that would render his position a relative one and reveal it as but contributory to the organic life as a whole would straightway menace the illusion of his personal prerogative and rob him of what is now for him the basis of all his experience and the sum of his personality. He does not see that his " experience," by reason of its inverted absolutism, wholly lacks the support of reality. He does not see that what he calls his personality is his successful collusion in the collective unconscious about him at the price of his habitual concession to impressions not primarily his own. This is why the psychopathologist is still futilely endeavouring to understand his patients from the static, personal standpoint of his own dogmatic

SOCIOLOGICAL IMPLICATIONS

absolutism rather than from the position of a relative and inclusive interpretation of consciousness. This is why the objective analyst remains always outside the real problem of the social disharmony represented in the nervous and mental disorders of the individuals by whom he is confronted. The truth is, he is himself a part of the disorder which in his unconscious absolutism he is presuming to treat in others. The tendency is one that exists among us all. For the taint of an absolutism within the social personality involves each of us equally as a contributing element in its fictitious structure. Hence the ultimate futility of our constantly shifting " methods." Hence the ever-recurring therapeutic fads that represent first one and then another absolute system of cure. But though each such system may for a while claim our support, in due course it fades again and is in turn succeeded by another in accordance with the varying phases of our social alternations. Our enthusiasm, as well as its decline, must after all be reckoned merely as the alternate reverberations of the social consciousness in response to the unconscious alternations of the bidimensional absolute which has its existence in the individual and of which the social manifestation is but a reproduction.

As the neurosis is generic, involving the social system no less than the individual element, the system of psychoanalysis, as well as the individuals composing it, is equally included under its indictment. From Freud, therefore, as from the rest of us there is due the acknowledgment of the inevitable part occupied by psychoanalysis in the systematization or unconsciousness that is the social neurosis. The private assumption of each of us to the contrary notwithstanding, we who have followed Freud could not possibly have been inspired in our work by a conscious interest in the disorders of personality represented in the social anomaly of the neurosis. Being ourselves unconsciously involved in the social neurosis about us, we have been urged forward through an unconscious or *personal* interest in order to divert our minds from our own implication in its *social* significance. To this end it has been unconsciously our endeavour to direct assiduous attention only to the specific manifestations of the neurosis as it exists in individuals supposedly other than ourselves. *In brief, we have been diligently occupied with the objective study of the neurosis in its obvious appearance in others as individuals presumably separate from ourselves, in order to escape the subjective acknowledgment of its actual presence within ourselves as contributory and interrelated elements in our common social consciousness.*

With each of us, the real motive has been the unconscious grudge of our personal involvement in a world-wide enslavement to an artificial precept such as can only oscillate between the alternations resultant upon our self-limited bidimension of " good and bad." When we can lay aside the incentives of personal self-defence and view our own reactions with impartial self-composure, we shall realize that it has been our own unconscious that first quickened the compensative defence-reactions which later culminated in the objective system we know to-day as psychoanalysis. For, with psychoanalysis as with other systems, its real incitement is found in the inevitable " come-back " that is the organism's response to its sense of affront before the illusion of the self-image. Again, it is the automatic alternation resultant upon a basis of counter-relatedness inseparable from the delusion of the personal absolute as contrasted with the relativity of the individual in respect to life as an organic whole. Again, it is the artificial presupposition of our own " rightness " that is the strongest determinative of our conduct, and to this secret autocracy that is our own personal absolutism we have rendered everything subservient.

Men like to say that God created them, but in truth it is they who have created " God." We like to employ this anthropomorphic image of absolute authority to our personal advantage. Rewarding the good and punishing the bad in accordance with the alternations coincident with the bidimensional aspect of an absolute Deity, this image of supreme authority represents merely the projection of the personal absolute based on the alternations of our own self-reflection. I do not doubt that beneath this vicarious image of a fanciful father-supremacy there ever remains the true and abiding principle that is the underlying reality of life. But, in the place of this principle of reality that is the unsponsored soul of man, we have timidly substituted such temporary cheats as are adapted only to lull our fancies with imperialistic dreams of personal empire. Indeed, in the personal projection actuating the social anomaly of religious belief the inverted bias comprising our own self-image has its strongest lodgment. It is here that the collective mind has tricked itself to its collective undoing. For in the current expression of our social inversion resident in this absolute arbiter of the moral law or of " good and bad " lies the very nucleus of our human pathology. And it is my position that the pretence, underlying the personal adjustment based upon early inculcated issues of self-interest and concealed beneath our specious determinants of " good " and " bad," is no less the underlying fallacy of psychoanalysis. For, in its attempt to offset neurotic disharmonies due to an unconscious repression of the sexual life of the individual, psychoanalysis has recourse to adjustments that are the mere *alternative* of repression—a repression legislated by the dictates of an equally unconscious and repressed society, be its expression opportunistic, sublimative, or *en règle*.

Thus psychoanalysis, likewise, presents a policy that is but a desperate alternation between the only two issues that are available on the basis of the absolute criterion such as inevitably obtains in our present bidimensional or pictorially constellated scheme of consciousness, namely, a policy in which the reaction of the individual can only be in the direction of the reverse or opposite extension. Hence, however personally displeasing to us, there is the need that we who are psychoanalysts somehow recognize that we, also, are unconsciously subordinated to the moral dilemma that is the reflection of our own self-interest. There is the need that we see clearly that psychoanalysis, too, is still under the domination of a falsely imbued impression of good and bad with its attendant issue in the alternations of an unconscious social resistance.

This illusory antithesis of getting or of not getting what one wants, this irreconcilable ache of man's unconscious is traceable again and again to the false assumptions of a self-reflective absolutism as arrogated by the individual as a single part or element in contradistinction to our organic consciousness as a whole. It is in the absolutism of the part that consists the dissociation of the whole ; it is in the relativity of the part that consists the integrity of the whole. Within the sphere of man's consciousness our fallacies of observation lie in the absolutism of the observer. On the other hand, in surrendering the bidimensional or pictorial illusion inseparable from the fixed position of the observer for the tridimensional actuality of our organic participation in life as an inclusive totality, we automatically yield it the full-dimensional component comprising the extension that is our confluent societal unity and which, in abrogating the artificial image of a personal and unconscious absolute, constitutes life in the encompassing scheme of the relativity of consciousness. In such a scheme there is offered to the dissociated personality, single and social, neurotic and normal, a readjustment that is fundamental. I believe it is only in the acceptance of the societal consciousness of man that there lies the ultimate step for each of us. For the principle of the relativity of consciousness is an organically unequivocal one. In its individual realization consists our societal integrity. In its societal realization consists our individual integrity. Only in the co-ordination of the two lies the fulfilment of our organic personality.

PART II

THE PSYCHOLOGY OF THE NEUROSES

Personally, I am more and more convinced that the cure for sentiment, as for all the weakened forms of strong things, is not to refuse to feel it, but to get to feel *more* in it. This seems to me to make the whole difference between a true and a false ' asceticism.' The false goes for getting rid of what one is afraid of ; the true goes for using it and making it serve. The one empties, the other fills ; the one abstracts, the other concentrates. Don't you think half the troubles of life come from being wrongly *afraid* of things—especially afraid of oneself ? (February, 1890.)

RICHARD LEWIS NETTLESHIP.

CHAPTER I

ANALYSIS OF FREUD'S DYNAMIC AND INDIVIDUALISTIC CONCEPTION OF THE NEUROSES

THE following pages are an endeavour to determine the conditions, social and individual, that constitute the health of the mental organism. What the health of the mental organism is, has not as yet been adequately described. On the somatic side, of course, one defines health as the harmonious functioning of the parts comprising the organism as a whole. But, as regards the constitution of the mental life in its totality, we have no such inclusive interpretation of the condition requisite to harmonious functioning. Although the psychopathologist is constantly engaged in efforts to restore the distorted mind to a condition of harmony and health, one finds nowhere a satisfactory statement as to just what constitutes the state of harmony which it is his avowed purpose to establish. Health, of course, is synonymous with the harmony of the whole. But from the point of view of consciousness we have not even determined as yet what is the organism as a whole or what are the parts constitutive of it. The psychiatrist is habitually preoccupied with the outer features of mental disharmony which the method of extrinsic observation has brought to his personal notice. It is evident, therefore, that his conception of consciousness is automatically withheld from a subjective inclusion of the organism in its entirety, and that it compasses only the particular aspect that falls within the limits of his own particular observation. It is this discrepancy which I should like, if possible, to isolate from its present personal involvement, with a view to the possibility of a clearer understanding of our mental problems. To this end my recourse can only be such an objective inquiry as may be the more hospitable because of its subjective inclusiveness.

In pre-Freudian days, as is well known, the psychopathologist who had to do with a nervous disorder turned quite automatically in the direction to which the patient pointed, or to the symptom indicated. Whether a paralysis, an obsession, a phobia or what not, this symptom or sign constituted for the physician no less than for the patient the exclusive focus of interest. Thus in the domain of nervous and mental disharmonies the entire field of inquiry occupied itself in earlier times with a mere obvious index of disease rather than with the disease itself.

With the advent of Freud the situation became wholly changed. Through his discovery that the disturbance was neither *what* nor *where* it appeared to be from the clinical point of view, Freud came to explain it upon grounds which led to a fundamentally altered conception of the hysterias and their kindred manifestations. Viewing the situation as a dynamic one, Freud regarded the symptom in question in the light of an unruly element within the central personality, whence, in his view, this central personality became, as it were, the controlling seat of government. It was Freud's position that this presiding principle must be held amenable for fostering within its domain so discordant an element as that whereof the symptom gave notice, and accordingly, it was to this central principle that Freud henceforth addressed his investigations.

This position of Freud's, in which he regards the essential mechanism of the neurosis as a symptom-substitution representing in substance a psychic transposition or a shift of affect from intrinsic source to arbitrary aspect, embodies the whole significance of psychoanalysis. It is a significance that marks the outset of our understanding of the real nature of the neuroses. For it was this conception that first posited as the background of consciousness an integral personality, from which, as a basis, it was sought to discover the factors operative in causing the division within it represented by the neurosis. But just as the enduring distinction of Freud's work lies in this conception of a central totality of personality constituting the substrate of the conscious life, so its limitation consists precisely in the erroneous position to which Freud assigned this totality of consciousness. I believe that the many inconsistencies and half-baked deductions of psychoanalysis, with the consequent deadlock to a truly comprehensive interpretation of the neuroses, are due precisely to this limitation of the conception of the neurosis within the bounds of the individual consciousness. When we have realized that this conception of a totality of personality is biologically tenable only *from the point of view of an inclusive societal consciousness and not of the circumscribed individual consciousness*, we shall, I believe, have taken the essential step toward dispelling the confusion and lack of coherence within the psychoanalytic system as it now stands.

As one looks back, it is not difficult to see how Freud's necessarily conventional, clinical point of view—the outgrowth of personal inclination and tradition—unconsciously bound him to a conceptual outlook that was necessarily circumscribed and limited, and how he was thus unwittingly led into a contradiction of the ultimate significance of the very conception which he had himself originated.

In the nature of Freud's postulate that a psychic transposition is the basis of the neurosis, his thesis assumes a breach in the integrity of consciousness. This breach within consciousness is due to the effort of a delimited area within it to establish itself as a separate, self-governing unit. His position envisages a conflict entailing a dissociation of the personality due to the secession of one or more of its integral constituents. Hence the real crux of Freud's thesis was the determination of the essential incompatibility between an *independent part* (dissociation) and the *coherent whole* (unification) within the sphere of consciousness—a conception which seems to me as beautiful as it is true. But in the bias of Freud's own individualistically circumscribed consciousness, with the inevitable separation or dissociation it entailed, Freud failed to recognize the implication of his own thesis. He did not see that he was himself unconsciously held within a position bearing the essential feature of the very disorder which presumably he was regarding from a non-partisan, unified point of view. He did not see that his own position was precisely that of a separate, delimited unit, within the totality of consciousness, represented in the dissociation of his own personal bias. There is here a consideration which Freud, and the rest of us along with Freud, have permitted to pass by completely unnoticed, due to our own unconscious embroilment within the limitations of our circumscribed individual consciousness. While theoretically advocating unification as the basis of consciousness, Freud was himself actually seeking unconsciously to reconcile with it a dissociation within himself. It is this self-circumventing illusion of the restricted individualistic consciousness which, if one may judge from the degree to which it has underlain my own work and that of others, is the essential fallacy of psychoanalysis.

In reality, then, Freud set out to account for the seemingly actual upon grounds of the seemingly actual. He did not see that the very medium of human experience, as *seemingly* actual and as commonly accepted by us to be actual, is in truth already biased by impressions that are only virtual. In short, Freud did not realize that our own so-called consciousness is unconsciousness. He assumed that the analysis or self-examination to which he subjected himself and his patients was disinterested and authentic in its inclusiveness of the personality as a whole. And all the while he failed to realize that the personality as a whole, as embodied in the self-limited consciousness of the individual, is itself imbued with all the prejudice of self-interest and with all the bias of dissociation constitutive of the habitual medium of our collective unconscious. As this habitual medium is actuated by individual tradition and separativeness, it is necessarily based throughout upon motives of personal preference. With an outlook distorted by personal preference (the unconscious wish), it is not possible to view the processes of life and its disharmonies with freedom and clarity. From a standpoint of private prejudice it is not possible to envisage private prejudice. Unconsciousness cannot compass unconsciousness. The wish cannot assail the wish. In our present mode of personalism and unconsciousness the attainment of consciousness is of its nature an impossible task. Thus the bias of Freud renders untenable the position of Freud when he assumes the abrogation of bias, since his position has itself arisen from the unsuspected bias of his own habituated or preferential mode.

It is this unconsciousness within ourselves which we psychoanalysts have let escape us and which necessarily gives to our work, for all its impressiveness, the conventional curtailment of the vicarious and unreal. As an illustration of what I mean, there is somewhere in the " Traumdeutung " an amusingly acute psychoanalytic touch in Freud's interpretation of the dream of a patient. This patient had on one day stoutly protested that dreams were not invariable wish-fulfilments, and on the following day she brought to Freud a dream in which she was represented planning a summer outing with her mother-in-law whom she cordially disliked. Here, she said, was proof that dreams were not necessarily wish-fulfilments, and a superficial glance would seem to give her the decisive score. But Freud was alert. " Quite the contrary," he replied with analytic acuity, " you have only furnished additional proof that dreams *are* wish-fulfilments, for it is precisely in your wish to prove to me that dreams are not wish-fulfilments that you have dreamed that you are going summering with your detested mother-in-law—a dream which could not more amply satisfy your wish to prove the incorrectness of my theory." So speaks Freud with triumphant naïveté, and, with a complacency that is no less naïve, we who are Freudians are still applauding with unstinted assent the subjective fallacy of his objective logic.

Like Freud, we have not seen that every dream of our own contains no less the identical wish to prove ourselves right. Like Freud, we have not seen that it is our wish that the dream shall contain the element of a basic and invariable sexual factor in substantiation of the thesis of us Freudians. It is the fallacy of the dreamer in the foregoing incident that she sets out with the absolutism of the personal premise; but so do we—the premise, namely, of personal "rightness." Thus we are in no different case from the patient whom Freud cites as manufacturing a dream to prove her position right. But while the wish of this dreamer—in its purpose in direct opposition to our own—stands out in sharp, unmistakable outline before us, our own wish—in its nature identical with hers, namely, the wish to prove ourselves right—remains enveloped still in the obfuscating mists of our own unconscious. There is here the organic inaccessibility of the wish to the wisher, of the dream to the dreamer. There is here the blindness of the unconscious preference with its basis in the personal absolute, and it is the need of us Freudians to recognize that the blight of its inconsistency is upon us all.[1]

How dominant is Freud's own individuating wish or personal preference one may realize who reads his essay on "The History of the Psychoanalytic Movement" and witnesses the bitterness of his feeling toward any who gainsay him. How strongly we share with Freud the influence of personal bias may be seen in our own bitterness when others would gainsay us. It is so with us all.

[1] "Psychoanalytic Improvisations and the Personal Equation," *The Psychoanalytic Review*, Vol. XIII, No. 2, April, 1926.

FREUD'S CONCEPTION OF NEUROSES

It is the morbid compulsion of self-vindication that underlies all "rightness." It is the habitual illusion of our own self-centralization, a less wieldy but more explicit term for what we have come to know theoretically—that is, in other people and as in no way touching our own personal feeling—as the unconscious wish-motive. For self-vindication and the unconscious wish are one.

And so, objectively, Freud is quite " right " in asserting that a basic sexual factor underlies the dream. Do not his own and his patients' dreams prove him so ? And Jung is, objectively, no less " right " in claiming that Freud is mistaken—that dreams are not primarily motivated by a sexual wish. Do not his dreams and those of his patients equally corroborate *his* view ? And so with Adler and his theory, and so with any of us and his theory. For notwithstanding that the theories of all of us are severally opposed one to another, yet all of us are equally " right," as may be equally substantiated by the dreams of each. The explanation is simple. The " rightness " of each is the wish of each and the wish is father to the dream !

CHAPTER II

FORMULATION OF AN ORGANIC OR SOCIETAL BASIS OF INTERPRETATION

WITHIN the various fields of scientific investigation, there is the established precept that we set out from the simplest assignable elements as a basis for all future inquiry. Of such, for example, is the ground-structure of the chemical and the biological sciences, and it is likewise upon ultimately irreducible units that the furthest abstractions of mathematics rest their foundation. But in our approach to the biological elements of consciousness we have proceeded upon no such soundly established principle. Unconsciously presupposing here and taking for granted there, we have reasoned from premises that have lacked the warrant of elementary support. Hence in the study of consciousness we have, in our unconsciousness, unwittingly slurred our obligations to the very first principle of scientific method.

This circumstance, however, is not one toward which we need feel scornful. Our blunder has been inevitable. In the study of the elements of consciousness a factor is introduced into scientific reckoning that completely reverses habitual perspectives, and to trace with scientific conscientiousness this inexorable reversal of the personal mode requires of the student very special laboratory qualification. For, in turning to the study of the basis of consciousness, we are ourselves the primary elements of our own inquiry. Ourselves unconscious, we have attempted to fold back upon ourselves and, from a basis of prejudice, to recapture our primary, unprejudiced basis. From a now sophisticated personal *adaptation* of consciousness we have sought to regain the native, un-

ORGANIC BASIS OF INTERPRETATION 115

sophisticated *principle* of consciousness of which our personal adaptation is the unconscious abrogation. Clearly, this task is of its nature self-contradictory. Only in the measure in which we realize that unconsciousness is our habitual mode and so allow it to cease automatically to dominate our lives may we come to study dispassionately the essential structure of consciousness through an unbiased examination of the primary elements of which it is composed.

Life has its beginnings in a continuous organic medium. Within this common organic medium our original infant organisms constitute identical elements. What we later regard as individuals are but corpuscles in a homogeneous, societal tissue. Organically, or from the point of view of their common and inherent affectivity, there exists no discrimination among these elements. Race or national separation, social or caste distinction have not entered into them. These are divergences that have no place in the organic origins of life. As integral members of an original organic matrix, the elements representing our primary infant organisms are no more differentiated psychically one from another than they are psychically differentiated from the life-source or the maternal organisms from which they have sprung. The mental life, being as yet wholly subjective and unaware, is simple, unitary. It is one with the organism's inherent feeling. Subjective feeling, indeterminate and unqualified, is, in the primary organism, the sum of experience, the compass of life. Primarily the organism's subjective feeling is its all. And as with the growing perception of outer objects life enlarges, this subjective mode is unaltered still. Our primary objective experience merges into continuity with inherent feeling. It is added to, included in the subjective life. So that in its incipient rapport with the world of objectivity, life maintains still a fluid, undifferentiated, confluent mode. For life is primarily affective. In the affect consists men's common ground. In the subjective affect lies organic bed-rock. Here in the common inherency of native feeling is the primal menstruum of our human consciousness.

But there suddenly comes an interruption to this state of unification. The parent, as spokesman of a world of unconscious collusion in the defence of self or the exploitation of separativeness, strikes in sharply upon this unitary mode of being with a wedge of interdiction that marks the beginning of a cleavage within the personality which the subsequent years tend increasingly to widen and secure.[1] With the sudden arrest of this early, unified mode through the entrance of the extraneous strictures of command and prohibition (suggestion or repression), the personality of the organism becomes automatically divided. For with command or reproof there is introduced the element of the ulterior. Organic harmony and confluence are no more. Into the life of confluence is now thrust the rude encroachment of personal motive—of motive based upon the outcome of promise or threat, of gain or forfeit. The inherent flow, the organic current of experience is now artificially checked. Henceforward expression is no longer spontaneous. Instead, a programme of conduct-with-a-view-to takes its place and becomes the dominant order of our activities. In the face of every summons the question must first be weighed —Will it be well or ill with *me* ? Upon the issue of gain or loss depends the response—the issue of gain or loss for the now separated, individuated organism. An adjustment to the ends of self-interest is demanded. Everything is at stake ; a fitting policy must be devised and the proper combination must be sought. Thus is obtruded self-consciousness, self-interest or that separation from its basic continuum that is incidental to the interruption of the organism's essential life, and with it a new mode of consciousness embodying a fundamental opposition to the primary unity of life now takes its rise.

[1] Consider the legend of the origin of the life of man as symbolized through the intuitions of the folk unconscious recorded in the Book of Genesis. For its discussion see " The Origin of the Incest-Awe," *The Psychoanalytic Review*, Vol. V, No. 3, July, 1918.

ORGANIC BASIS OF INTERPRETATION

Is it not clear that the condition here described is nothing other than a dissociation of consciousness, that this interpolation of the self-motive involves a division of the personality in which there is presented the identical reaction that we have come to know as the essential mechanism of the neurosis? If so, then life in our present mode of adaptation is throughout a dissociation. That such is actually the case is the position of the present thesis. For it maintains that division of personality, or the neurosis, has its basis in this incipient cleavage embodied in the separation of the individual element from its original organic continuum through the interdiction of the organism's early unitary mode, while integrity of the personality, on the other hand, is represented alone in the preservation throughout the growth of the individual element of its primary organic confluence.

Such a postulate is indeed very sweeping. It will be readily protested that it is too sweeping—that in effect it claims that the whole civilized world is in the grip of a mental dissociation, that it has its being, founds its organization upon a basis of unconsciousness. I can only answer that, however sweeping such a statement may seem in theory, this social implication of the neurosis is amply supported in actuality. For the unconscious reactions of the social mind about oneself are reflected unconsciously within oneself, the individual being but an element in our common consciousness. If one will permit himself to be sufficiently subjective in his own life to view with objective disinterestedness the reflections within himself of these unconscious reactions of the social mind, there will be little ground for protest against such an implication.

This indictment of the entire social mind, however, may rest upon no scant or uncertain foundation. We may not deal with so broad an issue with the personal conclusiveness of a merely dynamic or individualistic interpretation. Our approach must needs be genetic in its scope. We must take account of those integrations which mark the era of man's first awareness and which reach back to the nebulous sources of consciousness itself. For the thoughtful student will demand to know the phylogenetic origin of this universal tendency to interdiction toward her offspring on the part of the mother. Whence *her* self-consciousness, he will ask. One's answer must be largely intuitional, by which I suppose we mean that it must be gathered from sources that are coloured by intimations arising from one's own organic life.

It would appear that in his separativeness man has inadvertently fallen a victim to the developmental exigencies of his own consciousness. Captivated by the phylogenetically new and unwonted spectacle of his own image, it would seem that he has been irresistibly arrested before the mirror of his own likeness and that in the present self-conscious phase of his mental evolution he is still standing spell-bound before it. That such is the case with man is not remarkable. For the appearance of the phenomenon of consciousness marked a complete severance from all that was his past. Here was broken the chain of evolutionary events whose links extended back through the nebulous æons of our remotest ancestry, and in this first moment of his consciousness man stood, for the first time, *alone!* It was in this moment that he was "created," as the legend runs, "in the image and likeness of God." For breaking with the teleological traditions of his agelong biology, man now became suddenly *aware.*

That man's spirit should have quailed before the wonderment of so complete an emancipation is not surprising. Sensing his utter isolation in the face of so strange, so unwonted a realization, he could only cling desperately to the one visible and concrete sign of the prenascent world from which he had newly emerged—to the urgent and ineradicable actuality of *himself,* the one and only link that remained to bind man to the vast and hitherto uninterrupted continuum of his primordial past. Yet turn where he would, the organic hiatus had now been made and its inexorable breach yawned wide and inevitable before him. Unable as yet to endure the contemplation of his new freedom and the limitless expanse it spread before him, equally unable to recross again the gulf he had lately spanned and recover the paths of his original instinctiveness and automatism, the soul of man stood divided against itself. For man could now neither venture forth nor yet return again. In his division he could only grope blindly amid uncertain ways. Before him stretched the stern demands of consciousness and reality, behind him lay the fictitious decoys of a phantastic and immemorial preconscious. His choice lay between the two, yet he was incompetent to follow either. It is, it seems to me, the intermediate stage in man's development, comprised of these two contending issues and entailing the irreconcilable conflict of which each individual's experience is a recapitulation, that is the phylogeny of the unconscious. This is the experience of us all as it expresses itself in the self-consciousness that underlies the personal adaptation of each, through our gradually enforced awareness of the self.

Considered also ontogenetically, the development of consciousness, contrary to accepted tenets, has by no means proceeded upon a fluent and harmonious course.[1] In its very birth consciousness embodies a biological recoil—an organic impaction. Its very unfolding is an infolding, its begetting a misbegetting. For the rudiment of consciousness is self-consciousness. In its origin it is self-reflexive, self-relational. That is, consciousness in its inception entails the fallacy of *a self as over against other selves*. It is in this inevitable *faux pas* of man's

---

[1] The term "consciousness" is used by the writer in two different senses, the one having to do with the mental sophistication of individual awareness, the other with consciousness regarded as an inclusive racial principle. The reader must rely upon the context for the distinction between the restricted individualistic interpretation on the one hand and the organismic interpretation on the other.

earliest awareness, of his original self-consciousness (original sin), that consists the error or lapse in the process of his evolution. In this factor of development marked by the recoil of our self-consciousness or by the inference of our counter-relatedness is to be traced the momentary decline in the progressive curve of man's organic evolution. Yet such temporary recessions embody the operation of laws that are entirely within the order of our developmental descent. In the first dawnings of new and untried possibilities, it often happens that, as growth proceeds, conditions that are later to become assets in the developmental scheme are in their rudimentary phase very burdensome liabilities. The infant that has not yet learned to walk is wont to crawl with much ease and impunity, but with the finer adjustment of walking once acquired he may now move about his world in an upright posture with far greater agility and comfort than the movement of crawling could ever have afforded him. And yet many are the rude impacts and ineptitudes that attend the gradual acquisition of his new endowment. And so the developmental possibility offered man through his attainment of the stage of self-awareness is not less an onward stage in his evolution because in his awkward unaccustomedness he employs it to his own undoing. It is one of the glories of his growth which he may temporarily dim but not permanently extinguish.

With the further unfolding of the consciousness of man, or with his increasing awareness, there followed the recognition of the objective intervals between his congeners severally and between himself and them. His external senses of their very nature apprised him of such intervals, as, for example, those in relation to time and to space. With growing experience his perception of interval between himself and his fellows grew more and more insistent. It became indeed the basis of his operations. Besides, there were intervals which were not only spatial and temporal but intervals or differences that were attributive or circumstantial in their nature, such as

ORGANIC BASIS OF INTERPRETATION

vocal and featural differences, differences of sex, size, colour and of texture.

With this constantly growing, steadily deepening impression of difference, interval or separation in point of external characters, with this habitual looking out upon external or objective differentiation or *otherness*, something happened to the consciousness of man. That which happened was the *faux pas* in his evolution to which I have just alluded. For, through the suggestive influence of repeated observation of objective interval or discontinuity, man fell a victim to a trick of his own consciousness, and, from implications of disparity in the sphere of his peripheral contacts, he erroneously *inferred* differentiations in the sphere of his internal, nuclear, organic life. From data of observation in the field of his objective relationships he unconsciously drew analogous conclusions in regard to the essential continuities of his common, subjective consciousness, and so applied to the primary and inherent mode of his experience deductions which were warranted only with respect to the mode of his outer or objective awareness. From a difference of envelope he assumed a difference of content. From a dissimilarity of outer and accidental character he implied a disparity in the realm of his organic and essential life. *Thus arose the initial confusion accruing from the employment of objective method in terms of the subjective mode.*

It is my position that the fallacy involved in confusing the separate or objective with the confluent or subjective mode has become the very warp and woof of the collective mind, as it is the biological basis of the displacements characterizing the pathological references of the insane. Dealing cognitively (objectively) with our affects and affectively (subjectively) with our cognitions, we fail to envisage what is actually before us. Where there are two individuals—oneself, let us say, as compared with someone else—because of the dissociated *feeling* content with which each regards the other, our presumably objective judgment rests upon a complete subjective misconception. It is, of course, perfectly in order that people be demarcated by us one from another and from ourselves by characters that are external and accidental, and that this discrimination prevail even when such distinguishing characteristics are of a mental nature. But despite all such accidental differences, the original, inherent, organic life that is the underlying essence of any two individuals is common and identical. However different spatially, traditionally and characterologically, there is between them the essential bond of an inherent continuity, of an organic confluence.

It is interesting how the folk mind betrays its need of this underlying subjective unity in its effort to offset the objective tendencies of differentiation. In its desire to express its feeling of amity, its sense of mutual understanding, the habitual mind automatically employs the phrase, " It makes no difference." For example, if one has been unintentionally thoughtless of another, he is at once put at ease with the reassurance that " it makes no difference "—it being obviously felt that difference is the essential condition against which the social mind must preserve itself. Similarly we say, " It is no matter " or " It is immaterial "—a material or objective basis of relationship being evidently likewise sensed as an impediment to unity. There is the same implication in the disparaging intimation contained in the phrase, " He has an object in view." And more telling still is the coalescence of the two affiliated ideas of matter and disunity in the use of the single stem-ending employed in the words " object " and " objection," the evident implication being that *object* and *obstacle*, or *objection*, are subjectively indistinguishable.

It seems to me that even such seemingly trivial etymological evidences betray the organic intolerance of differentiation within the sphere of the subjective life. However habituated we may have become to the subjective inferences of interval due to the objective report of our external senses, beneath these outer and accidental demarcations there is the persistent assertion of an underlying principle of unification and continuity. In our own customary dissociated feeling we lose sight of this completely, and, because of the confusion of modes within ourselves, our judgment of others as being subjectively different from us reaches the point of actual criticism and resentment.

A child early illustrates this tendency to erroneous inference when he refers to inanimate objects about him—a toy or household object—a disposition to thwart his will. For example, he will grow angry at some intractable plaything and strike or abuse it in peevish retaliation. And it is the unfortunate habit of unwise parents—that is, of parents generally—to encourage the child's delusive tendency with some such corroborative remark as "naughty chair" (or whatever the offending instrument may be) and even to carry their complicity to the extent of themselves inflicting punishment upon the object in question.[1]

This tendency to erroneous inference in the mental sphere is the fallacy of an objective method of psychiatry, as it is the underlying misapprehension of the clinical approach of psychopathology generally.[2] Indeed, this misconception is responsible for many of the inadvertencies of reason that exist throughout our scientific ranks. It would seem, after all, that the people who know most are precisely those who suspect least. If the

[1] This mistaken tendency of inference has so far laid hold upon us as to mislead our perceptions even in respect to judgments concerning data which lie altogether within the objective mode. To cite an instance of homely type quite remote from the present argument:—when we speak of two buckets of water, drawn from a common source, in reality our concept is buckets of two waters. For the accident of their separation in space and of the demarcation of the bulk of each by the outline of its container leads the mind, habituated to the fallacy of subjective inference, to posit a difference or a *twoness of essence* where there is but a difference or twoness of outer circumstance or accidental condition. Hence there results a concept not of two buckets but of two waters, whereas the apparently two waters dipped from the same source are essentially one.

[2] "The Need of an Analytic Psychiatry," *The American Journal of Psychiatry*, Vol. VI, No. 3, January, 1927.

psychiatrist is asked what is dementia præcox, his answer consists merely in recounting the signs or symptoms " indicative " of the disorder. If he is directly confronted with the symptoms or indications of the disorder, he will tell you that they represent dementia præcox. With such a confusion in the mind of the psychiatrist one may well judge the confusion existing in the minds of people generally, and with this subjective confusion in ourselves one gains readily an idea of the kind of instruction which the student of psychiatry is now offered as a preparation for understanding the psychology of insanity! It does not occur to the psychopathologist to inquire what it is that constitutes the inherent condition whereof the specific symptoms as well as the generic term for them are but the pathological index. It does not occur to him to ask, in regard to this and other disease-processes, what it is that underlies the label as well as the appearances labelled. But unconsciously misled by the superficial or cognitive *aspect* of the real disharmony, he can only shift uncertainly from sign to countersign. The reason is that, lacking a societal encompassment of mental disorders, the psychiatrist does not recognize that a subjective condition is to be found alone within himself—that the condition for which, in his unconsciousness, he is now seeking the objective account is accessible only within the subjective processes of his own unconscious, as it is accessible subjectively only within the unconscious of mankind at large.

Because of this confusion within ourselves we fail to recognize that delusion is essentially of the affective mode, that its cognitive expression is but its secondary rationalization—a symbolic picture presented in lieu of the corresponding affect denied. It is this type of " reasoning " that is responsible for the tendency one sees everywhere within philosophical circles to make dark the things that are clear. Descartes' dictum, " I think, therefore I am," is the keynote to this cognitive fallacy. The tendency, as I said, even of us who are psycho-

ORGANIC BASIS OF INTERPRETATION 125

pathologists to evade the recognition of the element of unconscious replacement here—confounding cognitive form with affective actuality—is due, as always, to the bias of this self-same replacement within ourselves. Being social participants in the transposition of affect that is the societal neurosis, it cannot be otherwise. Hence this confusion between our perceptual and our affective modes is throughout a basic one, and as it is general in its origin it is necessarily general in its results.

We commonly accept the assumption that mysticism is an emanation of the Hindoo consciousness, when in point of fact the Hindoo consciousness is an emanation of mysticism. In truth, mysticism is a replacement that is not more endemic to India than to England or to America. For in mysticism there is expressed merely this underlying fallacy of reference that is habitual to unconsciousness generally. Mysticism is thus as symptomatic of our matter-of-fact normality as of the most occult form of transcendentalism. Psychologically, the normal mind is synonymous with the mystical mind. Such a replacement is, then, no isolated eventuality signalized in some sporadic neurosis or psychosis but, by reason of its ethnic scope, it underlies no less the genial illusion of the collective social mind presented in the form of amalgamated unconsciousness habitually disguised under the social symptomatology of our so-called "normality." Because of the automatic and unconscious transposition of modes that characterizes our mental processes at their present stage of development, the situation is one that obtains among us all. In the organismic sense we are none of us thinking clearly because we are none of us feeling clearly. This fallacy of implied subjective differentiation is the whole meaning of unconsciousness and the basis of all delusion. I believe that it is upon this deep-seated fallacy of affect incident to the development in man of consciousness or of self-awareness that rests the foundation of the social as of the individual neurosis.

The situation with us is indeed a serious one. Except

for one's faith in the ultimate triumph of the forces of integration over the disintegrative tendencies of our evolution, the mind could only despair at the contemplation of the vicious circle of mutual self-destructiveness in which our present attitude of unconsciousness involves us. As difference or discrepancy in the subjective or organic mode is, from the point of view of the continuity and cohesion of the species, self-destructive, the maintenance of such separateness entails for each individual a desperate loss of his sense of organic integrity. Under the blindness of the retroactive self-defence to which his erroneously assumed separateness inevitably drives him, he fights the more desperately to maintain his artificial individualistic oneness, and, the more desperately he contends, the further he defeats the acceptance of his true organic oneness. It is the inevitable fallacy of our disparate modes.

Freud, then, is right when in seeking to solve the riddle of the neuroses he addresses himself to the personality as a whole. But he is wrong in positing a personal or preferential localization of this central personality as he does when he places this integral consciousness within the bounds of the separative individual. This is to frustrate at the outset the aim of understanding the processes of consciousness through succumbing oneself to the very mode of unconsciousness which supposedly it is one's purpose to comprehend. It is an instance of one's intentionally honest effort toward self-understanding failing to escape the pitfall of personal preference in its very outreaching toward the unprejudiced and true. The separative or the personal *is* unconsciousness. Discontinuity and unconsciousness are conterminous. Thus we are again and again brought back to the impasse which is our refusal to realize that the individual, as a self-appointed, unconscious unit, is but a separate and dissociated *part*, that only as the individual accepts his place as an integral, confluent part in the common, societal personality does he become a conscious, unified *whole*.

ORGANIC BASIS OF INTERPRETATION 127

There is, then, the need to clear our vision through adopting the larger, more organismic viewpoint. There is the need to stand apart from the self and view it as the element that it is within the larger organism of mankind. From the organismic point of view the individual is as truly an element in the larger co-ordinated total comprising the ethnic organism of man, as the manifold cells comprising the individual body are elements in the larger whole constituting his individual organism. We have not as yet reckoned with the consolidated unity of this common societal entity. We have not reckoned with its organic urge in its influence upon human destiny. In our preoccupation with the dynamic or individualistic conception of the libido or of individual aggression, we have not reckoned with the genetic or organic urge that actuates the unitary race consciousness in its societal cohesion.

It is commonly taught by the schoolmen that self-preservation is the first law of nature. I do not believe it. I believe that the instinct of tribal preservation is by far the dominant urge among us. I believe that this instinct takes precedence over the impulse of self-maintenance to a degree that renders individual life insignificant in comparison. In face of the reflex assertion of the impulse of race-preservation the individual is brushed heedlessly aside. A group of miners will without thought descend one after another into a gas-filled chamber to rescue a fellow-workman from death and one after another share the fate of their comrade. We all know countless instances of this rescue-impulse as a response to the organic instinct of race unity.[1] Nor is it confined to these more

[1] An example of the blindly impulsive character of this instinct often recurs to me. I was standing with a lady on the shore of Lake Zürich. A sudden storm arose and we could see plainly that two young men in a sail-boat well out in the middle of the lake had lost complete control of their craft. To the crowd that had gathered on the quays it was evident from the way the sail was jibing from side to side that the boat would overturn. A number of launches began hurrying toward it. As the boat capsized, throwing the men into the lake, my companion, suddenly tearing off her gloves, dashed toward the water. I managed

sensational expressions of the impulse. The scientist in his laboratory toiling daily with indefatigable energy, receiving usually a remuneration that is not adequate to his actual needs and too often without even the sympathetic appreciation on the part of his environment of the significance of his quest, as it relates to the communal need he would serve, expresses equally this same organic instinct of racial solidarity. Yet I do not lose sight of the secret unconsciousness and separativeness that actuate also the unconscious and adaptive reactions of even the most earnest and gifted of these thoughtful, patient investigators. I am not unaware of the delusions of competition and petty jealousy existing even among the ranks of the scientific student. I am not blinking the facts of his personal vanity, of his pride of place and distinction. I will not deny how like a child he is when, on the day of college commencement, he is afforded the opportunity to parade to music in cap and gown and vari-coloured academic emblems in order that, having assembled with his colleagues, he may unite in praise of an archaic deity in thanksgiving for His all-wise discrimination in having personally called him to the best of conceivable institutions in the best of conceivable lands, etc., etc. But, notwithstanding the obviously disparate regression observable in these vestiges of obsolete nursery rudiments, there is yet, extending beneath it all, the surge of an earnest, unifying purpose that embraces the confluent needs of human growth as offered in interests pursuant of common, social ends.

It is the inherent urge actuating this common societal impulse, as contrasted with the narrower motives of

to seize her just as she reached the water's edge. On my rallying her and inquiring just what might be her plans with reference to two men a full quarter of a mile out in the lake and closely surrounded by competent rescue parties, she was unable to account for her impulsive reaction beyond declaring that she " just couldn't let them drown like that ! " Here was an individual with as goodly a share of unconscious egotism as the rest of us, but in whom at the sight of danger to others the self-instinct was completely subordinated to the organic behests of our common societal instinct.

separateness and self, that is envisaged in an organismic point of view. I believe that through this organismic outlook alone we shall come to embody the meaning of the neurosis in its true, impartial significance. In this conception we shall be in a position to view differentiation, under whatsoever form it manifests itself, as the fallacy of self-sufficiency, as the delusion of separateness that it is. Whether presented in the more restricted, individualistic expression of an hysterical hemiplegia, for example, or under the wider social aspect, let us say, of national militarism, we shall no longer study the mere manifest content embodied in the obvious symptom or signal—a focal hemiplegia or a focal militarism—but we shall address ourselves, in each instance, to the societal personality as a whole that underlies each and that comprises for both the organic totality of consciousness. We shall realize that in that totality lies the responsibility for the division among its elements expressed alike in both manifestations. We shall see that in these two seemingly widely dissimilar instances, one expressing itself within the individual man, the other within the nations of men, the situation is the same. In one, differentiation is caused by a breach in the neural continuity of the organism as symbolized by the inert, functionally disaffected segment within the individual; in the other, by a breach in the societal continuity of the organism represented in the functional anomaly of manic self-assertion and segmentation within the social body as symbolized in the separative reaction that has lately so disorganized the Western World. However different in outer form, in both reactions there is alike expressed an unconscious assertion of autocracy or the will-to-self as opposed to the confluent life of the organism as a whole. And it is only as we view these expressions, one individual, the other social, as identical reactions and study them in an identical spirit of interpretation, that we shall recognize the essential principle of our biology exemplified in them, namely, the inherent inviolability of the confluent life of the organism, both individual and societal. Only in this organismic outlook shall we come to understand the true significance of the neuroses in the sense of really encompassing the disharmony embodied in them.

It should be clearly understood that in the view of this thesis it is not a question of discrimination between the social and the individual, but between the societal and the individual societally conceived on the one hand and the social and the individual individualistically conceived on the other.

From this position we have yet to encompass clearly the neurotic disharmony, individual or societal. We have yet to encompass in its real significance what is the most blatant expression of its societal embodiment. Because of our dissociative, individualistic outlook we have yet to consider the psychopathology underlying the phenomenon of war. We have failed to interpret its psychology in the light of the mental attitude that underlies and actuates it. We do not realize that the settlement of war is properly the concern not of politics but of psychiatry. Here, as elsewhere, we shrink from unearthing the actuality of the interred affect, preferring to preserve its image in the fanciful balm of our own illusions. Our horror of war is thus centred solely upon the façade it presents and not upon the inherent significance of war. Accordingly, our concern is merely to alter the aspect, the cognitive form, the mental picture, and, under this altered semblance due to our bidimensional alternation, we still retain the same affect submerged in the unconscious grievance of national separateness and antagonism. There is here the subjective fallacy of the transposed affect and the ancient metonymy of all unconsciousness.

A conspicuous symptom of our societal pathology is the subjective illusion underlying the latent " belief " that diplomatic overtures between nations are competent to cope with the essential disharmonies which, from time to time, tend to issue in the social symptomatology of war, but which are, in reality, due to causative factors deeply rooted in the psychopathology of man's societal disunity. While not questioning the outstanding objective advantage of such superficial covenants as may secure to the social confederacies of nations at least a temporary cessation of their outward expressions of hostility, these surface amenities touch in no way the essential disorder. The real cause lies deeper and the real remedy must penetrate deeper. For the delusion of difference between nations, like the delusion of difference between individuals, is but the objective reflection of the subjective differentiation existing within the nation itself—a differentiation that is comparable to this same objective reflection existing within the individual as a subjective component of the national organism.

Just as the conflict underlying the neurosis of the individual is truly understood only through an analysis in the individual of the vicarious reactions that underlie it, so an understanding of the conflict underlying the neurosis that is societal may be attained only through an appreciation of the substitutive reactions of the group-mind as disclosed through an analysis of the group-consciousness.

Seen clearly, man's restlessness to-day is, after all, the restlessness of intercepted growth. The tremors we are experiencing at this moment throughout the political and economic world undoubtedly owe their impulse to the awakening of a new order of consciousness. In the seething undercurrent of discontent throughout the social organism at the present time there is seen the symptom of a repression that is no longer reconcilable with the growing consciousness of that organism. As in the individual personality a condition of repression that has become too long pent must inevitably break forth in an ultimate overthrow of reason, so in the collection of individuals comprising the societal organism the ultimate response to a too long sustained repression can issue only in a correspondingly overwhelming disruption of the social personality.

In what has just been experienced sociologically as the World War, man is afforded an organic warning of the impending disintegration which lurks unseen beneath the surface crust of immediate and temporary social adaptations within the depths of his unconscious. In that far-sweeping manifestation there are felt the first rumblings of a sociological disturbance that bodes the utter destruction of our old order of habituations, and in that desperate expression of man's social unconscious there is evident the need in which he stands of an earnest and far-searching self-analysis. For as overwhelming as is the catastrophe of the present war—and present it is—this catastrophe is but the detonator preceding the crash that is to come—a crash that has been gathering momentum within the unconscious of the race through centuries past and that will descend upon the world with inevitable fatality in the absence of a more societal and inclusive reckoning among us.

Without the recognition of the meaning of our disaffection, sociological as well as personal, without a more conscious realization of the social involvement of our personal separateness, it will not be possible for the creative forces resident within the personality of man to come into their natural fruition. But thus to encompass the organic disaffection that actuates the neurosis is *to include it within ourselves*. Thus to realize discrepancy is to make real within ourselves, where they exist in all their completeness, the division and antagonism of the disparate consciousness, be its countenance individualistic or social. Such a realization—such a comprehension of life in its manifold unconsciousness is a subjective, organic experience. The process is one that entails the slow divorce of self from the long habituations of our narrow domesticities, personal, familial and national. It involves the gradual sundering of the artificial sophistications of self-consciousness with which our childhood has been enclosed and in which were early laid the foundations of the dissociation that has now become automatic in the

ORGANIC BASIS OF INTERPRETATION 133

overwhelming impetus of its social involvement. The essence, then, of an understanding that truly encompasses the neurosis, consists in the recognition of our collective unconsciousness through the realization of a disaffection within and among ourselves as elements of a dissociated body-social.

CHAPTER III

THE ORGANIC SIGNIFICANCE OF THE UNCONSCIOUS

IN submitting a thesis which takes the position that the significance of the neurosis is its societal implication, and which lays the burden of its adjustment upon the societal mind at large, I fully realize that I am offering no welcome thought. The illusion of the separate self as all-sufficient and omnipotent is too obdurate not to regard with suspicion any attempt to dislodge it. Whatever the postulate, belief or argument, there lurks beneath it, in the mind of each of us, the unconscious determination to preserve intact the secret illusion of his own separateness. As long, however, as this affective fallacy underlies the reactions of our collective mentality, all efforts toward a reconstruction of society upon grounds of a more conscious and adult adaptation are futile. The adaptive and compensatory nature of the normal or collective mind occasions dissociation in all the activities arising out of it. With our mental outlook based upon illusion, our reactions are illusory. No matter how imposing in their manifest content, they are fundamentally spurious and undependable. For having been organically dissociated through the interdiction of the parent, normality is necessarily self-conscious and vicarious. This accounts for the ease with which the normal mind resorts to the replacements represented in mysticism. In the manifold expressions of mysticism the social mind finds its ulterior placations. This accounts for the habitual self-propitiations underlying its cherished superstitions and "beliefs," and explains the whole meaning of the man-made immanence represented in the vicariously projected image of invincible omnipotence we call "God"—an image with which we childishly seek to ally ourselves in order to sustain our impotent separateness. Men are tenacious of the substitution that is their "God" in a degree far beyond their suspecting. It is in vain that they pretend to throw Him off in the mere insolence of their reactionary "disbelief." In their very challenge is His sovereignty reaffirmed. For wherever there is dogmatism there is doubt, and beliefs that are denied are unconsciously not less fixed and ineradicable than beliefs that are affirmed. As long as there is unconsciousness so long will men be a prey to its tyrannical alternatives. Though they break or kiss the rod, it is upon them still.

Man will be slow to relinquish this symbol of God popularly employed by him as a defence against the free, unsponsored growth of his own spirit. It is a symbol, as are all symbols of the unconscious, that has been erected by us as a protection for the disparate self against the confluent life of our common organism. Indeed it is precisely in this collective illusion that is man's most desperate recourse. Yet, in our very extremity and in the very tenacity with which we cling to this illusion, there is to be seen, as always, a symbol for which the only warrant is the profound reality that underlies it. In so far as the organically true is denied, there inevitably ensues the vicariously false, and the insistence of the substituted equivalent is invariably the more intense in proportion to the urge of the organic need withheld. It is organic law.

Recalling the past, it is interesting to consider how conscientiously we have carried the biological method of research into the various objective fields of scientific inquiry. Yet, in regard to the subjective sphere wherein our own reality resides, we have persistently befuddled our perceptions through an unconscious adherence to the childish tenets of fear and superstition, instead of studying the phylogenetic account of our inherent mental descent in the spirit of objective disinterestedness. For, unconsciously yielding habitual perceptions the supreme place even in the laboratories of consciousness, as embodied in the researches of analysis itself, we have continued to preserve the unconscious image of self habitually disguised under our personal interpretation of God. Restoring the form of the idol from time to time by covering the rent with a temporarily stouter fabric whenever the straw has appeared, we have continued to maintain the self-flattering programme of our vicarious and self-protected image-worship. Men apparently do not yet begin to recognize that the socially consolidated aberration constituting their image of God is an illusion that is identical with the individual expression long recognized by psychiatry under the clinical characterization of " ideas of reference." Still seriously discoursing of the symbol called " God," they assume that their *image* possesses an actuality apart from their own imagining.

More significant still, however, is the fact that psychiatry too has its God. Objectively defining ideas of reference in others, we have failed to reckon with the subjective presence of this same replacement within ourselves. While we psychiatrists would carefully note the tendency to transposed affects within the arbitrary systems of the insane, we have wholly missed count of this same tendency within our own autocratic system. Among psychiatrists the favoured Deity is Dementia Præcox. The symptoms, reactions and prognostications assigned to the image implied in this arbitrary superscription attain with us to a quite endless category. And such is the subtlety with which the insidious tendency to the vicarious (affective displacement) secretly insinuates itself even into the courts of the elect, that individual personality is again and again led into the unsuspected trap that is our habitual confusion of the symbol for the reality that underlies it.

In truth " Dementia Præcox," the disease, is but the symbolic projection of dementia præcox, the actuality, ever resident in our generic unconsciousness. As it is the primary state of the infant psyche, its rudiment is preserved in the unconscious of us all.[1] The understanding and acceptance of this biological substrate of consciousness within oneself offers the only condition of its solution. In this subjective course lies the whole significance of a really organic analysis. To hold a theoretical, objective attitude toward the insanities is to remain under the thrall of the social unconscious. To preserve our own repressions by attempting to deny this preconscious factor within ourselves is merely to perpetuate this regressive trend under its present symbolic guise. Theoretical substitution is the big-stick of normality of which an objective analysis is the butt-end. To maintain the normal, psychiatric, adaptive outlook is to be repressed, vicarious, theoretical. And by our attitude of aloofness we merely preserve in unconscious form in ourselves the symptom-complex we stigmatize as dementia præcox in others. But we cannot alleviate a mental disorder from which we stand apart. It is only as we accept the testimony of its rudimentary presence within our own consciousness that its significance in the consciousness of others may become clear.

Of dementia præcox, the disease, psychiatry is in fact more a cause than a cure, just as mothers and doctors who habitually hold to a mental attitude of personal ministration and concern, however handy they may be in untoward emergency, are more an occasion than a remedy for disease in general. And so the real disorder, after all, is not dementia præcox but psychiatry. When the psychiatrist will have come to understand dementia præcox or the preconscious within himself, this objective figment of his own disordered consciousness will spontaneously vanish.

To-day, the symbol of the social mind that is called " God "—the symbol under which man has worshipped himself so confidingly throughout the ages—is gradually losing its symbolic adequacy and, as is typical when the

[1] " Character and the Neuroses," *The Psychoanalytic Review*, Vol. I, No. 2, February, 1914.

foothold of man's unconscious threatens to be dislodged, he is hastily replacing his shattered idol with an image that bears a new, a subtler and a more plausible disguise. Even in schools representing developments of the Freudian psychology and presumably devoted to impartial analytic inquiry into man's unconscious, we find this same unconscious self-worship shifted from the broken image of " God " to a merely revarnished symbol set up upon the same altar and called by the newer name of " Love." Though the form is altered, the substance remains the same. It is again man's self-love projected into the spurious objective that best lends to it the flattering security of the seemingly real.

I do not say that there is not in life an essential unity or love. I do not say that there is not for man an answer to the need he feels in his relentless but misguided pursuit of such an underlying reality. What I do say is that the unity he may find is the substance whereof the unity he is seeking is but the shadow ; that in his unconsciousness he has not yet begun to seek the reality that is the need of his essential, organic life ; and that, failing the reality which resides alone in the confluent, unified life of our common consciousness, he has pursued the temporary and personal satisfactions whereof such fanciful image-projections as " God " and " Love " are but hysterical replacements.

What is significant is the fact that, under however subtle a guise he may clothe it, every individual in the great confederacy of " normality " entertains and is actuated by some form of " belief "—a " belief " either in " God " or " Love " or in some other concept that is the emotional equivalent of these more general fabrications of our collective unconscious.[1] But in the image

---

[1] We overlook the fact that it is not the content of a belief but rather the mere condition of believing that determines its errancy or truth. The word *belief*, as has been said, is a derivative of the Anglo-Saxon *leof*, meaning *preference*, but we do not recognize that what one " believes " is merely what one *wants to think*. There are undoubtedly as many devout believers among the devotees of Science as of Religion,

fashioned of belief there is seen the inevitable process of compensation vicariously exacted of us by virtue of our denying the fulfilment of the organic reality of life. The dissociated mind can of necessity observe only dissociatively. In its repudiation of reality it resorts perforce to vicarious images of reality. It is for this reason that the normal mind is the mystical mind. In its organic disunity it cannot be otherwise. Although it seek under manifold signs and symptoms to conceal the tell-tale of its stigma, its blight is betrayed by countless evidences of its dissociation from the societal or organic personality. And it is not in the nature of the *object* that consists the element of the mystical in our human pathology but in the *mode* in which the object is regarded.[1] The objects of

and upon inquiry we should probably find that the pet *beliefs* of the scientist rest upon as unreasoning an attitude of mind as those of the religionist. The point is that whatever is thus believed in response to personal preference is arbitrary and doctrinaire, be it evolution, relativity, or God.

[1] It is really the element of secret emotionalism that constitutes mysticism. It is again a phase of the private alternative whereby we get what we want. What is called " intellectual mysticism " is but a secondary rationalization of this emotional element. But there is need of discrimination. While it is true that conceptions arising from intuitional inference may readily be begotten of emotionalism, yet the same inferences when based upon biological analogy cease to be mystical. Nietzsche's " primordial unity," because biologically inferred, seems to me a quite unemotional and inclusive conception. In the biological consistency that unites the most highly differentiated species with the lowest single unicellular organism, the mind straightway finds substantiation for Nietzsche's conception. Whereas the " metaphysical unity " of the religionists is, on the contrary, a wholly mystical conception. Through this postulate the mind is immediately involved in such vagaries as one connects with the doctrine of transubstantiation or with the flights of Annie Besant and her astral bodies !

But one can perhaps still more aptly illustrate the distinction in question by considering the totally opposed meanings—the one intellectual, the other emotional—contained in the word " vibrations " according as it is used by the scientist in regard to mathematically mensurable physical wave-lengths or as it is employed by the " hypersensitive personality " to describe certain sensations presumably recorded somewhere in the region of the epigastrium in response to subtle but invisible " psychic communications." In defining the term mystical one must not fail to include the attitude of mind that leads one scientist, who has failed to understand the investigations of another, man's mystical devotion offer an infinitely varied range. They may readily be presented by a host of images expressing the widest discrepancy in manifest content—for example, one's conception of the cosmogony, "the true artist," a scientific discovery, the "error of mortal mind," one's exchequer, "to-morrow" with its ever receding illusion of postponement, or a cult of mental healing with texts setting forth the ultimate solution of life; or, on the other hand, an autogenic sexual fetish, as one's body, the unreal image one causes to stand for one's mother, a favourite offspring, "God," or "the superlative woman." Among certain people a very popular vehicle for the mystical mode is one's "voice." To-day, too, there are people who talk in subdued whispers of the spiritual virtues of raw foods and who dilate by the hour upon the merits of lettuce—as though it were the millennium. Then there is to be noted the high place in mystical sanctuaries which the family escutcheon occupies among its votaries. There are people extant (I confess I am one of them) who still tend to entertain the belief that a reality underlies the social concept "good family." And—comedy of comedies!—such is the subtlety with which the element of the mystical or of vicarious self-worship evades the reality of consciousness that the very "sincerity" with which one comes to "relinquish" such objects of infantile illusion may itself actually rank among the spurious images of this identical category! Seriously fancying herself well on toward the goal of her analysis, if not quite arrived, one of my patients remarked to another: "I want nothing." It was spoken very gently, almost imperceptibly, so in keeping was the rendering with the spirit of its author. But it is evident that at least she wanted to be regarded as *not* wanting

to refer to those investigations as mystical. I am inclined to feel somewhat strongly on this point because of the fact that my conception of the primary biological unity of the organism and its influence upon the subsequent development of the personality has tended to be regarded quite arbitrarily in the light of a mystical interpretation. (See note 1, page 10.)

anything, else she would have felt no occasion to remark her detached state. But how exquisite the subtlety here ! Another says : " I want to get rid of *things*, that I may be more free." Getting rid of things or husbanding them may equally fall within the mystical or dissociated mode. As for one's " freedom " there is no object, unless it be one's " truth," that constitutes a more popular idol under which to hide the mystical fetish of one's secret self-worship. But whatever the vehicle, that which gives to it the hall-mark of the mystical is its quality of an inner, esoteric experience possessing an indefinable, transcendental meaning revealed alone to the peculiarly favoured possessor. Observe here the characteristic element of distinction, the factor of favouritism, the inseparable paranoid element of special delegation. For the object, after all, as every object of the unconscious, is no other than the self or the parent from the point of view respectively of the parent or the self, and our civilized world of boasted normality becomes upon investigation but a nursery of ungrown childhood, filled to overflowing with bogus Gods and goblins !

As the child lost in the street anxiously scans the face of every passer-by in the hope of discovering the features of his mother, so the grown-up, who has lost the quiet continuity of his organic life and flounders amid a world of dissociative habituations and ulterior ends, eagerly searches the countenances of all whom he meets, in the driving urge to incarnate anew the cherished image of *his* mother. The difference is that everywhere and in every one he finds her. And not his mother alone but his father, his brothers, his sisters, uncles and aunts, and with them (such is the magic of unconsciousness) the whole array of traditional furnishings reminiscent of his childhood's scenery. For as his images are born of his fancy, his fancy may create them at his will. Thus the world at large is but the family at large and the social *genre* but the mother.

In contemplating this identification of " the world "

with one's mother we come to sense more intimately the real significance in normality of the widely featured phenomenon of suggestibility. As suggestion is the affirmative expression whereof repression is the negative form, suggestion, like repression, is but the operation upon the individual of the will of the consensus, of which we all, of course, are the only too willing dupes. For just as our succumbing to repression is the individual's rejection of the consensual mind, so our succumbing to suggestion is the individual's acquiescence in the consensual mind. So that, whether the impetus be the factor of suggestion or of repression, whether it be offered in the positive inducements to " good " behaviour or in the negative disparagements to " bad " behaviour, in either case one is but fancifully subjecting himself to the domination of the parental will in the expanded guise of the consensual unconscious. Contrary to popular belief, suggestion is no clinical specific ; it is a social pandemic. The doctor does not wield it, it wields him. So that as suggestion and repression, or the will of normality (normality means " accepted rule " by the way), are but the will of the parent, it is the will of the parent that is really the " power " of suggestion. And as the influence exerted by suggestion, like the influence exerted by the parent, is based upon the mental precept of good and bad, suggestion like repression is necessarily separative in its effect. For its self-reflective tendency necessarily induces in us the inversion of self-worship. Again it is the discontinuity of the dissociative self in the separatism of its own unconsciously induced image.

When we come to contemplate this childishness in ourselves, we are naturally loath to admit that all our beliefs are but make-beliefs, and our privately cherished convictions of certitude but the compensatory assumptions of mysticism and dissociation. To the man who entertains the inner conviction that the girl of his heart is just the one woman in the whole world for him, it were futile to point out his inconsistency by recalling an identical "belief" maintained no less stoutly by him a few months ago in regard to his last year's beloved. It were as futile as to attempt to expound to a paranoiac, who has proof that he is descended from Napoleon, that he is the unconscious prey to unwarranted ideas of grandeur. Both of these esoterists will only look you blandly in the face and explain to you compassionately that " you just do not understand."

Truly, of the tissue of illusion is the fabric of unconsciousness, whether presented under the form of hysteria, mysticism or suggestion. All being alike dissociative, all are alike inaccessible to the arguments of an organic logic. And more and more it seems to me that when we who are psychoanalysts consider *our* unconscious preoccupation with the concept, the symbolic equivalent, the theory of consciousness as a substitute for the daily lived actuality of man's organic life in its totality, there is due the admission that psychoanalysis too, as it now exists among us, is itself no less an equivocation, a " belief," an hysterical replacement for the common, organic confluence of our societal life. Indeed, precisely because of its high claim as representing the court of ultimate conscious appeal, psychoanalysis requires to be brought to book more than any other of the manifold dissociative reactions coming under an indictment that envisages our collective, social unconscious. We who are psychoanalysts talk of the joyous enfranchisement of consciousness and growth as compared with the palsying limitations of unconsciousness and regression, when all the while we neglect to impeach the unconsciousness of our own lives and the narrow interests of personalism and self that govern them. Because in our own normality we are ourselves so comfortably ensconced in the social security of the collective unconscious about us, we fail to recognize our own embroilment in it. And so, in the impregnable solidarity of mere mass supremacy, our own assumed validity passes unchallenged by us.

To cite an example that is closest to me: I have

repeatedly held forth to patients concerning the potential joy inherent in adult love regarded in the light of the unifying principle of life, as though I myself participated in its subjective actuality in the simple, undifferentiated mode of my own daily living, when in fact I was only unconsciously exploiting the vicarious concept or symbol or theory of love, such as can only stand in the way of and obstruct the organic significance of love in its actuality. Thus, in spite of ourselves, unconsciousness makes disparate elements of us all. Indeed, it may more truly be said " because of ourselves " rather than " in spite of ourselves," for, in an organic sense, self (the separative entity) and disparity are synonymous.

But, however serious a situation that involves a worldwide neurosis, we may not take it tragically. The tragedy of it, after all, is only the unconsciousness of it. When we shall have truly analyzed the drama of the unconscious which now we but enact, there can be no tragedy, for the fabric of tragedy is woven merely of the elements of human " fate " in its embodiment of the unconscious. There is the need, however, to view our situation thoughtfully. Consciousness, in the sense of a true comprehension of life, will come into its own only when we have learned to look upon the humiliating spectacle of our dissociated selves with what enforced forbearance we can temporarily command. Our present attitude will continue to endure until more and more the disheartening sense of our disparities becomes accepted by us in an outlook that, having grown inclusive, has become our automatic and habitual mode.

Paradoxical as it may sound, consciousness has turned the heads of us all ! As it has turned them in a direction that has been inward upon our own image, each of us, as a result, has built of his individual organism a little separate entity unto himself—an entity which in its organic dissociation from life as a whole is necessarily wrought of a spurious fibre. Developmentally man is the biological snob *par excellence.* Scorning the slower accretions of growth that can alone imbue him with true biological culture, in his effort "to attain" he has attempted to pass too hastily from his humble category of vertebrate to the more socially elevated plane of "cerebrate." The result is that what he assumes to be cerebration is really but a fictitious brain-state that has become entirely withdrawn from continuity with his organic life. So that from the point of view of consciousness in the sense of an integral mental life—the especial mark whereby we claim prerogative over all other species—man is, by this very token, the least integrant of them all!

And yet, when we think of it, our predicament is really no shame to us. Consciousness is, after all, a very recent asset among us. That we should treasure it narrowly, personally, is but the inevitable entail of its slow, laborious evolution. It is as if, in our societal separativeness, our race had grown grey before its childhood had begun and we were now out of breath keeping pace with ourselves. For it is only our separativeness that has prematurely burdened us with the crushing weight of self-imposed responsibilities such as are the concomitant toll of our hallucinated self-sufficiency. Unlike the adult, the spontaneous joy of children is their whole-hearted participation in the free, impersonal radiation of life. Unlike ourselves, their personal importance has not yet defeated their impersonal significance. As yet they do not live under the curse of a dogma of conduct. Theirs is no creed of behaviour that is of one cloth with an enforced pretence of "goodness." Their lives are not a daily concession to fanciful needs of self-protection against an arbitrarily predicated world of "evil." Adult vigilance, however, early inculcates its delusion of separateness—of a self to be defended against other selves—and its dissociative influence is slowly imparted to the confiding mind of childhood. In a world of dissociation this universal suggestion acts with powerful effectiveness, and the child of yesterday, having once been inducted into the general guild of secret mistrust and compensatory behaviourism

K

and grown to parenthood, may be safely trusted to pass on without question the secret code of differentiation, self-distinction and disharmony to the offspring by which he is in turn succeeded.

When God called Adam and took him to task for going about naked (for eating of " the tree of the knowledge of good and evil "), asking him if he felt no sense of shame, Adam's prompt response was to betake himself to the bushes overcome with embarrassment. Whereas obviously the logical response on Adam's part would have been : " By no means. I am the outcome of your own handicraft and if there is any flaw in the product it is not for me to feel chagrin." As a matter of fact, Adam was in nowise different from the rest of us. But there he crouched, submissively answerable for the work of his creator and there he has got us all crouching ever since ! God, of course, employed the familiar parental recourse and intimidated Adam, calling from afar to him in his place of hiding. As was calculated, the strategy was completely effective and promptly brought Adam to his knees. All of which legend is but the allegorical statement of the simple organic truth that shame has first to be artificially induced in us before it can be experienced by us. Division or shame having been put into us, of course we feel division or shame.[1]

[1] There is a story reminiscent of juvenile days in my own home that is to the point. An older brother, then between four and five years of age, was being given his bath in the nursery as was customary in those days. Hanging above the mantel was a picture of the Sistine Madonna. The youngster being freed of his clothing ran skipping about the room. His governess happened to be present, and being duly horrified or, what is more probable as I remember her, acting in response to a sense of duty, she gently chid him for his lack of modesty, saying " Jesus doesn't love little boys who go about that way." The child looked up at the picture of the nude infant with doubtless a more discerning sympathy with Jesus' views than grown-ups are wont to attribute to the wisdom of childhood, and looking his would-be instructress quietly in the eyes he replied incontrovertibly : " He does it hisse'f ! "

If the story of my brother's life should ever be fully told, as some day I hope it may, it will help us realize the unerring fatality of an early enforced system of repression and its logical effect upon the individual's subsequent life as upon its close.

If we have become aware of ourselves and of our unprotectedness, it has been quite in the order of our evolution. But by the same process it is now high time for us to realize that there is no need of protection, and accordingly to come out of hiding and recognize that our fear and our self-protection, being alike identical with the myth of Adam's indiscretion, are alike induced in us by the identical process of an external word of repression or command thrust in upon an essentially inherent and consonant mode.

In the absence of our realization of this blunder into which we have fallen, from generation to generation we unconsciously repudiate the natural unity of our common life in favour of a life prompted by sophistication and disparity. Ourselves begotten of alien affects, our feelings in turn breed diverse cross-strains which can issue only in equally hybrid reactions. We refuse to see that the "evil," alike with the "good," is naught but the delusion of separateness extraneously induced in us through our artificial self-consciousness. This subjective division within us is the essential meaning of the all-pervasive bogey of our so-called incest-awe. As I see it, incest-awe is the organic inconsistency of this division within the organically indivisible sphere of man's essential feeling. Normality is unconsciously under its thrall because, through its organic disunity, normality has unconsciously placed itself under its sentence. Psychically normality *is* incestuous and hence its awe. The degree of its awe or guilt-revulsion is precisely the measure of its psychic inbreeding. The more organically unwelcome the infolding, the more organically outraged or neurotic the personality, and, accordingly, the greater the awe or feeling-conflict resultant upon our unconscious intimations of organic "guilt." Our sexual self-consciousness is the perennial fig-leaf of early tradition foliating anew in our critical Twentieth Century. It is the division of the self of behaviour from the self of spontaneity, of the self as disparate entity from the self as an integral element in our common organic life that is the meaning of the incest-awe as of the neurosis, in its social as well as in its individual expression.

When once we have assumed the broader organismic outlook, we shall see that, beyond a more extended compass of vision, there is really nothing of an innovation in this societal mode of envisagement. In respect to all systems coming under scientific observation, we have habitually entertained a biological conception of the relation *inter se* of the elements to their aggregate that is identical with the conception offered in the present theme. Hitherto the area generally considered has merely been circumscribed within narrower limits, that is all. When we shall have learned to move aside from our personal involvement in it, we shall see presented an organic phenomenon which upon examination consists of a dissociation within the societal organism. We shall see that this dissociation involves disharmony in respect to the mental and social relationships of the unit-elements or individuals that comprise ourselves and constitute *inter se* the larger biological aggregate of our common consciousness. Maintaining our impersonal angle of envisagement and turning to the idea of the sum of the more circumscribed biological aggregate constituting the individual, we see that this dissociation is, in reality, identical with the dissociation within the individual organism that manifests itself as impairment of harmony in respect to the physiological or functional relationships of the units or cells comprising *its* ultimate elements. When we lose sight of our place as common elements within the organic aggregate of mankind—as in the absence of an encompassing organismic point of view we must—we tend to separate arbitrarily the biological continuity of the two spheres, the individual and the societal. Because of our own subjective involvement we fail to recognize that the societal sphere, in the more inclusive sense, is the aggregate whereof the individual is the unit, precisely as in the more circumscribed physiological view the body cells are the units of which the individual is himself the aggregate. Between the two spheres there is a progressive continuity. There is no interruption of the organic transition from one to the other. For the psychological or the societal and the functional or physiological are continuous.[1]

It is evident that every bodily lesion consists of a *separation* among the elements of the impaired part. If among the cells of the liver, for example, there is produced the condition of disharmony or disease represented by a state of inflammation, there inevitably occurs some partition, some breach in or interruption of their concerted function, or of the function of the organism as a whole. The unfailing signal wherewith the individual is apprised of the destructive process is the reaction subjectively registered as *pain* or a sympathetic awareness on the part of the aggregate organism of the disordered condition of these elements constituting a part of itself. Such a disordered state or lesion being thus reported to the central system, as it were, the immediate response is an outcry of pain and a prompt recourse to remedial

---

[1] The biological (organic) continuity between the societal or psychological and the functional or physiological spheres is interesting in view of their obvious homologies as shown in the marked suggestive influences which we see passing over from the psychological sphere and affecting the processes pertaining to the functional or physiological sphere and doubtless operating no less in the reverse direction. One wonders without undue presumption how many so-called " organic " diseases are not primarily functional and hence functionally modifiable through the integral, societal agency of an organic analysis, provided, of course, that the separative process has not already crystallized into the static condition of structural alteration. At least it is clear that many so-called physical derangements need to be frankly regarded in the light of sheer somatic hysterias. See " The Psychological Analysis of So-called Neurasthenic and Allied States," *The Journal of Abnormal Psychology*, Vol. VIII, 1913–14, page 246, note 1.

An analogous condition is demonstrable in the physical universe in the fact that the phenomena of gravitation (such as planetary motion) and the phenomena of electricity (including the motion of light) have been proved to be so intimately related to one another as to be regarded now by the physicists " as parts of one vast system embracing all Nature."

aids. The organism as a whole, experiencing pain, reflexly demands relief, for the reason that impairment of the organism in any of its parts is a menace to its integrity as a whole. That is to say, when any one of us as an aggregate experiences pain in any part whereof he is the whole—when he experiences some local inflammation or separation within the elements of a part or organ within himself, he promptly directs his efforts toward its alleviation. But in the organic whole comprising the societal aggregate whereof he, as an individual, is the contributive element or part, the situation, as we shall in a moment see, is wholly altered. As related parts or elements within the larger organic aggregate, it is we ourselves who are the separative process—the circumscribed area of inflammation.

It is essential to bear in mind that the organic pathology of this biological lesion or separation that is the individual's dissociation from the inherent continuum of his organic, racial congeners is a condition that is conterminous with the individual's division or separation within himself. For organically there is no difference between himself and his congeners. Thus in respect to this societal lesion the individual element bears a twofold relation, an intrinsic and an extrinsic one. The element as an *individual* within the societal organism on the one hand is the *source* of the lesion. And on the other hand, as an organic *participant* in the confluent race consciousness, this same element or individual *experiences* the lesion as a menace to the integrity of his own organic consciousness or of his confluent life as a whole. The individual is thus the contained and the container, the stimulus and the response. Herein lies the unassuageable poignancy of the neurotic conflict. It is a conflict between the part and the whole, wherein the individual is the embodiment of both. Since he is unconsciously the part while inherently the whole, his conflict is one that is concomitantly individual and societal, for the individual and the societal factors are organically inseparable.

Just as in a comprehensive inquiry into the structural development of the organism it is necessary to consider not only the biological characters occurring in the development of the individual but also the corresponding characters observable in the development of the race, so in an organismic study of consciousness it is necessary that we keep in mind the essential parallelism between its individual and its phyletic trends. Analogous to what we know of the facts of comparative biology in the structural sphere, the organic consciousness of man, which we see expressed ontogenetically in the essential continuity of the individual personality, finds its phylogenetic expression in the inherent continuity of the societal organism. Accordingly, as the miscarriage of this primary continuity of consciousness is to be seen in the dissociation of the single personality, so the miscarriage of man's societal personality is correspondingly to be seen in the social dissociation of the collective unconscious. After all, the consciousness of the individual is but the consciousness of the race in miniature, and the personal dissociation within the individual is, therefore, only the miniature expression of the social dissociation within our societal consciousness. In other words, as one's individual organism is a replica of the social organism, the dissociation of the social mind is identical with the dissociation of the individual mind. For, since the societal and the individual factors of evolution are identical in their course, the social and the personal factors of dissociation are also identical. Hence the dissociation that is personal is necessarily social; the neurosis we study in the individual is necessarily concomitant to a neurosis within the wider social polity.

Let us now compare the difference in the subjective reaction of the individual according as he is himself the aggregate experiencing pain in any part of *his* organism, or as he is himself a part unconsciously contributing to the lesion within the organism comprising our common societal aggregate. As central system presiding over his own individual organism we have seen his prompt recourse to agencies of relief at the least trespass upon the integrity of any organ or part within himself. But observe the total reversal of reaction when he himself, as a single individual element, is the pathological instance threatening the integrity of the organic aggregate that encompasses him as a single individual element. Mark how he struggles *in blind collusion with* the disruptive process he unconsciously or separatively embodies. Such is precisely the behaviour of the neurotic individual and such is precisely the meaning of his " resistance." For in such a situation he seeks recourse to every conceivable avenue of evasion and of symbolic disguise in order to escape the protests of pain in the central inherent system resident in the common societal consciousness and experienced by him in its continuum with his own essential life. In the spirit of his behaviour he is exactly comparable to an individual who, on succumbing to a local disease-process, would seek to stifle the organism's premonitory pain in order to aid the toxic invasion and further its ravage within his own tissues! Such, however, in our unconsciousness is precisely the case with each of us. Each of us, in his misguided, ingrown self-interest, constituting in himself the pain and impairment that operate within and against the organic societal aggregate, contends in his self-protection not against but in favour of the disease-process which, from the point of view of the societal, organic life, is his own destruction. He seeks not its interruption but its continuance, not its remedy but its aggravation, precisely as the inflammatory process in any organ within the body seeks to maintain its separateness and prolong to a fatal issue the destructive process in the individual.

It is characteristic of separateness that it fights desperately for its own separative ends. Separateness, being destructive, must operate destructively. It would even seem that this self-destructive tendency on the part of the isolated component is the penalty imposed by the

SIGNIFICANCE OF UNCONSCIOUS

societal organism to safeguard itself against the tendency—among any of its elements as parts—to infringe upon the integral sum of elements constituting the organic whole. But if the separateness of the part is its own destruction, concomitantly the confluence of the whole is its own conservation. If the neurotic regarded individually, or as the embodiment within himself of a societal lesion, is an expression of separatism and pathology, the neurotic viewed organically, or as the embodiment within himself of the societal continuum, is no less an expression of confluence and health. If, in the first instance, he is himself the disorder that is his own separatism and unconsciousness, in the second he is the integration that is his own confluence and consciousness. It is this constructive aspect of the neuroses of which we have not yet taken account and of which we may take due cognizance only upon the basis of a wider, organismic interpretation of these disorders of the personality. It is the understanding of these disharmonies in the light of their congeneric significance, and their encompassment as morbid processes operating within the separative individual organism to obstruct the function of the societal organism as a whole, that is the significance of an organismic formulation of the neuroses.

CHAPTER IV

ORGANIC ANALYSIS OF REPRESSION AND OF THE FACTOR OF RESISTANCE FROM THE SOCIETAL VIEWPOINT

THE psychic phenomenon with which Freud was confronted in the very inception of his work was the element of repression and its concomitant reflection in the objective reaction of resistance. The resolution of this factor of repression or resistance Freud came very early to regard as the essential problem of psychoanalysis. But, as we have seen, Freud's conception of resistance was inevitably coloured by his own individualistic monocular, and in consequence it was not possible for him to view the neurosis of the individual in its societal implication. Lacking a societal basis of interpretation, he could not see that the resentment toward one's fellows comprising the individual's social resistance is merely the individual's objective evasion of the subjective disaffection within his own essential organism. Mistaking the mere symbol of the individual for the inherent continuity of individuality, Freud could not see the biology of resistance as the breach it is in the individual's continuity with life as a confluent, organic whole.

From an organismic viewpoint, the individual's reaction of resistance or his effort to project upon his fellows the pain of his subjective curtailment and repression only illustrates further the essential *sociology of the neuroses*. In the fuller light of a societal basis it may be seen that the mechanism of social replacement embodying resistance is purely symptomatic of the individual's constraint toward a surface rationalization of his own inherent grievance. His grudge is not personal, it is societal. It is not logical, it is biological. Residing wholly within himself, it involves only himself. His tendency to *refer* his grievance to the attitude of others is due to his own separative habituation and to his consequent effort to escape the *seeming* isolation of his biological responsibility toward it. And so the problem of resistance is central, not peripheral. Like its close kin charity (if not its very self in the garb of religious sentimentalism) the relinquishment of resistance is a benison that begins at home. It may not be inculcated through theoretical precept nor through the subtlest refinement of a technique based upon a system of analysis, but only through our actual participation in the societal confluence that is its underlying biology. Our very theory of resistance as an impediment to life is itself a resistance. For no formulation of life can function as life. It is only life itself in its organic confluence that may abrogate the separateness that is the essence of resistance. Whether in the societal or in the individual sphere, whether in the sphere we arbitrarily designate as psychological (mental) or in that we call functional (physiological), the question of health or disease hangs solely upon the issue as to whether the element—cell or system—functions integrally or separatively, congruently or resistantly. Under the limitations of a dissociative reaction toward the confluent, societal organism as a whole, such as constitutes our present socially affective mode, the individual organism cannot but react disaffectedly, and hence further the disruptive tendencies that breed disharmony within its own life. The dissociated organism can function only dissociatively.

If it is true of the world at large that each is against each, if throughout the tissue of the societal fabric every element is maintaining its own separateness against every other element, where may there be found a way to restore the condition of societal confluence that is the basis of man's inherent life? Clearly, if this separation from the organic life takes place within the individual, its reconcilement must take place also within the individual.

As, however, the individual is but a replica of every other individual—an organic world in miniature in the complex of sensations and emotions comprising his own personality—the reconcilement of the organic conflict within himself, or his own unification of personality as an integral part of the continuum uniting the whole, is also the reconcilement and the unification of himself with his congeners. Naturally, such a reconcilement cannot be the achievement of the individual as a separate social unit, but only of the individual as an integral element in the organic unit of our common life.

It is just here that there needs to be unearthed the essential fallacy of Freud, as of us all—a fallacy that has been the inevitable outcome of a habit of reasoning that is inseparable from the disparate social unit and its dissociative mode. Precluding within himself a participation in the organic societal mode, it was, of course, not possible that Freud should take account, in any inclusive organismic sense, of causative elements lying within this mode. Reasoning from the biased premises of an unconscious separatism, he could reckon only with elements falling within the scope of the separative mode, that is, he could only reckon personally—I mean in the sense of dissociatively rather than integrally.

In Freud's conception of the neurosis the condition embodies a repression of sexuality. That is, sexuality, regarded as synonymous with the sexual instinct, is posited as the primary factor of which the attitude of repression is a subsequent issue. In other words, sexuality or the "libido," as commonly understood (the separative will-to-self [1] in the view of the present interpretation) is in Freud's formulation the basic, antecedent element, and repression (whatever the occasion—lack of adequate outlet perhaps or the inadmissible character of the sexual impulse) is the organism's automatic recourse

---

[1] The Southern negro has a definition of libido that is biologically truer than that of either Freud, Jung or Claparède. He refers to inadequacy of the sexual life as a lack of " ambition."

operating as a result. So that Freud assigns the cause of a mental disharmony to the subject's repressed sexuality, and the basis of his analytic procedure has been very logically the endeavour to remedy the situation through an adjustment of the sexual life. Accordingly, it is the essence of the individualistic position of Freud that the neurosis is represented in life's repression of sexuality; while it is the essence of the organismic attitude here defined that the neurosis consists in sexuality's repression of life. In brief, according to the dynamic conception of Freud, the basis from which individual life takes its origin is represented in a heterogeneous substrate that is biologically discrete and " polymorph perverse " ; whereas in the genetic conception of the present formulation life traces its source to a homogeneous matrix that is organically confluent and unitary.[1]

In the light of a conception which assumed that the integrity of consciousness resides within the personality of the individual, Freud's confusion was inevitable. Yet viewed even from the standpoint of the individual, the factors of repression and sexuality can be regarded only in the light of organic concomitants. Under whichever of these alternate forms of reaction it may appear, both forms are the inevitable extremes of the dilemma due to the conflict that has been artificially created within the organism. Both are the individual's restless evasion and substitution following inevitably upon its separation from its primary organic source. Although repression and sexuality are organic concomitants, being simultaneous in their occurrence and in their efficacy equal and contrary, the factor of repression is dynamically the prior instance. This is true precisely in the sense that the pressure of my hand as I lay it upon the table is dynamically the prior

---

[1] It should be recalled that in the view of the present thesis sexuality as it exists socially among us is, in essence, narcistic throughout and that hence sexuality, including so-called *normal* sexuality, is, in my conception, a repression, and must be definitely discriminated from the spontaneous and biological expression embodied in the native instinct of sex. (See p. 10.)

stimulus, though the two elements involved—my hand and the table—are from the point of view of the respective pressures exerted by each, mutually coincident and equal. Considered in the light of individualistic consciousness (unconsciousness), repression with its actuation in the alternative of infantile fear or "goodness" and sexuality with its compensatory reaction in the alternative of infantile defiance or "badness" are inseparable and conterminous. For repression and sexuality are equally the *result* in the individual of the factor of organic disunity in the societal consciousness. There is the need to emphasize the fact that the reaction of sexuality as it abounds among us is currently confused with the basic instinct of sex. In point of fact sexuality is the direct antithesis of this organic expression.

The vast mass of the literature of sexuality embraced under sexology, with its voluminous representation of man's symbolic relation to life, will some day undoubtedly appear comparable in value to the equally formidable array of literary compilations that discourse of God and of man's extraordinarily complex relationship to Him included in a no less voluminous theology. As articulate in form, as sympathetic in treatment and as logical in development as both these themes undoubtedly are, it will ultimately be seen, I believe, that both are equally open to serious criticism and both on identical grounds, namely, that in respect to the matter of each, there is no matter there. I mean literally that, in default of the objective reality of the subjects treated under the two discussions by their respective authors, both treatises are in their nature utterly spurious. In Ellis as in Calvin, in Freud as in Aquinas, the sexuality envisaged in one system no less than the divinity envisaged in the other lacks a basis of reality. Both are vicarious rationalizations of the collective unconscious due to the effort to compensate its repression of the organic integrity of our common, societal consciousness. The concept "God" in the one instance, and its counterpart, obsessive sexuality in the other, are in the meantime made to serve the expedience of temporary symbols.

It is noteworthy that man is the only species of the animal world whose communal life requires for its regulation a system either of sexology or of theology. Concomitantly, one cannot but remark the far stronger co-operative instinct existing among the animals and the consequently incalculably greater societal solidarity of our less " conscious " kinsfolk as compared with our own ! [1]

Approaching the problem of the neurosis anew from the vantage coign of a more inclusive, integral background, I have come to regard the factors of sexuality and repression as standing to each other in a relationship that is the exact reverse of that assumed by Freud—the factor of repression being from this altered viewpoint the primary *cause* and sexuality the incidental *result* entailed by it.

To make clear what I mean, it is necessary to view the societal aggregate, with its basis in our organic consciousness, as an entity distinct from that of the separative individual unit with its basis in our dissociated unconscious. The element of repression is incident to the interruption of our functional participation in the unitary race consciousness. The separative, dissociated attitude of mind that precipitates the obsessive, dissociated and resistant individual is a development consequent upon this interruption. So that it is only as we come to recognize our need to include the sphere of man's integral organic life that the conception of repression as a factor anterior to sexuality may be understood in its biological import. To this end our conception of the organic

[1] One may find the objective evidence of this statement amply set forth in P. Kropotkin's *Mutual Aid, a Factor of Evolution*. Here Kropotkin traces in a very conclusive way the presence of the societal instinct in the lower animals and in primitive man. Kropotkin errs, however, when he reaches the levels of development expressed in the social organizations of man. For he fails to discriminate between the instinct of societal solidarity that is the natural cohesion of a species and the quite premeditated and ulterior expressions of social accord represented in the mutual self-interests of man's collective adaptations.

societal consciousness needs to acquire the coherency of clearer form and definition. We need to take account of the original, racial solidarity of man's consciousness and to consider the interpenetrations of common instincts and habits that originally ramified throughout the undifferentiated mental tissue of our common species, knitting its contributing elements into a unitary, homogeneous organism.[1] We need to form a clearer image of the uniform, co-ordinated *one-mindedness* of this primordial, " multi-cellular " organism that was man. In brief, we need to recognize the *individual* that was originally the aggregate consciousness of the race. For, to consider man's phylogeny at this period of his evolution is to consider a unitary organism. It is to break through the prejudice of the separative mode of individual men and reckon immediately with the unified principle of consciousness as a whole, from which only later there diverged the separative elements represented in the dissociated units we ourselves now comprise, but which unified principle survives to-day unaltered in the common unity of our confluent societal personality.[2]

Such is the parent organism from which we trace the course of our psychobiological descent. Such is the parent organism from which we trace as well our psychobiological dissent ! For it is evident that at a certain stage in the growth of this nuclear, racial organism there must have arisen those first faint stirrings which subsequently entailed man's earliest reckonings with the

---

[1] " An Ethnic Aspect of Consciousness," *The Sociological Review*, Vol. XIX, No. 1, January, 1927.

[2] If, in the flash of so brief an interval of time (speaking ethnologically) as fifty years or so, a plan were effected involving the complete segregation from one another of all the individuals comprising the societal organism of the species, the result, notwithstanding the many millions of years required for the gradual evolution of the race up to the present time, would be its complete extermination ! Such a consideration allows us to realize, at least objectively, how closely interwoven are the elements comprising our societal organism and how dependent is the integrity of the whole upon the organic participation of its parts.

FACTOR OF RESISTANCE—SOCIAL

nebulous beginnings of his self-awareness. This reaction whereby mind for the first time grew aware of itself was thus a societal reaction. It involved the aggregate, not the element. Its scope was ethnic, not individual. It was the primal awareness of man's organic consciousness.

In our unconsciousness we deny the reality of this biological phylum embodied in our organic consciousness and underlying the processes of our individual mentation. For this reason we seek perforce to appease our organic need through the imaginary solaces of a fanciful immanence that is but the unconscious *symbol* of the immanent and encompassing actuality of this common consciousness. In our unconsciousness we deny the collateral immediacy of our societal inclusiveness and for this reason we project the lineal image of indefinite extension composing man's dream of a personal life eternal. Denying our organic unity of compass, we compensate in a fanciful unity of duration. Denied his societal participation in a communal earth, man's need can only vent itself in the private illusion of a sectarian heaven. After all, life in its reality is immediate. Philosophy *ad infinitum* to the contrary notwithstanding, there is no " time " like the present ! When we can enter heartily into the realization of the " pseudo " quality of our mental unctions, we may begin to sense more closely the organic inevitableness of such symbolic equivalents as the generic folk-image of " God " and the infinite corps of His understudies, impressed one after another into the service of man's inverted narcism. We may, then, realize that nowhere is nature's abhorrence of a vacuum more vigorously asserted than in the organic intolerance of consciousness toward the voids of unreality. We may, then, understand how, upon the slightest suspension of reality in the sphere of consciousness, a symbolic surrogate will inevitably fill the rift with a punctuality that is automatic. This is reality's ultimate test of reality. It is the unfailing standard of the organism in its measure of the actual. Here is truth's **organic criterion.**

In their original organic commonness, individuals were complete and sufficient. They were undisturbed by the separative attitude of mind that mars our present development with competition and dissension. They did not spend their days in self-interested comparison. They had not yet come into the conflict of a self-conscious image-worship. In this sense—that the mental tissue of our common species was then undifferentiated—the aggregate consciousness of the race was synonymous with the consciousness of the individual. It was an organically unified consciousness.

Through the organic violation on the other hand, involved in the primal recoil of self-consciousness within this societal organism, there is to be traced the biological history of our mental and social disharmonies. Here, I believe, is to be traced the inception of man's collective unconscious and the phylogeny of the societal neurosis. Under the authority of this long-standing and consolidated system of repression the individual is born, and still under its shadow he enters upon the course of his development as an individual. It is this organized Mafia of societal repression, with its enormous weight of traditional and conventional authority—this repression within the collective societal unconscious, with its ready initiation of each new subject—that is the causative factor in the secondary reaction which we observe in the individual as "repression of sexuality." In our own unconscious fealty to the system about us we fail utterly to comprehend that *the repression which we observe in the individual is the result of a prior cause lying outside of the individual and that it consists of the repression within the collective, racial unconscious acting concertedly from without upon the now detached individual unit.*

It is important to distinguish between the social prohibition operating upon the discrete element or individual as a response to popular covenant, and the societal prohibition that operates within the confluent aggregate and is coincident with our organic separation from man's primary societal consciousness. The former is the result collectively of the latter, just as the neurotic repression is the result of it individually. For the societal repression is primary and the social reaction is a repression subsidiary to it.

To understand aright the essential conception of this thesis, it is necessary to have clearly in mind the basis upon which it rests. This basis is the distinction between the element that is societal and the element that is social, between the factor that is sex and the factor that is sexuality. It should be remembered that sexuality, whether in its social or in its individual manifestation, is here throughout regarded as an egoistic and infantile expression resultant upon the alternatives of secret self-interest secondarily induced in the individual in response to this same substitution and repression in the mind of the consensus about him. It is here held that the neurosis is a condition which indicts not the individual alone but society in general and that it consists in the substitution of this obsessive reaction of sexuality for the basic and inherent instinct of sex—that sex is an instinct that pertains not only to mating but to the unity of our congeneric life which, when unintercepted, is the function confluently of man's conscious and organic life.

If it is true that the societal repression resident within the race is the factor that is the cause of the individual's sexuality, it is evident that no amount of preoccupation with the individual factor or with the element of sexuality will avail to release a neurosis the source of which resides in the societal repression. The causative factor, then, that resides within the societal unconscious is the subjective factor to which the individual's sexuality (or its counterpart, the individual's repression) is the resulting objective response. As repression or sexuality of their nature constitute division, clearly they can have no place in the confluent subjective life. And as the neurosis is primarily a disharmony of the confluent subjective sphere, it is upon the continuities of this sphere alone that we must depend for the efficacy of an analysis that retains as its aim—the only logical aim of analysis—the recomposition or synthesis of the scattered elements of the personality into the organic unit of their original aggregate.

CHAPTER V

ORGANIC ANALYSIS OF REPRESSION AND OF THE FACTOR OF RESISTANCE FROM THE INDIVIDUAL VIEWPOINT

As the causative element in the neuroses is societal or subjective, an analysis that proceeds upon the objective tack of uncovering a patient's complexes is futile. If I am objectively interested in a patient's separative, dissociative expressions—in the infinite variety of his sexualities or infantilisms, it is traceable alone to the retention of this same unconscious mode within my own personality. In this situation the analytic procedure is such as bids fair to extend to an indefinite duration. But if, on the contrary, my own mode is organic and inclusive, my interest in the patient and my whole relationship to him will rest upon an organic, confluent basis. I shall be interested not in the dark secrets of sexuality which he may bring himself to divulge but in the delusion of separateness that leads him to suppose that my own sexuality or the desperate recourses of separatism and repression within myself are less dark than his own. Indeed, arguing merely from presumptive evidence, my absorbing interest in the subject of the neurosis would of itself make it a safe conjecture that my own reaction to the societal repression or my own sexual conflicts must have been by far the greater of the two. But neither is this the point. The point is that our sins are common because our lives are not common, and that the patient's sole need is his understanding of the causative factor in the reaction of separation and repression of the collective mind as it may be realized by him in the relationship of his personality to my own. My sole endeavour, then, will be directed to an understanding on his part of the cause of his neurotic separatism or of the societal repression which, in dissociating him from the congeneric consciousness common to us both, artificially creates his illusion of difference between us.

Lacking this realization of the societal involvement of the neurosis, there necessarily ensues a personal involvement in the analysis that invites situations which not infrequently attain to an acute crisis. The only remedy is the realization through one's own analysis of one's own societal disaffection. The only recourse is the complete reversal of one's own pictorial or introverted habits of experience. It will not be easy. To accept voluntary subjection to conditions involving involuntary pain will not become a popular pastime. But it is the only way in which we may be made aware of our social involvement in the societal neurosis about us. It is the only way by which we may come to take a conscious part *in* and not be an unconscious part *of* the analysis.

Never in the drama of human vicissitude has there been staged anything more ironical than the spectacle of an analyst's perplexity when the patient, having become by implication a " cure," fails to acquiesce in the principle she is now understood to illustrate. For presumably the time has arrived at which she (for the sake of dramatic interest let us say " she ") should naturally wish to withdraw from treatment. Unhappily, however, she entertains no such intention. On the contrary, in implacable defiance of analytical canons, she still stoutly maintains the unabated actuality of her neurosis and offers forthwith irrefutable vindication of her position in the sudden recrudescence of her incipient symptoms. In face of the undeniable testimony, the situation is untoward in the extreme. For at this point the patient's attitude toward the analyst is such as can be only adequately expressed by her in the language of the poet who wrote : " All the current of my being sets to thee," and in the interest of a busy practice, if to no other end,

FACTOR OF RESISTANCE—INDIVIDUAL 167

it is urgent that a channel be promptly provided into which to divert the stream! This is the real climax of the situation. Its tenseness is further heightened at this point by the introduction of that most delicate and difficult process in the technique called " analyzing the transference "! The fact is the transference will not analyze. It never does. That is the difficulty of this very delicate phase. At this juncture we cast frantically about for an " interest " for the patient, that is, an interest other than ourselves—marriage, art, social service, something, anything! The truth is, our analysis has failed of its aim, and in our extremity we are driven to seek shelter under the cover of a subterfuge. It is this subterfuge which consists in an effort toward what is called, in scientific phraseology, " the sublimation of the patient's sexuality " and is the closing act of our little comedy. As the curtain is finally rung down (the management is fortunate if it drops without a hitch), it descends upon a much perplexed psychoanalyst. He feels distinctly that something went wrong. He is not certain just what it was, but knows that, whatever it was, the fault lay entirely with the patient. But the circumambient gods, as one's fancy pictures, who from their remote recesses have witnessed until now with unsubdued mirth the transient episode of our unconscious charade, observing the wretched fate of the patient in her unanswered need, suddenly alter their mood from levity to grave concern as they thoughtfully remark one to another in their own wise way that the essential catastrophe, after all, is the unconscious of the analyst and that the real drama has but just begun.

However unpalatable the admission, here is the whole crux of the matter. We have dealt objectively with an inherently subjective situation. Our approach has been cognitive, not affective. It has been personal, not inclusive. Again we have merely looked out, not in. Again it is the illusion of the organic interval, and our problem has eluded us in the common fallacy of objective reference.

In a list of precepts for psychoanalysts ("precepts" for the elimination of repressions scarcely requires comment !) there is offered this naïve word of admonition : "Don't forget that the neurotic's chief dictum is : ' I am not as other men are.' " But here again the analyst characteristically fails to recognize that such a dictum is by no means the private monopoly of the "neurotic." He overlooks the fact that it is equally the tendency of us all and (what is of crucial importance) most especially of the analyst himself in the very utterance of his dictum. For in imputing to others this unconscious fallacy of self-distinction, he is in the same breath necessarily assuming the same distinction for himself—the distinction, namely, that he is himself in so far " not like other men " as to be privileged to tell them of the presence of this fallacy within themselves. Of course the analyst will say : "Well with me, you see, it is different." But this is precisely what the patient says, as it is what every one says. And here we come once more to the heart of the matter, namely, that as the neurosis is societal the self-distinction underlying it is necessarily the particular claim of every individual within the societal body. In this situation the analyst inevitably regards only the disparity of " the other fellow," a result which I feel to be typical of the error of the Freudian analysis.[1] But " who decries the loved decries the lover." In the true sense— in the sense of our organic life—there is no other fellow.

[1] A striking instance of psychoanalytic unconsciousness may be seen in the analyst's quite naive attitude toward his own unconscious need for such infantile pacifiers as he finds in the obsessive use of tobacco. That such diversions are no more adult than the use of the rubber ring or nipple of his infancy he does not for a moment suspect, the concomitance of such practices with the oral eroticism of his childhood having only a *theoretical* significance for him. The truth is, the psycho-analyst *wants to smoke*. Of course, it is not consistent with his teaching and if he is to have his way in the matter some process must be devised that will make it consistent. And so in his authoritarian suzerainty he forthwith decrees that the patient who objects to a smoke-filled room is a prey to unseemly resistances, and that his or her attitude of mind, not the analyst's, must be promptly looked into with a view to summary treatment.

FACTOR OF RESISTANCE—INDIVIDUAL

Our interpretation of his apparent differentiation from us is but our own projection of the differentiation within ourselves, just as his interpretation of our apparent differentiation from him is but his projection of the division within himself. It is this unadmitted division within each of us that has created the illusion of our organic separateness from one another. For this reason it is only as we accept the subjective task of realizing the spurious fabric of our own separateness and self-sufficiency that we may come to realize it within our patient by virtue of our inherent identification with him. Thus, to realize our division through participation with another is to pierce the delusion of our mutual separateness and unconsciousness and so to become mutually united again through the acceptance of our common organic life.

Based upon the organismic conception here outlined, clearly this subjective recourse can be the only logical position of the analyst. For, in the light of this conception, the neurosis or the separate mode was originally induced in the immature organism through the external suggestion of the individual in closest contact with it operating to dissociate it from its primary, organic mode. In consequence, the dissociated consciousness thus artificially induced can be restored to the mode of unification and confluence only by substituting for the superimposed suggestive contact—the predominant social repression embodied in the parent—the presence of a personality whose tendency is preponderantly of the confluent, societal mode. It is clear that in this conception the analysis of a patient, in the sense of his realization and acceptance of life, presupposes as a rigid organic condition the prior analysis and acceptance of life on the part of the analyst. In impaling the cause of this separatism, delusionally assumed by the patient to reside within himself alone but in reality having its residence in our common social repression, the analyst's preoccupation can only be with this same delusional arrogation of separateness as it occurs within himself. This means nothing less than that the life of the analyst must in its consciousness completely encompass the life of the analysand in its unconsciousness. This, I know, is a large demand. It is to realize in oneself a breadth of consciousness that embraces in its scope nothing less than the totality of unconsciousness in its entire social aspect. It is to include within oneself the collective unconscious or the far span of normality in all its separateness and sexuality. In brief, it is to open the way to a reversal of the unconscious situation now prevailing in which societal men encompass individual man, and to achieve the mode of consciousness in which societal man encompasses individual men.

I remember a young woman journalist coming one day into my study on the pretext of illness but in reality to look me over. She had been the rounds of the New York analysts, she said, having been "analyzed" by first one and then another, though I doubt whether any of the able physicians cited by her would have dignified the interviews in any such terms. But while herself unconscious, indeed quite paranoid, she made a remark which has since seemed to me highly significant. She said that we psychoanalysts appear actuated by an unconscious attitude of antagonism toward our patients, that we seem motivated by a determination "to get even." In the spirit in which it was made, the remark was obviously a projection and not a judgment, but I think the criticism is in general true—certainly it has proved true in my own case. For the analyst is either unconsciously pleased with the patient who gives him his confidence or he is unconsciously displeased at his withholding it. In other words, the attitude of the analyst is not uninfluenced by personal or egoistic predilection.[1] Here, then, is straight-

[1] Let me say at once that this nomadic young lady did me the honour to remark that she sensed immediately upon meeting me that *my* attitude was entirely different from that of other analysts. Of this she made haste to assure me at the outset. In thinking of it, a wince gives place to a smile as I recall the trustful complacency with which I benignly accepted as a statement of fact the cunning decoys of this

FACTOR OF RESISTANCE—INDIVIDUAL

way the factor of unconsciousness, of separation and hence antagonism in the analyst.

But if the analyst consciously senses the patient's situation, he sees without bias that the patient—being of a separative, unconscious mode—will, and inevitably must, act in every instance from motives of unconsciousness. If he confides in the analyst, he does so solely in the hope of winning for himself the good-will of the analyst (positive infantile affect or suggestion); if he is silent or evasive, it is because he doubts the advantage to himself of sharing his confidence (negative infantile affect or repression). The psychoanalyst who would reckon consciously with a patient's life may be moved by neither one nor the other manifestation. Both are outside the mode of reality. Both are expressions of dissociation. Neither attitude will touch the analyst affectively if he is truly within his own life. If, on the other hand, he is himself dissociated, whether normally or neurotically—in the collusion of the group-expression or in single isolation—and is ever seeking to reinstate in the present moment the mother-comfort of his own childhood, he will necessarily either receive the unconsciously motivated confidence of his patient with the unconscious satisfaction of self-interest (infantile egotism) or he will respond to his patient's unconsciously withheld confidence with the no less unconscious dissatisfaction of self-interest defeated (infantile egotism thwarted). In one case he manifests the sentimentality of unconscious sympathy and approbation, in the other the equally sentimental reaction of unconscious resentment and hate. In either case it is to be partisan, separative, personal, unconscious. This unsuspected personalism or unconsciousness within ourselves makes it easier for us to

seraphically unconscious individual, her flattering reassurances seeming to me at the time clearly to indicate the very rare perceptions of this unusually discerning young person! The aftermath as it has come to pass in the brief succeeding years enables me unhesitatingly to aver that my severely reproved colleagues were at least not more unconscious than I.

condone the personalism or unconsciousness in another, rather than understand it. Because of the greater significance to us of our own personal grievance as compared with our understanding of the impersonal needs of life as a unitary experience, our sympathy is automatically enlisted on the side of the patient's personal grievance. In brief, we prefer to sympathize with the suffering of an organism rather than with the organism that suffers. This characterological weakness in our analytic system renders the analyst an easy mark for the sentimentalizing reveries of the neurotic patient. It is thus a far cry from " Freud," the psychological conception as it tends toward the more unitary formulation and co-ordination of the problem of neurotic disharmonies, to " Freud " the father-complex as it tends unconsciously to dominate the consciousness of patient as of follower.

The admission that has eventually to be made without qualifying reservation is that the transference upon which we have laid such stress as an objective scientific phenomenon is in truth a state of mind subjectively induced in the patient in direct response to the attitude of unconsciousness on the part of the analyst himself. It is just here, in the dissociated attitude of analyst toward analysand, that there stands the inevitable impasse to the personal or individualistic analysis of Freud. Here is the futile revolution within a vicious circle that is the fallacy of its individualistic viewpoint. It needs to be repeated that the sexual or the personal, in the sense of the separative, is itself unconscious. Its primary source is the reaction originally induced in the organism by the disunity of the social unconscious as voiced by the parent. We shall be helped if we keep in mind that much of the confusion of psychoanalysis is due to the failure of psychoanalysts to realize that there is a distinction between the mother-image and the mother-organism. We must ultimately come to see that, due to the dissociative or bidimensional attitude on the part of the mother, the child automatically replaces the biological reality of the parent organism with

FACTOR OF RESISTANCE—INDIVIDUAL

the artificial *image* of the parent[1] induced by the parental command. Following the investigations of the last years it has come to be my definite conviction that it is this element of the pictorial and statutory, as reflected in the parent-image, that is the real impediment to consciousness and the sole meaning of " unconsciousness."

The suggestive instance (image) of the parental organism, due to the early influence of separatism operating upon it, savours wholly of a repressive, non-confluent attitude. It necessarily tends, therefore, through the gradual inculcation of the ulterior, separative, behaviouristic mode, to dissociate more and more from its original biology, the immature organism within its range. As the neurotic diathesis is induced through the surface diversifications of external suggestion infringing upon the original consonance of the organism, as unconsciousness is diversity of outer aspect in contrast with the concentration of consciousness and personality in its inner confluence, the resolving of the neurotic conflict lies in recalling the personality from its precipitation into the manifold quests of external compensations to the original integrity of its essential unitary life. In this process of rehabilitation there is abrogated the ceaseless urge toward the unconscious fulfilment of the *wish*, through the restoration of the native impetus of life in a conscious fulfilment of *function*. It cannot be too strongly emphasized that the original incitement to the neurosis is, from an individualistic basis, external. This reaction within the individual to a prohibition acting from without constitutes the whole significance of the attitude of separatism, of self-seeking and of self-defence that are synonymous with the repressed sexuality of the neurotic personality. But there is the need to recognize that this same attitude is also synonymous with the released sexuality which is " normally " regarded at the present time as a true expression of life. This so-called normal expression, however, in its obsessive self-seeking and in its obvious kinship with secondary

[1] See note 1, page 15.

dissociative reactions, stands at the very opposite pole to sex as the instinct of life in its organic significance.

The automatic release of the reaction of self-defence that is the reflex response to the irritant of organic prohibition is biologically significant. For with the extraneous interception of the organic mode or at the instance of prohibition, the individual is reflexly stimulated to a compensatory effort to replace this mode with the vicarious mode of self-defence. There is here the psychological concomitance between organic interdiction and organic recoil, between repression or curtailment of personality and sexuality or the retroactive impulse to individual aggression. In this connection it is interesting to note the etymological agreement of the ideas of defence and prohibition in the French word *défense* meaning prohibition. There is psychological warrant for assuming that the relation between these two words is more innate than accidental.

This psychological parallelism between repression or self-love and sexuality or self-defence, between the egoistic wish and the suspicion of interference with its fulfilment, underlies the identity of the phenomenon of homosexuality and that of paranoia. Students of psychoanalysis have tended to regard the reflections of these reactions as distinct manifestations, viewing them as contradictions rather than as concomitants, as opposites rather than as alternatives, as different phases of reaction rather than as different aspects of the same phase. Freud, for example, lays emphasis upon the factor of sexuality, giving it the place of dominant importance in the neurotic conflict, while Adler asserts that it is the factor of the individual's egotism that is of central importance in the causation of the disharmony. These seemingly opposed views are, in reality, the same. One envisages the somatic, the other the psychic aspect of a condition that is nuclear and common. Their seeming difference is merely the inevitable limitation of an objective and absolute mode of approach. In either case

FACTOR OF RESISTANCE—INDIVIDUAL 175

it is the symbolic manifestation that is confronted. Whether the reaction is represented in lust of body (homosexuality) or in pride of mind (paranoia), in both conditions the aspect contemplated is again the mere symptomatic index. In each is expressed but the secondary response to a deeper, more encompassing factor that has its substrate in our common consciousness. In each it is the semblance of the individual personality replacing the actuality of the societal personality. Each is the objective resultant of a subjective impediment to the confluent, organic life. In both there is represented but the superficial aspect, one expressing itself clinically in the symbolic anomaly of homosexuality, the other, in the symbolic anomaly of paranoia.

Thus far the interest of these anomalies, as far as psychoanalysts are concerned, has been their implication as it touches the psychopathology of the isolated or neurotic personality. Far more significant, however, is the bearing of these manifestations upon the psychobiology of the social organism as a whole. That these distortions of personality exist in a larval stage in the group-neurosis of "normality" is a circumstance with which the psychopathologist needs yet to reckon in his wider office of clinical sociologist. Naturally we have not yet begun to suspect the presence of these unsavoury elements, homosexuality and paranoia, in the unconscious of "normality," and as normality enjoys the security of mutual protective agreement among its constituents, the existence of these unseemly maladjustments within its ranks will long be treated by us with stolid disavowal. It is the distinguishing feature of the naïve countenance of normality that it experiences no need of self-questioning. A delusion that has become socially buttressed in the mutual reciprocities of its unconscious adherents is indeed impregnable.

Human consciousness, however, will not be understood nor a clearer, saner life opened to man until he has repudiated the unconscious, vicarious or separative as it exists in its securest, most widespread and most aggressive form, that is, in the *socially systematized delusion comprising the collective unconscious of our vaunted " normality."* For if normality, so-called, is in reality a dissociation existing under the protective mask of society, how can we who are normal or collectively dissociated comprehend dissociation in the neurotic personality? How can the actor be at the same time onlooker? How can subject and object co-exist in the selfsame content? How, in brief, is it possible for unawareness to envisage unawareness? Surely it is clear that the dreamer is of necessity partisan to his dream, and that the contemplation of a dream from within a dream is subversive of the very principle of consciousness. For knowledge being awareness *of* or *in regard to*, demands as its condition the two contrasting factors of a subject looking upon and an object looked upon. If normality is mere collective unconsciousness and therefore itself an artificially induced neurosis— if it is a condition of unconsciousness produced through the influence of external suggestion and therefore represents in itself a secondary dissociative state, how is it possible to fulfil the requisite condition of consciousness in respect to the two factors of subject and object in the matter of our consideration of the dreams of our patients? As my own work has in the last years come to adopt a more and more inclusive organismic viewpoint, I have become convinced that what we psychoanalysts *in our present personal and objective interpretation* consider " dream-analysis," and in regard to which we have taken ourselves and our patients so seriously, is utterly futile and invalid. I am convinced that, in the mood in which dream-analysis is now applied, it is itself the expression of an hysterical symptom—a cognitive replacement within the social unconscious comprising the arbitrarily assumed group-differentiation " psychoanalyst."

CHAPTER VI

THE DREAM AND ITS ANALYSIS IN AN ORGANISMIC INTERPRETATION OF THE NEUROSES

THE dream of the individual together with the individualistic analysis of the dream presents a most difficult and as yet untried field. There is here required a technique that is as elusive as it is unprecedented. For such a technique must include the unconscious complicity of the analyst in the social or image basis from which he analyzes. For it is only impersonally and confluently that we may understand what is personal and separative in another. To approach the dreamer's separative attitude of repression and self-defence toward the elements of his dream, in an attitude of our own that is socially no less separative and repressed, is to invite a situation in which we merely exchange the dissociative symbols of the sleep state for analogous symbols in the waking state. It is to replace refraction and distortion as they occur in the individual repression, with its symbolic wish-fulfilment in dreams, for refraction and distortion as they occur in the social repression, with its symbolic wish-fulfilment in " beliefs." For this reason, having come to view the unconscious in its waking and in its sleeping expression from the point of view of the common, organic mode, I have reached the conviction that the conception of dream-analysis as it has been entertained by us is throughout a misconception, that to speak at all of dream " analysis " from the personal or separative viewpoint is self-delusive. For our so-called dreams of the night are but the unaccepted realities of the day, the so-called realities of our day but the unaccepted dreams of the night. The night's reaction is individualistic, the day's reaction is social. Both are identical in their method as in their aim. Both represent the endeavour, through futile recourse to symbolic or " would-be " measures of recommunication, to adjust vicariously and upon a separative basis the organic outrage to life's inherent unity. It is the self-determined illusion of our societal disaffection. It is the lure of the symbolic in its mock pursuits of the personal and separative. It is the vicious circle of all unconsciousness vainly rotating upon the phantom axis of its own unreality.

In view of the repercussion of consciousness that is the essence of man's unconsciousness, the attitude that will best liberate us from our infolding tendencies of mentation lies in a conception that regards unconsciousness as a self-reflexive mode throughout. Such an attitude will clearly demarcate our tendency toward the peripheral or social distribution of the mental images comprising our *mirrored* affects as contrasted with the societal conservation of our *real* affects in the conscious fulfilment of our common personality. As long as we fail to realize this generic basis we shall continue to suffer from the delusion of our own organic disunity, and there will necessarily persist the vicarious shunting of affect into the distributive expressions of anger, duplicity and antagonism constitutive of resistance. Since our affects are organically common, if we do not permit them expression in universal confluence, they must inevitably seek an expression that is scattered and random. And so we need to recognize that we may not adjust our affective or subjective life through the study of the objective mechanism of the images or dreams that merely reflect it, but only through the subjective (conscious) reabsorption within us of the displaced and socially distributed affects to whose suggestion the dream, by day or by night, is the mirrored reaction.[1]

In an organismic view *differentiation is unconsciousness*. That is, the dissociated self or the separative element is, by reason of its organic anomalousness, necessarily at

[1] See note 1, page 56.

odds with self. For this reason there is inevitably entailed the universal conflict of unconsciousness, collective and single, that is man's disunity, social as well as individualistic, " normal " as well as " neurotic." Such is the disparity that is reflected in his dreams, sleeping and waking. The diversity of our fabrications, social and individual, is the diversity of our *selves*. Our complex is our complexity. In very truth " our little life is rounded with a sleep." We waken only to alter the form of our dream. Throughout the diurnal cycle the dream-state remains unbroken, and all efforts of analysis in our unconscious, separative mode are helpful only in accentuating the powerlessness of consciousness in its present state of differentiation. In the separative mode the elements of the personality are unassembled, and the result is an absence of organic coherence, of an essential unity such as may alone be the basis of a truthful inquiry into the unconscious processes of man's inversion. In my own case (the only case upon which any of us may occupy himself profitably is one's own) it has become clear that my attitude toward the night is predetermined by my attitude toward the day. If I have kept personal and repressed my real feeling during the day, the secret of my dissociation will be kept faithfully throughout the night, and upon waking in the morning such camouflage as will successfully hide my separativeness will have been already established by my own order prior to the waking moment.

It would seem that sleep is the beneficent leveller, that mentally as well as physically its function is restorative, that it is the solvent and the dissolvent of our fancied differentiations, of our artificial, fear-begotten defences against one another. It would seem that it is for man the opportunity of organic rehabilitation, that in this period of withdrawal and quiescence after the restless day of self-seeking and antagonism there is a palliative and conciliatory process at work.[1] After all, diplomacy and lying

[1] See note 1, page 10.

are wearying in their exactions, and in this period marked by an absence of social pretences and of the strain of our separative adjustments, consciousness undoubtedly tends to reassert its common, primal mode with images that promote and do not impede organic function—joyous images, expressive of common need, of organic participation, of concerted, confluent function. After all, our dreams are but the shadows our lives cast behind them when we stand in the light of our own personality.

It is only as we become one with this inherent personality through an acceptance of the unity of life in its entirety that the shadows comprising our dreams, sleeping and waking, may be truly resolved. Since our dreams of the night only tend to restore the equilibrium which the day has destroyed, our dreams are only in so far distorted as our day is distorted. In so far as the day is an evasion of the recognition of the infantile wish, with its corresponding entail of over-compensation and atonement, in so far does the dream reproduce again the identical wish of the day after having recourse to the extravagance and distortion requisite to its disguise. When in our day's reactions we shall have entered upon an organic, confluent mode of consciousness, our dreams will be one with the organic confluence of the day, furthering in their harmonious imagery the quiet process of the day's constructiveness. It will then be realized that sleep is but the day's diastole, that just as the period of diastolic relax following the rhythmic contraction of the heart has a function that is reciprocal and harmonious in relation to the systolic impulse, so in the rhythmic cycle of our day its period of rest is reciprocal and continuous with, not contradictory and opposed to, the constructive function of the day's activities. The dreams of the separative mode, on the other hand, only occlude and congest the avenues of our sleep-consciousness. These obstructive travesties effect a complete deadlock due to the confluent organism's ineffectual effort to arrest and clarify these separative trends that are reflections even in sleep of the unlived, fear-ridden, organically discordant experience comprising the day.

With our present habitually tutored day, the very approach of our awaking automatically prompts us to don a costume of disguise before we rise to move again amid the tedious maze of masked players who, like ourselves, have lost the reality of life's organic meaning. As long as one's feeling is thus resolutely set against the surrender of his artificial defences, as long as one fears to remove the mask of pretence covering his personality, no amount of intellectualization, of mental analysis, of theoretical " truths " (I have tried them all !) will avail to lift his repression and admit him to the simple reality of his common, organic feeling. It is in vain that we seek the truth. Truth, as it is customarily conceived, is but the theory whereof life, as it may be lived, is the reality. To seek the truth is again to pursue the phantom of our own mental imagery. For reality disappoints all formulation. No symbol may stand for equivalence but only for equivocation. The lesson the psychoanalyst has yet to learn is that reality has no substitutes, that no *seeming*, however plausible, may replace that which *is*. It is this lesson—the very lesson we presume to teach our patients—of which all our work is as yet but an empty recitation. Accordingly, no amount of intuitional or theoretical acumen on the part of the analyst can do other than thwart a patient's need of self-realization. Such intellectualism on the part of the analyst is the substitution that is *his* neurosis. Recourse to intellectuality is his concession to the socially current repression and substitution which in our collective unconsciousness we credit as normality, never once suspecting, in the strength of our numerical security, that *normality is but the collective dream-state of man's waking life.*

Because of the psychological identity between the dream that is our day, with its dramatization in the objective furniture of cubic actuality, and the dream that is our night, with its scenic reproduction in flat, pictorial outline, an individualistic analysis in the sense of an encompassing realization is of its nature precluded. Only as we can come to stand apart from both, and view them in their proper light as symbolic phenomena divorced from life, may they be assessed in their true relation and thus analyzed in the only sense that gives meaning to the term. But this is not a merely mental process. This is to actualize organic life in our daily experience with such sincerity as to realize within ourselves the spuriousness of our habitual, dissociated mode. It is so to include the dream outside the dream, constituted of the separative day with which the separative night is enclosed, that we shall have automatically entered upon the mode of self-unification which is one with a societally unified, confluent consciousness. The essential mark of such a mode of consciousness is that, in its subjective consonance, it regards with an equally objective clarity the vicarious processes of the day and of the night.

Our attitude of the day is amply illustrated by our attitude toward our dramas. As our lives are based upon unconsciousness, our dramas as well as our dreams are also necessarily based upon unconsciousness. Since the logic of the dream is inverted, it is essential to reverse the dream's unconscious motive in order to understand its fallacious sequences. The drama equally represents the interplay of unconscious motives. Based thus upon the inverse processes of unconsciousness, its logic is also necessarily inverse. And so in order to understand the drama, its motive must likewise be observed in its reverse trend. In other words, the drama and the dream are identical in their essential mechanism. When the psychopathologist is confronted with the drama of *actual life*—the inverse process represented in the neurosis—his immediate recourse should be to intercept as far as possible the inharmonious development of the patient's life history and, having completely reversed its underlying motive in the light of conscious perspectives, to unravel its meaning through carefully retracing dis-

THE DREAM AND ITS ANALYSIS 183

coverable inadvertencies of development to their logical source.

In this function the analyst's attitude toward the human drama presented in the neurosis of his patient becomes identical with his attitude toward the dreams of his patient. One would naturally expect that his attitude toward the drama of the stage would be equally logical. But a societal analysis fails to justify this expectation. For such is the elusive tenacity of the seemingly actual, as it appears in the dissociative recourses of the social mind, that the psychoanalyst, too, continues to regard the bidimensional *aspect* of life presented in the drama as a conscious form of art. In consequence it comes to pass that a train of unconsciously destructive events which he deplores as an expression of life in the clinic is applauded by him as an expression of art in the theatre. The same untoward sequences, which in clinical retrospect are *viewed* with compassion, are in the process of their theatrical portrayal *experienced* with delight.

I do not see how such inconsistencies between our collective and our individual reactions to unconsciousness are separable from the present confusion that exists between the objective and the subjective spheres of consciousness. Because of this confusion, in our dissociation we take pleasure in participating in the dramatic representation of the identical processes of unconsciousness which, subsequently contemplated as actuality, we interpret only as pain. This inconsistency between our subjective and objective reactions accounts also for the many discrepancies in the psychiatrist's personal attitude toward the dramas of the clinic and the drama within his own home. It explains how it happens that we, who are seemingly competent to trace an individual's neurosis directly to the influences that have unconsciously surrounded him as a child, will yet unconsciously surround our own children with these selfsame influences. Surely never was the " other fellow " so abused and ourselves so tricked as in our psychiatric clinics when, in our self-conscious formulation of the occasion of his confusion, we deem ourselves less unconscious than he.

As it is the especial métier of the unconscious to convert the actual into the seeming, its subtlest attainment is the conversion of what is most actual into what is most seeming. If of realization itself it may effect a semblance, it is the ultimate achievement in unconscious ventriloquy. If of analysis itself it may make a pseudo-analysis, it has secured its entrenchment through a technical recourse that is wellnigh impregnable. Through such a strategic manœuvre one often attains a quite faultless analysis of a dream, when all the while the realization is but seeming. As the dream is but the reflected image or " negative " of yesterday's duplicities and introversions, an attempt to capture and " analyze " it from the retrospective standpoint of the replacement and introversion of the day, is but to retain unaltered and unalterable the unconscious embroilment of one's self-delusive introversion. Yet, with the practised dexterity of our habitual sleight-of-hand methods of analysis, we still pursue the futile industry of our objective dream-trapping, idly endeavouring to drag the travesty of the day's distortions embodied in the dream into the self-conscious analytic dissecting-room. In truth, the real need is that we surrender the analytic dissecting-room and all its paraphernalia of symbolic technique to the common reality which underlies it, realizing that its artificial displacements constitute the sole function of the dream parody. For set what snare we will, a dream cannot be taken alive. The chasing of dreams is like the chasing of rainbows. One may no more behold his *real* self in the mirror of the dream than in any other reflecting surface. The image reproduced may be never so lifelike but it is not life. As with birds on the wing, so with our dreams; we cannot capture them except we destroy them. The attempt to do so is to repeat without end our habitual offence against the organic grammar of life constitutive of the double negative of all unconsciousness. Again it is unconsciousness within unconsciousness, personal preference within personal preference, unconsciousness *unconscious* that is the baffling complicity in our self-dissociation.

This self-involvement of the neurosis, this *unconsciousness of the totality of self* makes of our individual enfoldment a wellnigh inscrutable situation. In such a situation the individual's efforts of self-help—the recourses of personal rather than of societal outlooks—become comparable to the efforts of a man who would attempt to lift himself by his own boot-straps. This it is that comprises the dream within the dream of all individuation—of all separateness. Of course, it quite naturally seems to us, in our now differentiated mode, that the attainment of a position of relative inclusiveness is a humanly impossible task. Yet, if we are to attain to a true recognition of our *societal dissociation*, we may do so only through the acceptance of the basic actuality of our common, organic confluence. Such alone is the essential recourse of a fully awakened consciousness.

Whether we will or no, we are thus brought back again and again to the essential fallacy of our day's dreams as of our night's—to the illusion of personal causation or of individual sponsorship that is at the heart of man's dissociation, both neurotic and normal. In the presumption of his self-determined hypothesis of good and bad, of hope and fear, the individual is assuming unconsciously the supervision of the universe, and the constant endeavour of his thoughts as of his dreams is to keep secret the traces of his personal presumption through the subtle projections of the disguised image. Some call it God, some call it evolution, but no matter what the collective title under which our private prerogative is symbolized, it is in reality but the cheat that is the personal illusion of a central causality resident within ourselves.

I know that in this subjective statement of the disharmony of consciousness there is presented a trend that is wholly unacceptable to the symbolic or absolute logician ; but, on the other hand, the objective statements of the absolute logician are with equal validity unacceptable to the relativist. According to the objective logic of the mental absolutist the fact of our very existence is theoretically untenable. In the unconscious determinism of men's personal prerogative, the postulate, as is generally known, is that the universe in which we have our being was either created by some agency existing outside itself or it was self-creative. Of the two alternatives either is impossible, but the vital fact remains that here we are ! The logical untenability of a position that limits itself to these commonly accepted alternatives may some day offer sobering consideration to our unconscious absolutism. For the present there is grave need that our absolute or theoretical logic yield place to the relative logic of a more organismic point of view. In the world of physical phenomena prior to Einstein it was impossible for physicists to proceed with further creative extensions because of the limitation of their underlying conception. So in the sphere of human activities around us, as long as we continue in our present objective fixity of thought, it will not be possible for life to unfold because of the set limitations of unessential attitudes of mind that block all essential creative expression.

CHAPTER VII

THE BIOLOGICAL SUBSTRATE OF THE NEUROTIC CONFLICT IN ITS ORGANIC SIGNIFICANCE

IN studying the neurotic diathesis one recognizes the existence of two marked reaction-types more or less clearly delineated one from another in mood and *tempo*, though they equally sustain the same central *motif*. The vicarious method of dream-analysis described in the last chapter as having all the appearance of adequacy, when inherently it is invalid, is especially characteristic of one of these two types of personality. The two types may be distinguished by the contrast between their specific reactions to the original repressive incident occasioning the organism's primary dissociation.

I am not in sympathy, however, with the *implication* in the discrimination of types demarcated as " introvert " and " extravert." These terms imply, as they are meant to imply, an essential difference of type rather than a circumstantial difference of reaction. In general the extravert is rather approvingly regarded in the light of a " jolly good fellow," as contrasted with the introvert whose disaffectivity, on the contrary, tends to be regarded with an undisguised slant. As if the jolly good-fellowship of the hysterical type, with all its aggressiveness and ebullience, were not as truly a substitutive alternative resultant upon repression as is the reaction of his more silent, ingrown confrère of the opposite type! As if the affable, effervescent type were not as truly " shut-out " as his psychological vis-à-vis is " shut-in " ! Psychiatry has a great deal to say about the shut-in type of personality but it has nothing to say about the shut-out type of personality. Yet of the two the latter is by no means a less serious form of dissociation, and certainly it is by far the more widespread in its results.

There are, then, two types of reaction to be discriminated. There is the type of individual who upon the initial stimulus to defence has recourse to a tactic of unconditional retreat. He simply withdraws *in toto*, and his attitude toward his congeners is thenceforward completely negative. He no longer sees nor is seen by them. They are so far outside his ken that their existence is not for a moment admitted by him. Excluded from the range of his actualities he does not even concede them an hypothetical status. Such is the *autocentric* individual. This personality is the subsequent precoid, if in his withdrawal he does not even so much as pretend acknowledgment of the external world; he is the later psychasthenic, or normal of the socially detached type, if he adopts the more temperate policy of a seeming *rapprochement*. In either case, enclosed within a system all his own, he lives entirely apart from the world of actuality, ruling alone (and of course supreme) over his self-determined cosmogony.

Then there is the type of personality whose course is the exact opposite of that just described, the difference of reaction being due to the modifying conditions, " constitutional " for aught I know, that attend the repressive occasion. With this type of personality, due to the fact that the arresting instance overtakes him, as it were, in the open, retreat is automatically barred. He is surprised in the act, discovered with the goods in his possession. Detection and apprehension are here simultaneous. Unable to deny the actuality of the situation, his instinctive recourse is in the direction of a desperate effort to palliate the attending circumstances. Resort to an alibi being out of the question, he seeks to exculpate himself by adopting a policy of a more or less truckling servility. He would atone his offence by propitiating his accusers and so winning a recommendation of leniency. Such is the *allocentric* type of personality. This type may be seen

THE BIOLOGICAL SUBSTRATE

either in the so-called normal individual of the socially adaptive reaction or in the definitely efflorescent or hysterical neurotic, according respectively as he succeeds in conniving in the social pretence and unconsciousness about him and thus saves his own neck, or as he fails in his effort at social compromise—the process flatteringly known to-day as "sublimation." In this event his failure of adaptation is due to the stronger urge within him of the factors that are allied with the underlying communism of his organic consciousness but which in his mental dissociation he is unable to co-ordinate with his innate experience.

Viewed biologically these two types represent, as I see them, a functional over-emphasis *in the individual* of the reactions pertaining to one or the other of the two fundamental co-ordinated systems underlying the biology of man's confluent life and determining, when in balanced relation to one another, the integral health of the organism. I refer to the cerebro-spinal and the sympathetic nervous systems. The opposite recourses of behaviour, manifested in the two psychological types just cited, represent, I believe, the two extremes of reaction resultant upon the disturbed balance between these two systems coincident with the factor of repression.

In the preconscious form of life [1] preserved among the animals, there has occurred no break between these two fundamental systems. In the feline series, for example, one observes the same graceful, organic undulations in the movements actuated by the voluntary muscles or in the reactions presided over by the cerebro-spinal system, as occur in the rhythmic and harmonious co-ordinations that characterize the function of the internal viscera controlled by the sympathetic ganglia. With man the picture is a very different one. Upon the introduction of suggestion or repression and their concomitant interdiction to his inherent feeling, there resulted an organic cleavage within his personality. Coincident with this artificial

[1] See note 1, page 10.

summons to an adaptive and ulterior response, the spheres of reaction corresponding to these two systems within the organism of man were henceforth divided. Affective responses within the organism's subjective nuclear life, with its physiological substrate in the vasomotor and visceral reactions (sympathetic system), were no longer correlated with affective responses which, having their substrate in the nuclei of the brain and spinal cord (cerebro-spinal system), pertain to the objective, external adaptations observable in the organism's voluntary activities. Hence, from this moment forward the co-ordination between the two systems became automatically impaired, and there could no longer be the smooth, uninterrupted confluence of function that originally united the two systems into a single co-ordinated unit.

The disintegrating effect of this artificial cleavage between these two reciprocal systems occurs only in the constituent that marks the adaptive cerebral reactions or in the segment or terminal mediating the relationships *socially* of the individual elements *inter se*. In the central or visceral system the organic unities remain intact. Here in the depths of man's organic being, actuated by his involuntary, instinctive life, the disparity of separateness cannot enter. Here is unbroken continuum. Here the organism is susceptible to no interstitial flaw. In this central, involuntary system which is organically common and confluent throughout the species, the extraneous element of repression with its reaction in disparate, ulterior quests is automatically excluded, for in its native inherency the organism is one and indivisible. It is the peripheral portion of our organisms with its specialization into the external sense-organs, through which is mediated our recognition of objective difference or interval and through which occurs, as has been said, our consequent inference of intrinsic differentiation. In the peripheral system, therefore, the fallacy of separateness due to this biological fission may be enforced with seeming success.

THE BIOLOGICAL SUBSTRATE

In a word, it is only in our social and external relations that the fallacy of organic differentiation works havoc in any positive or active sense.

In this generic schema is probably represented the physiological substrate of the schism within the organism caused by the impact from without of the trauma of repression, and there is represented as well the basis of the resultant contrast of reaction-types in accordance as the repression tends more strongly toward one or the other side of the divided reaction.

Replacing essential continuity with mere contiguity, or the unity of our organic life with the superficial gestures of an outer code, the *normal* of the hysterical type may rub surfaces, as it were, and play desperately at the game of vicarious unity. We see this everywhere exemplified among the devotees of normality in reactions that are apparently confluent but that are, in reality, determined cerebrally or peripherally in response to the division within the unitary organism of man. Such are the expressions to be seen, for example, in our religious hobnobbings, our spurious social covenants, our ingenious political and economic affiliations, and in the superficial flatteries and connivances common to normality generally. How definitely such vicarious reactions are an infringement upon man's organic life is readily seen in the unfailing equalization that follows swiftly upon them, exacting their inevitable toll in the ultimate retributive penalties of national and industrial wars, of social and political dissension and in the world-wide expression of disaffection that marks the social periphery of our self-plumed "civilization."

On the other hand the *neurotic* of the hysterical type, by reason of the greater sensitiveness of his organism, is held within the grip of this organic conflict. It permits him neither to fawn nor to defy whole-heartedly, but because of the irreconcilable urge of this inner conflict it keeps him ever torn between its two extremes. As an expression of the allocentric reaction he lives within a system that is divided against itself, sensing throughout life, only intuitively, the unassuageable pain of his division.

In direct contrast with this reaction the autocentric type lives within a system that is completely dissociated from the common, congeneric life. But, though the system is in itself uniform throughout, he suffers no less the affliction of his life's incompleted cycle because of his organic separation from the socially reciprocal, peripheral system. The allocentric seeks in vain to atone to himself for his extradition from the co-ordinated organism in the spurious compensations of a peripherally (socially) separative system. The autocentric would annul the pain of his separation from the co-ordinated organism in the futile appeasements of a central (individual) system which, in its insulation, represents no less his complete dissociation from the world of actuality. The one would repair the organic breach within him through recourse to conciliations that lie exclusively within the social sphere (peripheral dissociation). The other would resort to reparations, which, being wholly enclosed within the *ego*, embody exclusively the individual factor (central dissociation). In brief, the allocentric sees himself as *picture* in the world outside of him. The autocentric sees the world outside of him as picture *within* himself. If the conduct of the latter personifies the smoke-screen, the conduct of the former is typical of the red-herring !

Here again we witness the vacillations between the social consensus and our personal resistance to its behests, between the opposed factors of suggestion and of repression, of personal advantage and of personal disadvantage, due to our unconscious alternatives of good and bad. In the disorganization pertaining to these two reciprocally dissociated spheres—the cerebral and the visceral—our unconsciousness consists, in either case, in the individual's inability to realize a unification of personality comprised of the balanced inclusion of the two through the co-ordination of the organic and the conscious spheres of his experience.

THE BIOLOGICAL SUBSTRATE 193

It is my view that in the phenomena of repression or of sexuality artificial symbols are substituted for the natural gestures represented in the innate feelings of life and sex. In substituting the manifold symbols of expression for the natural gestures of spontaneous feeling, there is manifested a dissociation of the consciousness of man of which the union of his nuclear and peripheral fields of feeling (affectivity) is the biological basis. Just as the gesture is the motor expression of its concomitant sensory reaction, so is the symbol the motor expression of the sensory *repression* concomitant to it. As the gesture is the organic accompaniment of reality, the symbol is the vicarious barrier against reality. We find the sponsorship for the symbol in unconsciousness or in a mode that is personal, systematized, repressed, while the gesture has its sponsorship in a mode of consciousness or in a confluence of feeling that is impersonal, societal, organic.

If one may speak of ethnic modes, it may be said that in what is called the period of Greek thought—with its preference for form to substance, for " the good " conceived rather as beauty than as truth, for life felt more in its outward line than in its inner meaning—there is ethnically reflected the allocentric or peripheral type of reaction. A close sympathy with all that pertains to this early period of Greek culture is certainly characteristic of the strongly marked types of this reaction.

On the other hand, the era of Christ and of the psychasthenic reaction of Christianity, with its lugubrious reversal of the Greek *motif*, is a mode one finds preeminently adapted to the autocentric type of character, with its apotheosis of the symbols of love, of truth and of the spirit. Said Christ : " The spirit is more than flesh," thus controverting the tendency of the Greek ideal, and an ascetic Christianity has flocked to him. But in the eidolon of Greek as of Christian there is offered again but the symbol. In the organic incompleteness of each there is presented only the inadequacy of the letter, of that which serves as a sign. In the first it is form, colour,

N

substance; in the second it is the word, the concept, the spirit. To-day there are not wanting indications that there awaits man a period that is confluent of the two in which these symbolic or separative racial modes shall become absorbed in a unification of word and of substance. This moment of man's organic realization within himself of the integrity of life in its totality will usher in a sociological renascence when man's life will embody a mode in which the spirit *is* flesh.[1]

The contrasting systems here denoted as allocentric and autocentric, corresponding to the contrast between the cerebral, peripheral or social mode of reaction on the one hand and the visceral, central or nuclear reaction-type on the other, merely mark anew a very old and commonly recognized division. Here in this more physiological envisagement of it there is offered merely a different conceptual basis. There is an analogous division in the experimental psychologists' discrimination between motor and sensory. Doubtless also in the contrast more rhetorically defined as romantic and classical there is contemplated the same division of types, not to mention the contrasted reaction-types popularly known as temperamental and phlegmatic.[2]

It is needful to remember that the allocentric type of individual is, within the peripheral division of his cerebro-social system, as truly self-centred as is the autocentric type within the central, visceral division of his sympathetic

---

[1] Perhaps this distinction of type has its societal counterpart also in the opposite psychological reactions embodied in the esoteric tendencies of Catholicism with its markedly autocentric organization, as compared with Protestantism's more allocentric trends. The difference between the two types of reaction is also seen in the broad geographical contrast that separates the consciousness of Asia from that of Europe.

[2] See discussion of opposed reaction-types independently determined by M. Geiger, " Neue Complicationsversuche," *Philos. Studien*, XVIII, 1903, pp. 347–436 and also by myself, *The Determination of the Position of a Momentary Impression in the Temporal Course of a Moving Visual Impression*, The Johns Hopkins Studies in Philosophy and Psychology, No. 3, The Psychological Review, Psychological Monographs, Vol. XI, No. 4, September, 1909.

THE BIOLOGICAL SUBSTRATE 195

system. The difference is that the allocentric embodies dissociation in his seeming adaptation toward the social dream that is his day, and the autocentric in his seeming adaptation toward the individual dream that is his night. Every psychiatrist is familiar with the facility with which the dementia præcox patient may analyze his own dreams. But what avails his facility? He is by very virtue of it not less but rather more shut in, for his " analysis " is but the trick through which he subtly evades the social demands existing outside his own centrally dissociated mode. At all times he holds the stage of his self-determined drama, viewing the spectacle of it not as onlooker but as producer. What he permits you to see is but a play within a play, conceived and enacted within the theatre of his own mind. And so in the autocentric type embodied in the psychasthenic personality—the reaction of the type of normal or neurotic that is related to the precoid in its extreme expression—one may be led quite far from the touchstone of reality by reason of the very simplicity and quite genuine correctness of his " analysis." And so no less with the allocentric type and the equally plausible decoys of *his* illusory system. What is needed is our realization that in the projections of one as in the *intrajections* of the other there is equally embodied the identical purpose of self-withdrawal from the common medium of reality.

Most significant of all is the need that the psychoanalyst realize, on the one hand, the peripherally determined tendencies of his own socially compensative reactions or of his own allocentric normality, and, on the other, the centrally biased trends of his own insularly compensative adjustments or of his own autocentric adaptation. Failing to accept, through his own analysis, the possibility of the completely theatrical or symbolic nature of the so-called actualities of his own day as they tend to be expressed in the immediate moment at hand, he may himself easily succumb to the fallacy of a too ready credence (analyst's wish-fulfilment) in judging the validity of a patient's presumable self-envisagement. This unconscious alternative which we trace again and again throughout the varying manifestations of the mind of man, whether in its single or in its collective expression, whether in the immediate reaction of the individual or in the remoter adaptations of the race mind, is equally the unconscious actuation underlying the system of psychoanalysis.

It would seem to mark some strange miscarriage in our sociological progress that a dualistic system, such as psychoanalysis, should have arisen as an emanation of Jewish thought, when one considers the essentially monotheistic tradition of the Hebrew consciousness. In this sense the sociological reaction of the Hebrew mind manifested in the dualistic principle of Freud, as exemplified in his basic theory of psychic ambivalence, would seem to denote some inadvertence in racial perception. Monotheism with its principle of a universal immanence of good is clearly a sublimation of the unitary preconscious mode (autocentric), just as the dualistic theism of the Gentiles, with its basis in the alternatives of good and evil, is the sublimation of an irreconcilable unconscious mode (allocentric). May it not be that unconsciously psychoanalysis is a Semitic repudiation of the basal law of Moses and of its preconscious principle of an underlying unity, precisely as Christianity is an unconscious repudiation of the same unitary precept as exemplified preconsciously in the teachings of Christ ? May it not be, too, that these unconscious alternatives now actuating the dualistic systems of Jew and Gentile will ultimately resolve themselves into an organic monism of accord which, in the societal encompassment of each, will become equally understanding and inclusive through the united consciousness of both ?

CHAPTER VIII

THE DISTINCTION BETWEEN SEXUALITY AND SEX IN RELATION TO UNIFICATION AND ORGANIC MATING

IN the impatience of the industrial laboratory to meet the public need, it happens not infrequently that, through an omission of adequate qualitative tests due to the unusual haste of production, an inferior grade of material is distributed such as would not have been produced under more temperate circumstances. The time has come to acknowledge that through a like inadvertence many of the products of psychoanalysis are seriously open to criticism upon the same grounds. Owing to overhasty construction and to a lack of requisite tests of their genuineness, an appreciable deficiency has occurred in the quality of the material produced. Due to this occasion psychoanalysis is answerable for engendering in the public mind certain conceptions which are utterly without a basis in fact. Coupled with this want of moderation, certain publicity experts have disseminated a wide range of literature embodying a mass of disastrous misapprehension. In mere zeal for a market they have circulated it broadcast amid all manner of suggestible, because unconscious, individuals and communities. Unconscious doctrines, however, cannot be promulgated except from unconscious sources. When psychoanalysis has achieved a sufficiently impersonal and far-reaching outlook to apply to itself in reality the same tests which it is now applying to others in theory, it will realize the need of recalling, as far as is possible, the many conceptual products of its overhasty output and of offering instead a more scientifically controlled and a more adequately tested summation of views such as are suited to serve as an ultimate interpretation of human consciousness.[1]

There is a characterological aspect of human consciousness which psychoanalysis has yet to consider. By character I do not mean the habituations of personal bigotry. I have in mind a characterology that is racial and that furthers the conscious integrations of man as expressive of his societal life as a whole. Thus far, instead of regarding the personality of man as a societal aggregate assembled of the elements comprising individual men, psychoanalysis has tended to create artificial divisions within this organic unity. Unconsciously influenced by a division based upon the bias of its own arbitrary alternatives, psychoanalysis has assumed contrasts of behaviour which completely lack the foundations of an organismic inclusiveness.

Perhaps the most unwarranted of such conceptual contrasts, because most harmful and far-reaching in the confusion it entails, is the artificial discrimination connoted under the terms homosexuality and heterosexuality. From an organismic viewpoint the alternatives presupposed in such a distinction are traceable alone to the unconscious ambivalence within the psychoanalytic system itself. From an inclusive position it will be seen that in the systematization underlying the contrasting concepts homo- and heterosexuality, the psychoanalyst himself has fallen a prey to the contrasting images of hope and fear, " good " and " bad," underlying the alternatives of his own absolute system.

In a situation that is organically false, an organically false reaction is the inevitable response. As long as sentimentality—the unconscious projection of the flattering likeness of one's own ego—dominates, as now, all clinical procedure, the tendency to inversion or image-substitution that underlies the psychoanalytic system itself will necessarily render what is now the purely

[1] " Psychiatry as an Objective Science," *British Journal of Medical Psychology*, Vol. V, Part 4.

fanciful isolation of the so-called homosexual complex inaccessible to consciousness.

It is the tacit assumption among psychoanalysts as among sexologists generally that the condition described by Freud as unconscious " homosexuality " deserves recognition as a true biological phenomenon, and accordingly they tend to concede it place in the social scheme. Since the analytic approach is not societal, the analyst necessarily gives to the homosexual inversion a position that is positive and static. Whether the case is regarded as " curable " or " incurable " it is customarily treated as an objective disease-entity. Many instances of so-called " analysis " that I have known have consisted in nothing else than overcoming through suggestion (consensual assurance) a patient's social resistance to this type of adaptation, notwithstanding that to this end there were pressed into clinical service the external adjustments of active heterosexuality. This conception is as unfortunate as it is unnecessary. The adaptation of the homosexual disorientation within the societal consciousness is organically as impossible as is the adaptation of the disorientations of paranoia in the organically societal aggregate. " Normally " the adaptation of both phases of inversion are a commonplace, but that it is so is but an added commentary on normality and its collective unconsciousness.

That the natural expression of sex is the union between man and woman is indisputable. The concomitance between the sex of man and the sex of woman is self-evident. Being organic, this reproductive convergence of the male and female of a species is a process that occurs spontaneously and without intervention. No dissertation is required to establish this view. There is, however, the need to set forth clearly a factor entering into human behaviour that is not spontaneous and to render conscious the conditions now obtaining unconsciously among us through the artificial intervention of this extraneous factor. When we spoke of the reactions of the child to the early influences of inducement and prohibition (suggestion and repression) corresponding respectively to the mental images of good and bad, we saw that " good " coincides with the individual's personal advantage as reflected in the social approval about him, and that " bad " represents his personal disadvantage as likewise reflected in his social surroundings. In the presumptive absolute of our arbitrary images of good and bad, the system of behaviour thus unconsciously begotten in us assumes sponsorship even of the primary and organic instinct of mating. Not even this fundamental impulse of our human behaviour is safe from the infringements of our self-reflective alternatives of good and bad with their attendant measures of individual advantage. Accordingly, the organic and inherent impulse of mating is henceforward seen from the point of view of personal self-interest. A common, societal instinct of reproduction experiences thus the inversion of a secret, personal aim.

This secret element of personal advantage and acquisitiveness that has come to mar the free and natural expression of man's mating impulse is fully attested in the covert self-consciousness that characterizes his " in-love " attitude. In the alternative attitude of good and bad that necessarily limits him to the issues of advantage or disadvantage for himself, man no longer approaches the essentially unitary instinct of love with unity in himself. Either there is the response in the individual that is " good " in that it concedes the social exaction (positive suggestion of self-advantage), or the response that is " bad " in that it repudiates the social consensus (negative suggestion of self-disadvantage, i.e., repression). In the first instance the individual accepts the alternative of the socially approved adaptation of heterosexuality, in the second the individual's reaction issues in the alternative of the socially repudiated adaptation of homosexuality. In either alternative the factor of psychic inversion and self-interest is equally decisive. In the first it is presented in the form that is the individual's response to the consensual suggestion, in the second it is presented in the form that is his response to the consensual repression. What is significant is the fact that, as each type of response is an alternation on the basis of the social suggestion or the social repression answering, in the first instance, to the desire of personal gain or approval and, in the second, to the fear of personal loss or disfavour, both types of response, in returning upon self and self-interest for their satisfaction, are equally *ego-sexual*.

As is universally the case with reactions based on the unconscious contrasts of good and bad, in the choice of either alternative there are preserved the elements actuating both. In the heterosexual alternative there is the unconscious presence of the homosexual component, in the homosexual alternative there is the unconscious presence of the heterosexual component. The reason is that the underlying factor that equally determines each of these seemingly opposed reactions is the deeper unconscious inversion of man's ego-sexuality with its inevitable alternatives of self-advantage based upon our artificial differentiations of good and bad.

The conclusion is unavoidable that we shall have to reconstruct entirely our conception of the interrelationship of man and woman in respect to the instinct of sex. As has been said before, hetero- and homosexuality are purely fictitious discriminations. Like the distinctions presumably expressed by the conception extravert and introvert, they embody no discrimination *in kind* whatever, but are terms for the alternative aspects of one and the same thing. As the concept connoted by these terms may with advantage be replaced by the concept connoted by the terms allocentric and autocentric, so the concept expressed by the terms heterosexuality and homosexuality may with propriety give way to a concept such as we may correspondingly express by the terms *allosexual* and *autosexual*—terms which do not indicate a difference of content between two reactions but merely an alternation of aspect in one and the same reaction. With a view, then, to what I feel will afford a clearer and more encompassing outlook upon the problems of our human adjustment, both individual and social, I shall, wherever convenient, dispense with the term " homosexuality," because of the needlessly misleading stigma it imposes upon the individual, and use instead of *homosexual* the term *autosexual;* correspondingly, instead of the term *heterosexual*, with its equally misleading social implication of " right " comportment, the expression *allosexual* will be used, it being understood that by these contrasts I mean the dual alternations of self-love due to man's unconscious repudiation of the organic instinct of sex in favour of the personal inversions of sexuality.

Sexuality is the *effort* of conjunction of peripheral and visceral spheres, but because of the interposition of the personal or self-reflexive element, with its necessarily inverse aim, there results on the one hand (socially) the mere apposition of periphery with periphery, entailing an inverse erotism or autosexuality in the form of narcism (self-reflection), or unconscious homosexuality proper ; and on the other (centrally) the mere (psychic) enfolding of visceral with visceral, entailing an inverse erotism in the form of autoerotism or ego-sexuality proper. Sex, on the contrary, is the spontaneous, effortless and non-personal conjugation of the organismic poles comprising male and female. This distinction between sexuality and sex explains the ulterior quality of a sophisticated and self-conscious " in-love " state representing *contrast*, in replacement for the organismic love-state representing *identification.* Hence sexuality is but the temporary self-appeasement of a reciprocal adjustment, whereas sex is the permanent self-realization of a mutual co-ordination.[1]

[1] Narcism (homo-erotism) is a reversion of interest representing a sexual reaction to the pictorial affect or to the personal image. Auto-erotism (ego-erotism) represents an arrest of the individual's sexuality due to its impact with the personal image or with the social self-reflection about him. Narcism embodies the reflection of the individual's erotism in its social phase. Autoerotism is the absorption of the individual's erotism in its personal phase. Autoerotism is thus central and represents the retroversion or interception by the organism of its

A consideration that cannot fail to be of interest to the psychoanalyst is the obviously complementary relation of the two types, the allocentric and the autocentric, in respect to one another, and its undoubted significance as regards the instinct of mating among the more conscious personalities such as we should expect to follow the unifying process of analysis. The marked unconscious affinities observable between the two types I take to be a fact of general recognition among psychoanalysts if not among the laity itself. But unconscious affinities, being infantile or adaptive in character, are obviously attachments of an ego-sexual nature. It is an organic corollary, however, which in its social implication is unconsciously blinked by psychopathologists, that an individual who is infantile or unweaned or ego-sexual is in his objective sexual interest also *de facto* ego-sexual—ego-sexuality here being nothing else than the extension of the ego-sexual or autoerotic mode into the sexual objective of another individual. If, as would appear, normality is the expression of the unweaned and unconscious mode of society generally, it is not to be wondered at that the admission of this fact has been so generally suppressed, since there follows logically the distasteful conclusion that, unconsciously, normality or society in general, which includes us all, is ego-sexually constellated.

Accustomed as we are to think so much more readily in objective than in subjective terms, the conception of ego-sexuality as the determinant of the relationship between persons of the opposite sex, or the conception of our supposedly " normal " or " heterosexual " society as being in essence ego-sexual, has not yet entered the analytic consciousness, nor is it likely to do so without a violent storm of social protest and " resistance." But the typical expression of sexual union, as it exists among " normals," is redolent of this inverted bias. The folk-

efferent interests. This occurs in the individual inversion expressed in the sensory images of dementia præcox. Narcism is peripheral and is expressed in the social inversion pertaining equally to the motor images of homosexuality as to the sensory images of paranoia.

reaction of the social mind represented in the custom of marriage, if clearly confronted, reveals throughout the umistakable signs of this alternative. If we note carefully the countenance of this social reaction, we cannot fail to observe that its instigation is based upon the mutual desire to mollify, to " please."

Hence, marriage is for the most part a process of mutual adjustment of the ego-sexual claims upon one another of the two parties involved. After all, the " oneness " of marriage is an achievement due to the pooling of the private unconscious of the two parties to the arrangement. It is the permanent coalition of the unconscious of both, collectively, with a view to the temporary guarantees of each, severally. For marriage is an arrangement in accordance with the terms of which each party to the covenant secretly withdraws from his organic place as a societal element, in exchange for his fanciful sovereignty as a circumscribed domestic aggregate! That is, in marriage two unconscious elements have merged into a single unconscious entity. Through the self-reflection one achieves in his unconscious mate, through the self-reduplication he achieves in his unconsciously begotten offspring, one's family is again but the unconscious of the individual freshly reinforced through a subtle recourse to symbolic replacement. It is the substitution of the single, self-limited social group for the all-inclusive, organic consonance of the societal aggregate. Thus the social cluster comprising the family is but the *symbol* of the societal unity comprising one's own confluent life. The transaction is, in reality, nothing else than the unconscious reinstatement of the early childish mode of separateness, fear and dependence, such as actuated the mental bias of one's own domestic traditions. In the marriage and homemaking of each of us there is but the unconscious transmission of the marriage and home of our parents.[1] For

---

[1] While a student of Jung's in the early days of psychoanalysis, at the time when Jung was the very organ of Freud's genius, the clear emanation of his spirit, I remarked to him one day that I had come

SEXUALITY AND SEX

as the child is nurtured amid a codified system of opinionativeness, this self-reflective (suggestive) habit about him engenders a self-reflective habit within him. Having early formed an image of himself in the social reflection with which he is surrounded, he begins early to examine his own reactions from the sector of this habitual self-reflection. It is in this reflection of the self that consists the repercussion of consciousness constitutive of self-consciousness or the manifestation we unconsciously personify as *behaviour*—an off-hand term for a reaction which we have not yet begun half adequately to analyze.

As self-consciousness is of its nature personal and adaptive, it does not lend itself to analysis on the static basis of a merely adaptive and personal premise. Its true analysis is the realization on an inclusive basis of a genetic and relativistic principle of consciousness. In the mere match-making of our pictorial affects, human relationship has become throughout artificial. It is this private impersonation of affects which we have substituted for the common unity of our real affects. In this mutual comparison of reflected impressions our relation to one another becomes a superficial and meaningless balancing of one affect against another. This artificial substitutive quality has entered even into the expression of man's mating and reproductive impulse, and it is blindly venting itself to-day in the merely mutual attritions of our so-called sexual life. But this suggestive, substitutive image-systematization of sexuality is the direct antithesis to the unification and spontaneity of sex. Where there is unity of spirit, the symbol of unity expressed in bodily congress assumes a totally different significance. Sexuality is the mere apposition of bodies in place of a unity of spirit. In this apposition of the personal is the very abrogation of personality. It is the

---

to the conclusion that the neurotic individual inevitably married his mother. Jung's reply, alert as a flash, was characteristic of his brilliant, inclusive scope of vision. " I have come to the conclusion," he said, " that *every* individual inevitably marries his mother."

mark of sexuality that it is autocratic and exclusive ; it is the mark of sex that it is relative and inclusive. This bidimension or image-substitution of sexuality is the psychological mechanism of our sexual resistances. For resistances, after all, are but the irksome oppression of our habitually enforced adjacencies. For this reason marriage is habituative, suggestive, inverted.

Wherever conditions require the isolation together of any two normal individuals though of the same sex, over a protracted period, there appear very unexpected phenomena in the mental reactions of the two with respect to one another. These reactions may be noted not only where their isolation is due to the accidents of circumstance, but also where it is due to voluntary withdrawal from habitual associations in the mutual interest of a common pursuit. The observation is noteworthy that, in such instances, the dreams of each individual show a persistently autosexual trend whose invariable object is the other, while, on the other hand, the fancies of their days' dreams disclose a no less persistent criticism and repugnance on the part of each toward the other. It is the more interesting that this identical ego-sexual reaction (secret antagonism) is found also in two persons of unlike sex under the mental conditions of isolation involved in the mutual pursuance of self-interests represented in the bilateral attitude of marriage.

It is not inevitable that marriage should be the expression of inversion we make of it at present. Marriage is inverted or ego-centred not because of an organic necessity but because, in its mistakenness of form or its violation of the organic inherencies, marriage, like all mere external forms, is not biological but symbolic. In the present stage of society's arrested growth marriage is not the outcome of a mode of societal confluence but of a mode of personal preference. It is the unconscious enforcement of a self-predicated want, not the conscious acceptance of an organically determined need. When I speak of marriage, I have not in mind the permanent union of man and

SEXUALITY AND SEX

woman that is biological and true and that is the natural basis of our human society. I refer to the *mental attitude* toward marriage that we have come to substitute unconsciously for marriage itself. In place of the bipolar position of man and woman, we have substituted the bidimensional attitude of male and female. Because of this mental attitude of "marriage," people whose lives might be mutually necessary become, on the contrary, merely inevitable to one another. It is again our paramount image of self with its resultant reflection in the bidimensional picture. But whatever is pictorial is personal, whatever is personal is factional, and wherever there lurks the unconscious element of the factional or separative, union is organically interdicted.

Glancing even superficially at the obvious aim toward the mutual exchange of egoistic satisfactions and at the give-and-take of superficial coquetries and accommodations generally characterizing the marriage relationship, there is ample evidence of the completely infantile, undeveloped, ego-sexual nature of the motives determining such unions. If one considers the large number of women who are supported by men in the capacity of sexual partners, and observes their obsessive self-ornamentation, their voluptuous exaggerations of dress and manner, their liberal use of perfume and cosmetics with which to enhance their personal appeal, and considers correspondingly the large sums of money contributed annually by their votaries in maintenance of such sexual commodities, the ego-sexual character of such mutual arrangements is not far to seek.

In contrast with this state of affairs in the sexual life of "normals," it has for some time interested me to observe the unconscious autosexuality invariably presented by neurotic individuals. The unconscious character of it, whether latent or actual, always manifests itself in a privately repressed, unsatisfactory form or in a form that invariably entails conflict. It has long seemed to me that this repressed and tormenting expression of the tendency to the enfolded satisfactions of autosexuality, or to the unconscious extension of one's ego-sexuality to others of one's own sex, is but the aim of the personality toward an organic unification deflected into the symbolic form represented in *bodily* identification or in objective likeness.[1] It has further seemed to me that such a symbolically distorted urge, if converted into its true meaning, would issue in an organic identification representing a completer, more conscious order of union. I am not unmindful that in the fixity of our own symbolic substitutions our tendency is to make such organic conceptions needlessly difficult of assimilation. In a paper read before a psychoanalytic meeting several years ago[2] I gave expression to this same view, and my meaning was so completely misconceived that I was actually quoted subsequently as having said that I considered neurotic autosexuality (I then suggested the use of the term homo-phyllism) to embody a "higher expression of love" than that represented in allosexuality. Such a statement could not be otherwise interpreted than as an outspoken advocacy of homosexuality! It is, of course, not to be denied that the union *typified* in the allosexual relationship is alone an adequate expression of sex-unity. But it is adequate only as organic unity or conscious love, not as sexuality or self-love, the basis on which at present it very generally rests.

Biologically, autosexuality cannot be other than essentially infantile and regressive in character and as such it runs counter to the basic aims of analysis. But emphasis should be placed upon our need of recognizing to what a very large extent actual autosexuality exists under the objective symbols of allosexuality. Marriage, I repeat, as it largely obtains in the present stage of

---

[1] The word *like* is from Anglo-Saxon *gelic*, compounded of *ge*, meaning together, and *lic*, meaning body.
[2] "Convention in Psychoanalysis and Its Interpretative Inhibitions," a paper read at the Eighth Annual Meeting of the American Psychoanalytic Association, Atlantic City, May 10, 1918.

society, fairly teems with this infantile mode of sexuality. As the dominant impulse between " lovers " with their coy, infantile aim of secret self-satisfaction amply attests, the relationship, under whatever guise of exterior circumstance it may be concealed, is necessarily egoistic or autosexual.

I feel sure that sooner or later it will be recognized that allosexuality and autosexuality are synonymous, that these seemingly contrary adaptations are really but alternate aspects of one and the same thing. Sooner or later it will be seen that, while the neurosis entails in every instance an autosexual undercurrent, it is an expression of autosexuality that is organically intolerable, and that the social adaptation underlying normality is equally the unconscious expression of a collectively assimilated ego- or autosexuality. Thus our pseudo-normality is an unconsciously conceded (socially assimilated) inversion to this infantile mode of sexuality in substitution for the original organic instinct of sex. This is why it has seemed to me that in the neurotic reaction, for all its distortion, there is presented a progressive urge of evolution—that in the very distortion of the neurotic personality there is the premonition of a type of a clearer, more conscious social order. In his distorted effort to assimilate to himself a vicarious, objective (bodily) likeness, the neurotic expresses symbolically, unconsciously, an inherent urge toward a subjective, organic identification. In this view normality with its allosexual reaction is psychologically more autosexual than the reaction we recognize as unconscious or neurotic autosexuality. Although this repressed expression is symbolically the more infantile and regressive of the two, yet, of the two, it is potentially far the more competent to the truly complemental relationship whose fulfilment is merely symbolized in the allosexual adaptation as it commonly exists among us. What really underlies the conflict of the neurotic or the unconsciously autosexual is his organic urge toward a completer oneness of life.

His autosexuality is but symbolic. It is a disposition the essence of which is what I have elsewhere called "homophyllic"[1] and the organic culmination of which can be realized only in the unification of the complementary systems embodied in a corresponding monophyllic union.

In the beginning of my analytic work I fully believed with other psychoanalysts that there was a condition of neurotic or "unconscious homosexuality" distinguishable from what I then believed to exist conversely as "heterosexuality." I was too theoretical, habituative, academic, too limited in the freedom of unsystematized observation to recognize that sexuality, as it now exists socially, is everywhere of one cloth, that all sexuality being narcistic is "homosexuality," that it is of its nature an expression of the infantile desire of self-supremacy, of self-seeking, of self-gratification, that, in a word, sexuality is synonymous with autosexuality or ego-erotism. As homosexuality is but the projection socially of what is ego-sexuality individually, sexuality or ego-erotism is the very essence of homosexuality or homo-erotism. But, like the rest of my confrères, it was my habit to refer the question of health or disorder of adaptation to the artificial distinction between heterosexuality and "unconscious homosexuality" respectively. In other words, my criterion of health and growth was formerly the merely unconscious conventionalization of sex, the mere procuring for it, as it were, the external formality of the social blessing. It is only in the last years that I have seen in its fuller clarity that health is essentially unity and identity of personality as contrasted with the introversions of an unconsciously alternative adaptation. Only in the last years have I seen that as life and sex are one, so are self-worship and sexuality one, and that the real contrast as seen in the light of the health and growth of the organism, whether individual or societal, is the contrast between the organic

---

[1] See note 2, page 208.

instinct of sex on the one hand and the introversions of sexuality on the other.[1]

It is the unerring test of unconscious autosexuality that the quest that manifestly registers itself under this artificial form of expression can find its answer only in a realization which, in its true sex determination (love), is latently the precise reverse of this expression. In the attitude of lust and autosexuality toward the male there is presaged love or sex toward the woman ; in the attitude of lust or autosexuality toward the female is the earnest of love or sex toward the man. On the contrary, it is the unfailing test of the delusionally systematized autosexuality (ego-sexuality), which is social or " normal," that the quest thus recorded in its manifest content can find its satisfaction only in the no less manifest " reliefs " of a *seemingly* opposite sexual determination (allosexuality). In the self-lusts (autosexuality) of the male,

[1] In a recent meeting of psychopathologists a paper was presented which described the results of a questionnaire that had been distributed among the students of one of our prominent American universities, the object of which was to learn the nature of the sexual life of the college students. The figures compiled from the answers submitted showed in the author's view a surprisingly high percentage of masturbation and homosexuality. But what is of interest is the fact that in the interpretation of the author of the paper, as well as in that of every member who participated in the discussion, the concept of masturbation was restricted solely to personal practices on the part of the single individual, while the concept of homosexuality was confined entirely to the manifestation of sexual interests or activities occurring between persons of the same sex ! Apparently it was not suspected that these manifest expressions of autoerotism or homosexuality are the least widespread or significant forms of its occurrence, that the really important and far-reaching expression of these disorders of instinct occurs in the latent form represented in the symbolic substitutions of heterosexuality as commonly practised, for example, in houses of prostitution. Yet these latter expressions were avowedly regarded as real expressions of heterosexuality and, accordingly, its devotees were naively interpreted as presenting a psychological adaptation which showed a frank contrast to that of their " homosexual " confrères ! It is hopeless to expect any scientific understanding of anomalies of reaction that pertain to our subjective life as long as scientists themselves persist in confusing the objective appearances under which these anomalies are disguised for the subjective actuality of these anomalies themselves.

his objective is the body of the female with her autosexuality or self-lusts ; in the self-lusts (autosexuality) of the female, her objective is the body of the male and his self-lusts or autosexuality. In the satisfactions of these objective conquests lies the whole meaning of sexuality, as in the inclusiveness of a subjective unification lies the meaning of love.

The type of union biologically natural and fitting is that between man and woman as unified personalities. But in the present repressed, vicarious, infantile state of the individual and society, such a union is as yet in very large measure merely a type. To make of the union of personalities something more than a type—to make of it an organic reality—there is needed some such unification within each through the personality of the other as would be realized in a relationship representing the union of the two complementary systems, the peripheral and central, the societal and individual. The separation of these two systems we have seen to be the response to external repression from without, and in the re-uniting of these artificially separated complements there would be re-established the originally confluent organism, individual and societal, such as alone embodies the free and unified personality.

Union is not a thing of body in the contrasts of male and female with their artificial dissociation from life. The female in her rôle of costly *objet d'art* and the male as collector of such wares do not approach in this mere surface affinity a consummation even remotely akin to any such organic reality. No man or woman ever understood the other's body who has not understood the other's mind ; no man or woman ever understood the other's mind, who has not understood the body of the other. It is only in an organic identification such as is inclusive of both that there is fulfilled the united understanding, in both, of the mind and body of each. Union is of personality as realized in man and woman through the fulfilment in each of their identification with life in its totality, the one (male or female) embodying the peripheral, societal,

SEXUALITY AND SEX

allocentric complement, the other (male or female) the internal, central, autocentric complement, the two divided personalities realizing in the welding of each with each the organic unity of both.

In saying "male or female" I am advisedly avoiding assigning specifically either sex element to either organic rôle. In general the societal or peripheral rôle and the visceral or central rôle would seem analogous to the respective rôles of male and female, in the fact that the former is more fittingly adapted biologically to the external demands of life as hunter and provider and the latter to the more retired, enclosed conditions of life pertaining to the functions of conservation and maternity. There is the further parallel that in the female the reproductive organs are organs of receptivity, lying deeper, more centrally within her organism, while those of the male are more contiguous to the external skeletal tissues and are invasive in function. Nevertheless, because of the frequent transposition between the two sexes of the traits supposedly specific of each—a far more frequent transposition than the conventional division between the sexes affords opportunity to observe, the woman being often the more aggressive, the man the more retired of the two—to assign forehandedly one or the other complement to one or the other sex is arbitrary and without warrant. This is true particularly in respect to the distinction between the neurotic exaggerations of type described as auto- and allocentric, in which the conventional psychosexual differentiations are practically indeterminable.

These and kindred reflections lead me to feel that the term "opposite" sex is subjectively an unfortunate misnomer. To the neurotic especially, whose life has been crippled through repression in response to external opposition, all "oppositeness" is felt as a menace. Consider the inhibiting intimidations to the subjective child, resulting from the implied oppositeness between teacher and pupil, that characterizes the attitude of our prevailing pedagogical systems. Consider to what extent our systems of education are really barriers to education. In the very idea of oppositeness the child is instinctively revolted. His organism shrinks from it as from a blow. It is under such circumstances that, in his sense of the oppositeness of the sexes, the individual's unconscious recourse is to the sex that is not opposite his own. Yet here too, as we have seen, he has only turned to the objective symbol of unity, and the inherent opposition remains. For the symbol of unity or that which stands instead of unity is itself opposition. Thus in the neurotic's unconscious recourse to this symbolic or autosexual form of identification the opposition or separation is only accented anew.

Organically, or from the point of view of personality, woman is not opposite to man but each is the complement of the other. As in a current of electricity the flow between its two termini is dependent not upon their opposition but upon the functional confluence between its positive and negative poles, each being incomplete in the absence of the other, so is the relationship of sex between two organisms ; it is confluent and not opposite, it is of the nature of complement and not of contrast. And so the need of the neurotic, as of the normal individual, is such a completion of his personality in the organic complement of his mate as is co-extensive with his unification with life in its organic compass.

In the symbolic unification or unconscious autosexuality represented in an objective likeness or bodily identification there is but the short-circuiting of a true organic unification. Where it has occurred in personalities of a high intellectual or social order, the phenomenon has tended to be accounted for through recourse to a conceptual accommodation that is more generous than scientific. A plea has been advanced for the acceptance of the comrade-love of such individuals on grounds of the high character of the expression of their inverted tendency. To this end there has been invoked the conception of an " intermediate sex." But in this undoubtedly hospitable

SEXUALITY AND SEX

envisagement there is to be seen the sentimentality that is as always but inverted sentiment. The conception of an intermediate sex is the creation of an intermediate imagination. An intermediate sex is a biological solecism. It represents the attempt of a divided mind to reconcile a divided state of feeling that is prior to it. It is again the arbitrary assumption of opposition and the vicious circle of separateness and unconsciousness. As for the high order of many of its representatives, there is no high order of infantilism or autosexuality. The existence of a high order, moral and intellectual, of this type only imposes upon its representatives the greater societal obligation to understand and encompass its meaning. Their need is to relinquish the infantile distortion of life symbolized in this inverted bias of their unconscious autosexuality, and concurrently to enter into the organic realization of their innate consonance. It is only when this organic inherency has become disturbed, whether neurotically or normally, singly or societally, that there occurs the reflex effort toward vicarious restitution, resulting either in the exaggerations of self-assertiveness or in an over-emphasized self-derogation representing respectively the spurious bravadoes of an alternative maleness on the one hand and the artificial propitiations of an alternative femaleness on the other.

As has been said, because of our objective, perceptual attitude toward one another, our contacts, whether mediated through visual, auditory, tactile or other stimuli, are necessarily superficial and attributive. This superficial registry of stimuli includes also the sphere of our sexological responses. Thus in civilized man the sexual reaction, in both male and female, is restricted to the superficial sexual zones. Because of man's repression of this essential sphere of his feeling, the natural flow of the sexual impulse is artificially intercepted. Hence the genital stimulus in man is limited to the superficial tactile organs. It does not radiate to the deeper visceral structures constituting its nuclear terminus—in the male the rectal, prostatic and crural zones, in the female the rectal, the deeper vaginal zones and the cervix uteri (the homologue in the female of the prostate in the male). It is because of this intercepted radiation of the natural sexual response that there has arisen the necessity for the formulation of an "anal complex"—a complex that is regarded by psychoanalysts as existing quite sporadically in certain neurotic individuals and that is by no means recognized as a condition common to the race of civilized man! For naturally with the interception of the sexual impulse at its nuclear pole, or with repression of the visceral sex zone, there can only result in its stead a "complex" and along with it such artificial sexual adaptations as have been described as intermediate. In addition to this repression of our organic sex feeling there has occurred a corresponding compensation in the sphere of the mental and social life, which in the woman has led to the social adoption of the rôle corresponding to the *mental image* female and in the man to the *mental image* male.

Among the lower orders of animals the distinction between male and female entails no organic opposition. In one and the same organism this bipolar condition is undifferentiated and self-contained. On the other hand, with the mental sophistication connoted under the distinction man and woman we have come to assume the presence of an artificial opposition between the male and female organism. With the male element or organism we demand the mental and physical attributes we arbitrarily posit as "man," with the female element or organism we demand the mental and physical attributes we arbitrarily posit as "woman." Thus we repudiate the polarity that is confluent of the two elements male and female and exact of the organism we discriminate as man that it repudiate the characteristics we discriminate as woman, and of the organism we discriminate as woman that it repudiate the characteristics we distinguish as man.

SEXUALITY AND SEX

This arbitrary, unbiological dictum necessitates that a " man " shall repress the female component within him notwithstanding that his organism is compounded of it along with the male element. Conversely, it makes obligatory upon the woman that she repress the male element within her notwithstanding that it is a no less constituent factor than the female element in composing the bipolar quality essential to the unity of her organism.

With this artificial condition and its edict of enforced repression there often occurs such a one-sided development within the organism that the result is the exaggerated reaction we see in the bilateral extremes we have described as good and bad, as saint and sinner. It is interesting to observe, though, that upon analysis one discovers within the repressed sphere of the sinner's personality all the factors that constitute the personality of the saint, and that within the repressed sphere of the saint's personality, there are disclosed all the elements that constitute the personality of the sinner.

Such findings as we owe to our deeper penetration into individual psychology make clearer the superficiality of our normal, social distinctions. They afford us reason to believe that when psychiatry has loosed itself of its superficial acceptations we shall find that wherever the bipolar life of the organism, male or female, is permitted to fulfil its natural expression there will be no longer the repressed or unconscious instigation to such exaggerated distortions or over-compensations as now issue as a result of the organic repression of these artificially dual phases. We shall then recognize that the " intermediate sex " is a fallacy due to discriminations that arise from a disregard of the inclusive nature of sex. What is really apprehended by the term intermediate sex is the *composite sex* whereof the unification of personality within every individual, normal as well as neurotic, is the inherent embodiment. It is in this concomitance of the social and nuclear systems that consists the organic co-ordination of the individual element. Without it there is lacking the organic correlation of the societal aggregate such as is the essential biology of man. The organismic postulate here proposed sets out from the conception of a *principle of primary identification* within the original psychic organism as the biological basis of consciousness.[1] Upon this principle rests the biological significance of the unity of personality that comprises the consonance of life, individual and societal. The essence of the neurotic diathesis, socially and singly, is merely the reflection within the individual of these surface diversifications of external suggestion or repression, as more and more they infringe upon this original consonance of the organism. This gradual replacement of our original unity and inherency by the external inducements of the extraneous and alternative is the whole significance of unconsciousness. This, in reality, is the meaning of the manifold dissimilitudes of men as compared with the unified personality of man.

If, in the androgynous personalities represented in such autocentric types as Buddha, Plato or Christ, there is manifested this unifying urge of the inherent organism of man, so the allocentric personalities of Socrates, of Napoleon and of Nietzsche are equally expressive of this same composite urge. If this unifying urge of man's common sex incited the genius of an Hypatia in centuries past, it has directed no less in our own times the creative impulse underlying the genius of George Eliot or of Olive Schreiner. In the contemplation of such genius we see presented the unity and concentration of personality that is the real meaning of the artist as contrasted with the extraneous dissipations and diversities of the average reaction-type. It is this unity of personality that is the source of the artist's creativeness as it is the inspiration

---

[1] " The Genesis and Meaning of ' Homosexuality ' "—a development of *the principle of identification or the primary subjective phase of consciousness*. See *The Psychoanalytic Review*, Vol. IV, No. 3, July, 1917.

of his genius. This composite quality of the sex life explains the gentler intuitions we often find in the personality of a man. There is undoubtedly the feminine in man though as yet he stands in fear of it. It does not wrangle or contend. It does not calculate success. The feminine in man is the artist in man. It is because of this that there can be in the societal unity of the artist's intuitive instinct no place for the illusion that is called " the public." To him " the public " is but the collective repudiation of the common soul of man—a repudiation that corresponds to this same disavowal within the private soul of each of us. Unmoved by its clamorous demands, the artist feels within these manifestations of the public mind the common soul that underlies it, and senses within it the pain of denied needs identical with his own. This is the unfailing intuition of the artist. It is because of this sense of the unity of life that no artist was ever yet successful, that his triumph or his failure are above all public concern.

And so by " the artist " I mean the quality of personality that is enticed by no external advantage, that entertains no indirection, is unmoved by the inverse compensations of egoism and the unconscious wish. Such a quality is organically, societally self-contained and subsists without object. It does not sue for favour nor seek to please. In this confluence of the personality of the artist as of the neurotic, in this creative concentration of man's genius, whether articulate or denied, is embodied the societal instinct that is the composite life of the race. This organic integrity of personality that is the composite life of man and that is organically inseparable from the unifying urge embodied in the impulse of mating has its clearest intimations in the affirmations of the artist as in the frustrations of the neurotic. In the unifying urge represented in these two opposite extremes of reaction—an urge which shall neither impose nor accept an adjustment extraneous to the inherent personality—is expressed the demand for a self-realization in a unification which, being organic, is all-inclusive.[1]

Only in such a conjunction will man realize his original mode of societal confluence. When such a conjunction will enable him truly to realize in the instinct of mating the deepest need of his being, union will no longer as now be *represented* through juxtaposition in the mere physical symbol of bodily interpenetration, but it will *be* through unification the societal reality of an organic intussusception.

[1] It is not by accident but by some inner, intuitive design that man has adopted the symbol he employs as the sign of infinity. In the mark of the mathematicians—consisting of two circles that are one, one circle that is two, wherein is neither beginning nor end—is expressed the character of the infinite and all-inclusive in a form of conjunction so complete as not to be susceptible of possible increment.

CHAPTER IX

ULTIMATE RESOLUTION OF THE SOCIETAL NEUROSIS IN ITS SOCIAL IMPLICATION

THE first demand of our organic completion through a unification with another is a unification within oneself. From a basis of a divided self one can look out only dividedly. From a separative mode one can judge only separatively. If the individual embodies a symbolic replacement within himself, others about him appear to him necessarily also as symbolic replacements, and the degree of his resentment toward his own separateness is the measure of his resentment toward theirs. After all, the only implacable enemy of man is his own unconsciousness, and the reconcilement of himself to himself the severest test of his essential personality. Its realization is born of a patience that is not virtue but encompassment.

Man, in his unconsciousness, stands ever by himself and for himself. In the separateness of his personal resistances toward the societal organism as a whole, the individual has become marooned within his own insular habituations. But this isolated attitude of mind is a condition which, in our interpretation, is societally anomalous. Though originally imposed, this condition now automatically imposes itself upon the social personality. Thus far this organic disaffection of man has sought alleviation in the social convivialities that are but the syndicate of men's collective unconscious. Men have sought to appease their personal isolation through the accommodations of mere objective agreement. They have substituted the symbols of social fraternization for the actuality of man's organic consonance. Within the unconscious of man his secret disaffection has remained unaltered still.

So often this statement that every man is for himself alone has brought the rejoinder: " But why may he not be ? Surely such selfishness is natural to man." But is it ? I do not think so. Of course I have not in mind the individual's effort of preservation in the interests of his natural life and growth. I have in mind the private differentiations due to man's *mental attitude of self-distinction*. In the conservation of interests incident to the individual's instinct of physical preservation, man's native experience entails no secret *self-conscious* design. But it is the tell-tale of man's mental attitude of personal separatism that he is constantly under the necessity to *pretend* that he is not separative or for himself. This universal pretence reveals a biologically specious condition of life for which we feel a universal need of concealment. For whatsoever attitude of mind is not openly compatible with the personality imposes a division of the personality. A socially divided personality is a socially insecure personality. Back of the social mind that pretends it is not concerned exclusively for self lies a basis of social fear and distrust. Pretence is division of personality, and division of personality is fear. If the pretence and the division are social, the fear is social. The effort of numbers or of the social consensus to combine in support of their mutual fear is unavailing, for a consensus begotten of fear is an organically spurious consensus. At the heart of it lies a secret division. This is the travesty of normality with its secret soviet of fear.

The analyst or the psychiatrist whose outlook is objective fails to regard this consensual fallacy in its social as in its personal implication. Being of the social unconscious he cannot contemplate the social unconscious. Being himself divided he cannot realize his own division. We all prefer the satisfaction of seeming together socially to the reality of being together organically. We like the seeming integrity of the social unconscious because it

RESOLUTION OF NEUROSIS—SOCIAL

conceals our own disaffection. It is only this seeming security of numerical preponderance, however, that affords us comfortable protection against the aberrations of the isolated, non-conformable or neurotic personality. Nowhere is the autocracy of unconsciousness more blindly cruel than in the mass impetus of our social consolidation. We are not unaware of the resistance of the individual to the social consensus, but we have yet to discover the resistance of the social consensus to the individual. The psychopathologist has offered interesting formulations regarding delusions of persecution, but none whatever regarding delusions that persecute.

The group work that has been gradually developing among my students and myself has consisted essentially in a reversal of this habitually objective course of the psychiatrist. Instead of studying ideas of reference objectively as expressed in the individual, we have studied ideas of reference subjectively as they occur socially among ourselves. Our experience as a group has led us inevitably to the conclusion that the personal analysis is a self-contradictory process, that only as the individual realizes through his societal experience the futility of the personal or private basis is it biologically possible to be truly in harmony with a healthy and constructive environment. If our position has any value and significance it is because it has come to us through the daily test of an actual living experience, and because as a societal experience it cannot fail to extend itself societally to others also.

Let it not be thought, however, that our efforts toward a social analysis have proceeded upon a smooth and untroubled course. If the individual has his " ups and downs " in the effort to unify his consciousness on the basis of a personal analysis, he meets no less with alternations of satisfaction and depression according as his resistances surge or ebb in his efforts toward a social unification of consciousness. If the individual analysis presents a situation that is unconscious and bidimensional, a group analysis presents a condition that is equally unconscious and bidimensional. In the bidimensional reaction of the individual toward the personal analysis, he tends, as we have seen, toward a permanent fixation upon the analyst which shows itself alternately in the mental reaction of "love" or of "hate." But in either the personal or social situation he tends to hold tenaciously to this new object of his infantile affect in the secret hope of ultimately reconciling and amalgamating it with the love that underlies still the original mother-image. Unhappily, it is the invariable failure of the personal analysis that the patient carries his secret purpose to a successful issue. For either he remains fastened between the old and the new love-objects in a consolidated image-fixation upon the analyst, or else he returns to the original love-image afforded by the parent or to its surrogates, with or without the collateral aids of sublimation.

In the actual experience of our group analysis the tendency was essentially no different. But there was an additional recourse in the group analysis that is precluded in the personal analysis. In the personal analysis there is a bidimensional attitude toward the analyst that alternates constantly between infantile docility and infantile resentment, between sentimental approbation at one time and outraged disillusionment at another. But this alternation always occurs, of course, within one and the same individual. In the social analysis the situation is expressed quite differently. It was my experience that this diversity of reaction within the group led at first to the formation of reaction-clusters within the group, so that one unit became consistently docile toward the analyst and resentful among themselves, while the other unit became hostile toward the analyst and docile toward one another. Both alternations (resentment or docility) were, of course, equally spurious within each group of reactions.

The practical outcome in each sub-group was very different however. In the cluster that united against the analyst, a confederacy was formed that presented all the features of unconsciousness we have seen to characterize the collective reactions occurring everywhere throughout the domain of our normal adaptation. The psychology of this reaction, as we know, is the collective pooling of the unconscious of its members severally, with a view to the mass support afforded each individual within the unit separately. The result as it occurred in this cluster was a temporary deadlock and a corresponding re-adoption of the normal level of bidimensional standards, personal and social.

In the cluster in which the sense of resentment was limited to inter-reactions among its own members, while as a unit all held an attitude of friendliness toward the analyst, there was offered a form of group-unconsciousness that at least lent itself to progressive analysis and resolution. But here again there was discoverable the secret pooling of unconscious motives of personal interest and self-protection that in no way differentiated this group division from the former, that did not separate the " faithful " from the " unfaithful," nor absolve the " docile " any more than the " resentful " from a secret complicity in the collective reaction that is the mass neurosis of normality.

It should be remembered that the plan of group analysis was adopted not because I had *a priori* found in it the logical solution of the neurosis. Not by any means. Neither had I inductively reached conclusions that led to any such logical determination. Not even theoretically was there at hand anything of the nature of a *logical* solution. A dissociation is not logical and its solution could not be logical. The neurosis is not a matter of the intellect and the process of its unravelling could not have been intellectually predetermined. As thought and affect are processes that occupy essentially different spheres, to *think out* a solution for a disorder of affect is self-contradictory. To attempt to do so is beyond the range of organic possibility. All that I had in mind in our group undertaking was *to obtain affective conditions shared in common that might afford a basis for the observation of affective conditions withheld separately.* It seemed to offer the opportunity to secure a relative and societal background against which the individual would be enabled to view in impersonal perspective his own hitherto absolute and personal evaluations. Up to this time I had for years worked on the group conception in the absence of any tangible background of experimentation. There was now needed the practical substantiation of this group conception in the actual assembling of " analyzed " individuals into an organized social aggregate. While the programme of group analysis entered upon by my students and myself came into an intensive application with the beginning of the year 1923,[1] it was actually the summer of that year that marked the active inception of our experiment as an organized unit, our group having then its first opportunity of a practical test in the daily contact of its members; so that we were still at this time only feeling our way toward the ultimate outcome of an analysis involving more than two or three individuals.

In my view the really significant finding that has resulted from our close mental association as a group has been the opportunity of demonstrating through group experience the practical significance of the very unexpected disclosure upon which I chanced some years ago in my conception of the bidimensional image and its influence upon the reactions of consciousness at large. It is this conception which has proved to be the real foundation of our work. I am convinced that an adjustment of consciousness, whether analytic or conventional, whether of the laboratory or of the street, will ultimately demand that we bring to book the very origins of our mental and social systems of " thinking," that we challenge our customary values of mental adaptation at their very

[1] The reader is reminded that this book was outlined in 1923. From that time to the time of publication (1927), the group analysis, proceeding along the lines indicated in this chapter, has further substantiated the thesis here stated.

foundation. Our problem resolves itself into one that shall challenge in every detail the fixed basis of an arbitrary and unconscious position of absolutism as contrasted with the fluent evaluations that alone pertain to a basis of conscious relativity.

Upon the basis of our prevailing personal criterion first inculcated through the alternative precept of good and bad, the mind of every individual existing under our present social system is disposed toward a dualism of outlook that renders every affective judgment of the individual irreconcilable and self-contradictory. For a basis that rests upon a mental *standard* or criterion of evaluations is necessarily moralistic and divided. A moralistic command entails a moralistic interdiction. Every affirmation contains *in itself* a negation that is equal and contrary. That is, every criterion *of its nature* entertains its opposite. Whatsoever I must be or think or feel, I must at the same time also not be or think or feel. Whatsoever I believe, to that precise degree I likewise disbelieve.[1]

This is not so simple. It is not by any means so simple as we tend to make it. It does not merely mean, as we would like to think, that if I love good people I do not love bad people. Not at all. That would be obvious and a matter of fact. It would leave our absolutism quite intact and our criteria quite unchallenged in their fallacy. It means something far subtler than this. It means that if I love good people I *do not* love good people. It means that in the measure in which I love an object, in that measure I hate that object. It means, in sum, that, within a system of absolute measures, my concept " love " as my concept " good " is throughout fanciful and artificial, that, in disturbing the natural equilibrium of the organism, my mental criterion is resisted by a counter-judgment, which, being fanciful and artificial, tends in a precisely reverse direction at one and the same time. It means that every mental image, arising on the basis of our present

[1] See note 1, page 53.

absolute criterion, possesses unconsciously an ambivalent value. *Stating the proposition in psycho-dynamic terms, every affective mental image is counterbalanced by an opposite image having an attractive force that possesses the quality of all bidimensional (or pendular) motion and accordingly it acts with a momentum the direction of which is at every moment precisely equal and reverse to its own impulse.*

After many years in which I have been delving into the processes of the unconscious and striving to unearth its intricate mechanisms, I have come upon no phenomenon that has seemed to me of such basic significance as this illusory mechanism of unconscious dualism and conflict that underlies our absolute criteria of values, individual and social. Through Freud we have learned that a psychic ambivalence underlies the neurotic processes of the individual, but we have not yet learned that an equal ambivalence underlies the processes of the social unconscious. Furthermore, while Freud has shown that there is this ambivalence of motive underlying the individual process represented by the neurotic conflict, it remains to be seen that each term within this ambivalent outlook is itself likewise ambivalent—that psychic ambivalence necessarily presupposes at all times an essential condition of ambivalence that repeatedly doubles upon itself. For, if we will examine either term of our ambivalent proposition, we shall find that it too is based on opposed valences. That is, on our present absolute basis of evaluation, every term of our subjective judgment necessarily divides and re-divides with its very inception. Not only does the contrast between love and hate represent ambivalence, but love contains in itself an ambivalent motive, and hate contains in itself a motive that is equally ambivalent. And so, to whatever subjective determinant we may turn, there is inevitably this inseparable element of contrast due to our own subjectively bidimensional basis.

As regards the neurosis of the individual, we have learned through Freud that an unconscious system of

RESOLUTION OF NEUROSIS—SOCIAL

images, operating to inhibit spontaneous thought and action, is the essential meaning of this disorder. Of course, Freud attributes such disorders of development to an associative inadequacy resident in the individual organism. But in the study of the social unconscious upon the inclusive basis of a relative method of approach, we shall recognize that an identical system of images operates to hinder the spontaneous expression of the social organism; that as there exists a neurosis of the individual that is due to an unconscious system of personal images, so there exists a neurosis of the social mind due to an equally unconscious system of social images; and finally that the latter condition within the social consciousness as a whole is the primary and essential disorder of which the individual manifestation is but a subsequent and secondary symptom.[1]

It is not possible to speak of the group basis of analysis that has become the central feature of my own work without calling attention to a bidimensional situation that has made itself felt within the ranks of psychoanalysts themselves. Moreover, this situation has forced into prominence a hitherto unrecognized impasse within our psychoanalytic interpretations, precisely because of the inevitable conditions of an individualistic basis of analysis. The outstanding theoretical feature of Freud's position toward his patients has always been a policy of "hands off." With the inception of psychoanalysis it has been the signal position of Freud, and subsequently of us all, that the patient shall be left free of all domination or direction or suggestion, that in order that he come into a sense of adult responsibility toward his social environment generally he must come into a responsibility toward his own mental processes as they relate directly to the analyst. This policy of non-interference is one which those of us who have attempted to follow the psychoanalytic programme have adhered to with strict conformity. But it is clear that the analyst becomes automatically the

[1] See note 1, page 15.

all-engrossing criterion (transference) of the patient's unconscious and that unconsciously the analyst assumes toward his patient a corresponding position of personal criterion. So that, however sincere our intention, there has resulted what is perhaps the weakest point in our psychoanalytic technique, a point that has warranted the most severe criticism of our work, namely, that treatment by psychoanalysis continues for a far too long and indefinite term.

To offset this embarrassment recourse is now had to a procedure whereby the analysis is brought to a conclusion at a certain definitely assigned period—a period to be determined by the analyst according to the circumstances in each case. The change proposed, then, is from a course of indefinite to a course of definite duration; from a procedure that, at least theoretically, places upon the patient the responsibility of terminating the analysis to a procedure that definitely takes this responsibility from him and places it in the hands of the analyst. But, in proposing that the analyst shall at an assignable moment in the analysis peremptorily determine upon a definite period at which the analysis shall cease, and in formally pronouncing that from this moment on the patient shall be cured, we are confronted again with the deadlock of the bidimensional and alternative. In this recourse we are merely resorting again to the legislation of suggestion and, unconsciously falling a victim to the pictorial concept " cure," we are in no sense meeting the issue. For in the criterion of the suddenly achieved " cure " we are not less the unconscious victims of an illusory and absolute criterion than we were victims of a criterion that is illusory and absolute when we presumed the position that the patient must at all hazards be left in a position of freedom toward the analysis.[1] In my view, this proposal

[1] We are warned, of course, that this new shift of technique will arouse in us unprecedented resistances. But let us be wary lest we capitulate too easily to this ready-to-hand ogre of " resistances " ; for by the same token we have been warned throughout these analytic years that we must expect unprecedented resistances to the former dictum of

RESOLUTION OF NEUROSIS—SOCIAL

of psychoanalysts themselves that we no longer assume a policy of non-interference but that we offer instead the arbitrary suggestion of spontaneous " cure," there is sounded the death-knell of psychoanalysis as administered on the basis of the personal analysis. This does not mean, however, the death-knell of the basic position of psychoanalysis as deducible from the principle first enunciated by Freud. On the contrary, if we would enlarge the application of psychoanalysis to include the wider scope of our societal personality, there would be realized the necessary advance toward the full significance of Freud's essential principle.

It is admittedly a part of the purpose of the present thesis to show that there do exist conditions which make treatment through the method of psychoanalysis, as it is at present, needlessly long. But to reduce the length of treatment calculated to adjust the distorted mind would seem as unreasonable as to curtail the length of treatment intended to adjust the distorted limb. As Freud remarked long ago, no one would question the validity of the orthopædist's method because of the length of time it requires. Why then all the outcry because of the length of time often required by the psychoanalyst's method? It is my own feeling that if there are conditions which make the method of psychoanalysis needlessly long, what is required is the analysis of these conditions. I believe that under these circumstances the method will automatically adjust itself. But to shorten a course of treatment because it is long seems unintelligent to me. It seems merely shifting from one unconscious condition to its equally unconscious alternative.

Let us examine more closely the real alternative here. The fact is that by reason of the dualistic basis existing in the personal analysis, the analyst necessarily invites the

---

psychoanalysis—a dictum which imposed without parley or mitigation a rigid analytic policy of non-interference. Our inconsistency is but another instance of the automatic illogic of the alternative, of the inevitable compulsion of the personal criterion.

indefinite continuation of the analysis on the part of the patient, no matter what he may theoretically say or do to the contrary. For the analyst is himself the victim of an unconscious criterion represented in his personal standard of "cure." That is, he entertains for the patient an image of self-dependence obtainable alone through psychoanalysis. But in this standard of "cure" he entertains a wish-motive that is self-contradictory. For, in wishing to cure a patient through a process of self-dependence, the analyst, because of the involvement of his personal wish toward the patient, necessarily presents his cure through processes that interfere with self-dependence. It is again the bidimensional dilemma of the absolute or personal criterion, and an absolute criterion necessarily involves a wish-motive of two terms either of which unconsciously invites its opposite. In his personal criterion the analyst would both release a patient with a view to the patient's self-dependence and at the same time retain a patient in order to make sure that his self-dependence is complete. With one gesture he would detain him while with the other he would set him free. This is undoubtedly an awkward deadlock. This is the very contrary of a cure that aims at self-dependence. For the analyst, whether in detaining or dismissing a patient, is acting for him. But, on the basis of the criterion of the personal image, there is inevitably this alternative. It is unescapable.

This solicitous attitude of mind, I concede, has undoubtedly tended to extend the course of the analysis to an indefinite duration. But does the alternative—the arbitrary manifesto that a certain time limit shall peremptorily conclude the analysis—really settle the issue? Does it not rather sustain than remove the dilemma? Of course, a theoretical assumption has been invoked that is calculated to warrant this procedure upon psychological premises—the premises, namely, that the analysis consists in the fanciful reproduction of the birth experience, that the trauma in which the birth culminates physiologically must be psychically reproduced through the trauma of sudden separation of the personality of the patient from that of the analyst. But does corroborating the illusory and symbolic dramatization occurring within the neurotic mind assist such a patient in disabusing his mind of the fallacy of the illusory and symbolic? In this alternative of a predetermined period for a patient's withdrawal from analysis are we not merely having recourse to the more decisive position of the father as contrasted with the more lenient and compromising attitude of the mother-image? Further, in what we call the mother-father alternation are we not again merely projecting the dualistic criterion that is our own personal and contrasting basis of evaluation?

In my own work I have had an opportunity to realize convincingly the completely illusory and arbitrary character of this mother-father alternation. This has been shown in the fact that patients undergoing analysis with me have turned to my assistant, Mr. Shields, in the thought that they would find in him a less severe analyst than in myself, while patients who were being analyzed by Mr. Shields have turned to me in a similar hope. Needless to say, in either case, the patients were equally disappointed in their quest. Yet this alternation would have continued indefinitely had not a solution been found elsewhere, namely, under conditions of a social analysis in which a personal attachment is not permitted the conditions of lodgment necessary for completing the personal illusion of permanence and fixation.

I have come to the definite conclusion that in the individual analysis the neurotic patient pulls the wool over the eyes of the analyst and inevitably comes out the victor, because unconsciously the analyst is inevitably on the patient's side. Besides, to show sufficient interest in an individual to sit with him in personal conference daily or three times weekly (whatever the routine may be) is to indicate to the very susceptible emotions of the neurotic patient that his presence is personally desirable.

The situation is only interpretable on the part of the neurotic patient, with his unfulfilled personal emotions, as the implication that those emotions are fully reciprocated personally on the part of the analyst. For with whomsoever we enter into a personal situation of mutual secrecy we are in a situation of mutual complicity. In the secrecy and confidence of the individual analysis, in which there is the close, private, specialized relationship of one individual to another, there is the tacit disavowal in each of the commonness of the socially prevalent quality of all unconsciousness. As long as there is a private and personal system resident within the analyst, he necessarily corroborates the private and personal system resident within the patient in front of him. The fallacy of the private system is the illusion of personal secrecy. Clinically, it is the secrecy of unconsciousness that is the backbone of unconsciousness. Though a patient divulge in minutest detail all the data entering into his unconscious experience, he yet retains his unconsciousness if he retains a sense of secrecy toward it.

In our group activity, as we have seen, there were several, who in refusing to meet the organic demand for a social amalgamation of their personality, were forced unconsciously to seek the protective regression afforded either in family, in friends, or in some form of defence-reaction that led to the isolated activities of mere social or normal connivance. On the other hand, others, with no less motive of personal defence-reaction, sought protection in the alternative of family union which they contrived to secure among themselves, and unconsciously assumed collectively that I, as the analyst, could be arbitrarily delegated by them to the rôle of *pater-mater noster!* As I have said, there was thus formed once more an unconscious cluster, a cluster, however, that was no less an unconscious form of social encapsulation than the first.

Biologically it is the natural process that with the growth of their strength offspring become less and less

RESOLUTION OF NEUROSIS—SOCIAL 235

attached or dependent upon the parent and that concomitantly there is more and more aptitude for equal give-and-take activities or play with their fellows, at first with brothers and sisters and later with those of their congeners with whom chance affords association. Of course, though, if the parent has a mental background that attaches the child artificially to him through the image-suggestion of omnipotence, then, on the basis of our present individual and social adaptation, the child cannot find in any of his contacts a natural medium of association. Although the child may leave his natural parent and associate objectively with his congeners, he carries with him the image of the parent, and naturally he foists this image upon all with whom he comes in contact. At the same time all who come in contact with him equally foist upon him the image of *their* omnipotent parent. Our position is that *as this image is not personal but social it cannot be personally but only socially resolved.*

The point would seem to be that the child cannot look for companionship in the mother or father as long as he holds the mother or father in the light of an image or criterion. Neither can he come into simpler relationships with his fellows on the basis of this criterion of the mother-image without investing the personalities of his associates with an equal image or criterion. The difficulty of the personal analysis is the preservation of an image-situation the while one endeavours theoretically to dispel the image. But in the natural give-and-take of human beings in their work and play activities under conditions of social analysis, there is afforded the reality of a social equalization that renders untenable the secret and obsessive fixation with which we merely *look on* one another from the background of the bidimensional picture.

The result of our group affiliation, to express it symbolically, has been a family of "good" and "bad" children, of whom some desired to run away from home while others were content to remain beside the family hearth. Socially, the result was a bidimensional division or alternative that exactly parallels the division or alternative within the individual. But there is this significant difference between the personal and the social analysis In the individual the component that is unwelcome may be permanently repressed, while in the alternatives represented socially it is possible to stimulate these components into repeated recognition through the constant clashing resultant upon placing the opposed elements, represented by the alternate issues, under conditions of socially irritating contrast or competition. In the social analysis there is no letting sleeping dogs lie. Once the unconscious of one alternative reaction has been set upon the other, the fight is to the finish. There is not the private recess of personal secrecy into which one may retreat. There is not the recourse to self-partiality that allows a smoothing over of unpleasant reminiscences and a successful substituting of more flattering condolences.

According to our group or social conception of the neurosis it is assumed that the causative element in the production of these disorders is social or phyletic and that the correction of these disorders must proceed upon a social or phyletic basis. Our position is that the individual cannot be healthy whose consciousness is the outgrowth of an unhealthy social mind about him. It, therefore, becomes the essence of our group conception that the disorder of the individual presented *manifestly* in the individual's " symptoms " may only be corrected through the analysis of the social processes constituting *latently* the individual's collective medium.[1]

As we first learned from Freud and as has been corroborated through researches in psychoanalysis made independently of Freud, the neurosis is synonymous with the repression of the instinctive life of man, and in the prevailing interpretation of psychoanalysis the remedy lies in the successful adaptation of the personal satis-

[1] " The Group Method of Analysis," *The Psychoanalytic Review*, Vol. XIV, 1927, " The Laboratory Method in Psychoanalysis," *The American Journal of Psychiatry*, Vol. V, No. 3, January, 1926.

faction of sexuality expressed both in direct physiological release and in the equivalents of sublimation. It is our position that this interpretation is far too narrow, that in interpreting the neurosis as due primarily to disorders within the sphere of man's reproductive instinct, there is left out of account the disorders of instinct due to the obstruction of man's tribal or congeneric life and to the consequent interruption of the creative expression of his personality as a societal unit. Our feeling is that sexuality, as it now exists, is very generally of an over-stimulated or obsessive character, owing to the undue and greatly aggravated insistence that has been vicariously brought to bear upon this sphere. In the absence of the natural outlets of man's societally instinctive expressions through the common avenues of concerted work and play, the function natural to the physiological process of reproduction has been overburdened and inflated out of all proportion to its primary significance. While, as a consonant part of the congeneric instinct of man, sex is an undoubtedly powerful urge, in the self-interested and bidimensional bias of its autosexual, personal quest, this manifestation has become but a symbolic exaggeration of the natural instinct of sex. This exaggerated condition is due secondarily, however, to a repression of the reproductive faculty of man as naturally expressed in the creative interests of his common societal activities. As our give-and-take expressions among our fellows develop into activities that are reciprocally creative, in the same measure our obsessive drive toward the satisfactions of sexuality, whether repressed or indulged, will cease to dominate human personality in its present completely unconscious and bidimensional image insistence.[1]

[1] It should be clearly explained that *group analysis is not my analysis of the group but that it is the group's analysis of me or of any other individual.* In our laboratory usage, " group " does not mean a collection of individuals. It means a phyletic principle of observation. This phyletic principle of observation as applied to the individual and to the aggregate is the whole significance of group analysis.

CHAPTER X

ULTIMATE RESOLUTION OF THE SOCIETAL NEUROSIS IN ITS PERSONAL IMPLICATION

I WELL recognize that in its matter this essay offers little that is new. What I have sought to do is rather to speak of our human reactions in the large from the basis of the altered consciousness of the handful of men and women whose group experience, as gradually it has grown and gathered strength and cohesion among us, has permitted the more subjective or societal realization of these reactions. But though it is true that there is little that is new in the matter of this essay, yet, in so far as the collective differences existing among us as a group have been allowed slowly to diffuse themselves gradually into the solution of our common acceptance of one another, it seems to me that in its mode at least our position offers an approach that brings us a step closer to the increasingly urgent problem of our human adjustment.

After all, the intrinsic mode underlying our conception is the real significance of our conception. To understand our position the reader's only recourse is to repudiate the bidimensional alternatives of extrinsic moralities based upon precepts of a personalistic or self-restricted behaviourism. For the position of this thesis will be little understood in the light of the accustomed interpretations of the conventional social mind. Because of the unconscious bias of its own mental absolute it will appear to the social polity that, in the altered attitude here outlined, the social polity is threatened at its very foundations. In its tenacious hold upon habitual prepossessions the organized consensus does not realize that these foundations are already tottering. It will not see that in order to further the replacement of the already disintegrating structures of our present social system, a more widely envisioning concept of the organized consciousness of man must needs be invoked. In some way, though, there must first be brought home to each of us the realization that there can be no true unity within the societal organism as long as we are a prey to impressions that are but the give-and-take reflection of mental attitudes existing mutually in one another. As long as we fail to identify the tyranny of mental attitudes within the social unconscious with the reflection of similar tyrannical mental attitudes within the personalism and defection of each of us, man cannot rise to the reality of an organized social consciousness. As long, for example, as we fail to understand that when a mental attitude in others pleases or incenses us, it is necessarily but the reflection of a corresponding mental attitude in ourselves, we shall continue to praise or punish such mental attitudes, together with the acts resulting from them, with the mere retaliative measures of personal reward or redress. So that our attitude will continue to be, as now, the mere pro-and-con reaction to impressions determined by the unconscious self-reflection of our own " good and bad."

It is precisely this illusion of mental oppositeness that we need to dispel. Harmony will follow automatically once we have accepted in its societal significance the affective unity of life. With this realization there will be no further need of the restraints of an alternative principle of morality which, in its bidimensional legislation, aims to establish merely a temporary balance between essential opposites. With the elimination of the individual hope-fear alternation the whole incitement to personal infringement will have been removed. What inducement will I have to cheat a man if he is myself ? Or betray a woman if she is I ? To what purpose will I seek to enslave another to my whim (call it love, marriage or what you will) if between us there is the acceptance of an organic compliance that allows the realization in each of the common unity of both ? Why would I seek to outdo anyone in the invidious competitions of what is called " success," if I know clearly that success comprises only the self-reflective distinctions existing within the unconscious of the social mind in response to the spurious incentives of the personal alternative as it exists within the unconscious of the individual mind ?

Our prevailing personalistic basis is not applicable to an organismic viewpoint, because a policy that is self-reflective in the unconscious is self-contradictory in consciousness. Unity or consciousness of personality is organically preclusive of whatever is personal or unconscious in the personality. For every wish that is attained an equal disappointment is incurred. For every satisfaction that is secured a corresponding denial is imposed. To fulfil one's wish is to abjure one's reality. Asking is its own postponement, as striving is its own defeat. This inner homology between desire and its non-attainment is alike the hope and the despair of atoning to oneself unconsciously or personally for what is one's need consciously or societally. As with compulsion-replacements elsewhere, the real occasion of prayer is one's unanswerable attitude of mind in prayer. In the self-compensation of man's want as an individual organism, he necessarily repudiates his inherent consonance as a societal organism. Thus our personal dearth and our personal plenty are organically the same. As the part embodied in one's personal wish (unconsciousness) is intrinsically opposed to the whole embodied in one's societal unity (consciousness), to desire is at the same time to fail of attainment as well as to covet. This is the paradox of our personalism and unconsciousness, as it is the impasse of the personal absolute underlying it. In the personal opportunism of the unconscious wish we would fancifully summon the processes of life to ourselves in place of contributing our individual function as common participants in the reality of these processes. Our contradiction, after all, is the

RESOLUTION OF NEUROSIS—PERSONAL

division within ourselves, and the real impasse as always is the self-image embodied in the delusive alternative of good and bad.

I know, of course, that much that I have tried to set down in these pages has been said many times before and by those more competent of expression than I. Indeed, in its objective envisagement, the recognition among us of differences, personal, national and international, has become a commonplace. Even in the columns of our daily news items, these conditions of societal defection are mentioned time and again in the casual tone of the matter of course. Among the current comments one reads, for example: " The task of saving civilization seems rather hopeless when it doesn't promise an immediate and private profit "; " When a statesman says he despairs of the world he means that he despairs of getting what he wants "; " All nations seem agreed that chaos may result unless other nations forsake their evil ways "; " Civilization is just a slow process of envisioning more rights to fight for "; and so on without end.

But no amount of objective observation, however astute, will avail in clearing personal outlooks. Too easily is one's mere observation, however right and seemingly true, the embodiment of secret self-satisfaction and detachment. Personalistic observation, far from resolving the affective illusion of the onlooker, serves only to accentuate it. Dissociation within another individual that is observed by us but that does not quicken us to a realization of our own implication, automatically embeds us still deeper in the fixity of our own unconscious personalism. There is need to withdraw from our accustomed observations and to include within ourselves the dissociation that seems to lie outside of us but that is, in fact, the unconscious projection of our own dissociation. In this affective illusion of the onlooker, we are ever hoping merely to convince others of the disinterestedness of our interference with them. A disinterested interference is biologically impossible. To wish to convince others is to be unconvinced ourselves. True disinterestedness consists alone in our own self-realization.

The familiar French saying, " Tout comprendre est tout pardonner " is, like so much that is proverbial, *almost* true. It has assembled the right elements but in the wrong order. It gives to the letter dynamic priority over the spirit.[1] It is hysterical replacement refurbished in the condensation of the epigram. It is but the literature of the neurosis. If we transpose the equation in such manner as to convert intellectual values into their organic terms, the proposition resolves itself into a form that is, I believe, much nearer the answer to the problem of our human pathology : To forgive all is to understand all. I have only this in mind in saying that the neurosis is societal, that it is common. This is what I mean in saying that differentiation is unconsciousness and that the factor of societal repression or the societal factor of separatism is anterior to the separatism of sexuality or to the factor of our individual repression. As the societal and the individual are organically one in mode, the unification of the individual is at least a step toward the unification of our societal consciousness. This is all I have in mind in speaking of consciousness as the encompassment of life. It is a mode of consciousness that is inclusive and that reconciles within itself the disparity that is social.

All this I had at first " in mind " only. It was, I confess, a theory with me and, like all such substitutive re-

---

[1] I hold that the word " spirit " employed in its biological connotation belongs to the legitimate equipment of the laboratory. Because the religionists have carried it off and perverted it to sentimental uses, I shall not surrender the claim of the scientist upon it. And so by " spirit " I do not wish to indicate anything akin to the ghostly itinerants reputed to stalk o' nights, nor to that beneficent impulse that moves people to cheer the afternoon of life by " doing good " when the infelicities of age or infirmity have dulled the edge of less salutary proclivities. Neither have I in mind any philosophical concept whatever, nor least of all a conception savouring of a religious purport, all of which seem to me equally apparitional. I mean merely man's innate, unprompted or unchecked feeling as expressive of his organic life. That which in man responds to natural beauty, actual or inferred, is of the sphere of the spirit as I use the term.

RESOLUTION OF NEUROSIS—PERSONAL 243

placements, the theory held for me only an unconscious or symbolic significance. There was lacking in myself the recognition that the theoretical is identical with the symbolic. And so my position in stating that the theory of analysis is the neurosis of the analyst has lacked its personal acknowledgment within my own consciousness. Truly, unconsciousness cannot envisage unconsciousness. Secret separateness cannot encompass secret separateness. The division of each of us is the division within himself. The real grudge is one's own grudge. After all, there is only one vice and that, paradoxically, is the virtue of being better than other people. Yet so tenacious are we of this our solitary shortcoming, that we will acknowledge all other " faults " rather than disclaim this one. But the task of ourselves as the task of our patients is the recognition of our own personalism and resentment. It is to forgive all *within ourselves*, that we may understand all within others who are societally no less ourselves. It is to realize that the whole intricate problem of our " understanding " is but the retributive fabrication of our own unforgiveness.

It is just here that the repressed and isolated individual resolutely balks. Such a solution, he declares, offers nothing for him. He does not discover in it an advantage for himself. Quite true. In his unconscious sense, there is nothing for him. His self-seeking is itself the very kernel of his delusion. It is only in the disparate bias of his arbitrary individualism (I do not say individuality) that he can apprehend anything so dissociative as an advantage for himself as a separate individual. It is only as the wilful, defiant, separative child that he is, that he would seek the treasure of life for himself, that he comes demanding a governmental form embodying a system of monarchical autocracy whereof he is to be the supreme ruler, when, in truth, life is of its very essence an organic democracy and the individual an element in its societal confluence. In the quandary of his organic involution the neurotic, if one might so crudely express it, is literally "hell-bent" on attaining heaven. He does not see, for he will not see, that life and 'self are irreconcilable. On the contrary, with every available device, with every recourse of subtlety and with ever more enticing symbols, he seeks to decoy the common, free gift of life into the circumscribed and artificial confines of his own self-bias.

In this deflection of his mental outlook he is far from the basis from which his experience originally set out—the organic basis in which the secret of life is its commonness and in which the commonness and the joy of it are one. As the analysis proceeds, synchronous with the gradual acceptance on the part of the patient of his mistakenness and of his growing responsibility toward this mistakenness through the widening of his societal outlook, there comes his automatic awakening to the realization of the inherent confluence of life in its utmost fulfilment. It is a slow process this that demands our reversal from an habitual attitude of disparity and separation to one of participation and confluence, from self and unconsciousness to consciousness and life, but it is the inevitable task of an analysis that bases its procedure upon an organismic conception of consciousness in its relative inclusiveness.

I am under no illusion as to the futility of reckoning upon any far-reaching assent to such a thesis as this. I know well that a thesis which confronts the securely entrenched ranks of the social unconscious is, in general, predetermined to defeat. In this unpromising outlook, however, I am not dismayed. Were I guided solely by personal inclination I would endeavour at least to narrow the scope of a challenge such as this. I would, for instance, absolve myself from the obligation of recording so sweeping and unwelcome an indictment as that which lays to the door of normality in the large the imputation of auto-sexuality and infantilism. To many, such a statement will seem extravagant, bizarre, unwarranted. So that, if I would propitiate my readers through the presentation of a more acceptable thesis, I should naturally wish, if I may not wholly withdraw this statement, at least to palliate its implications.

. But as this statement seems to me essentially true, as it is the very crux of this thesis that unconsciousness is social and not individual, that the collective unconscious is the anterior factor to which the individual factor involving the neurosis is but the reflex response; as the central issue upon which my entire position must stand or fall is the conviction that the *responsibility for the neurosis rests upon the societal consciousness in its ontogenetic phase within each of us;* and above all, since my indictment of the social unconscious is one from which I am no more exempted than others, to withhold such a statement would be nothing other than the hesitation to affirm my real conviction and so retain the servility and introversion of my own social unconsciousness. This position is precisely the expression of what I believe to be the essential embodiment of the neurosis, and my wish to keep silent would be nothing else than my own unconscious wish not to relinquish the neurosis in which I share as a social element within it. Upon closer view, my unconscious fear becomes merely my wish to save my own individuation and unconsciousness at the expense of the participatory, societal confluence that alone constitutes consciousness.

This, as I think of it, is interesting, for upon reflection it grows still clearer that my reluctance would be again the neurosis within myself or the retention of the very separateness I am presumably undertaking to observe. After all, my irresolution would amount to my withholding not the statement but myself. It would represent my preference (as always it is my preference unconsciously) to withhold myself from my organic place as a confluent part in the societal aggregate. Instead of being one, therefore, with every other element comprising it, it would mean that I preferred to retain the illusion of my own disparateness, phantastically hoping in my dissociative mode thus to comprise in my individual self the self-possession that alone pertains to the acceptance of one's share in our common, societal aggregate.

And so I have come to believe that, however unwelcome the imputation, it is only the societal indictment as it applies to oneself personally that affords the real opportunity of release from the neurosis of society. It is the illusion of differentiation that is the essence of the neurosis. It is the fallacy of our personal separateness that is the meaning of our societal discord. Through our mutual analyses and also in the contacts of our daily living as a subjectively organized group, we have come to realize that this subtle attitude of disaffection is extraneous to the essential life of man. Affective conditions recognized as results outside of us are affective conditions unrecognized as causes within us. Subjectively, societally, they are the same. From a relative or organismic basis there is no difference. Just as cosmically or in the objective universe there is no absolute time and space, so organically or in the subjective universe there is no absolute cause and effect. As objectively time and space are "relative to moving systems," so subjectively cause and effect are relative to organic sequences. Accordingly, our need is to recognize the implication of the unconscious not as directed against others nor against oneself, but as including oneself equally with others in constituting together in our common life a single, societal unit.

There will, I know, be much misunderstanding in regard to what has been set down in these pages. If, by chance, the conventional artist should read this thesis, he will tell you that he understands and that he accepts it fully, on the ground that he finds its full realization within his own intuitions. But the artist will be mistaken. Should the conventional scientist read it, he will tell you that it is not possible to find substantiation for such a thesis within the scope of his authenticated formulations and that therefore he cannot understand or accept it. But the scientist will also be mistaken. Both will be quite right objectively, but this is, in itself, to miss the meaning of a conception that is essentially subjective.[1] This thesis has been felt and written from an intrinsically relative mode, and it is only from an intrinsically relative mode that it can be felt and understood. As yet the artist knows feeling only in the absolute form of the images that exist within himself; as yet the scientist knows feeling only in the absolute form of the images that exist outside himself. The one lives within the dreams (fanciful formulations) arising within the personal system that is individual; the other lives within the concepts (theoretical formulations) transmitted to him from the personal system that is social. Yet I do not doubt that among both artists and scientists, as well as among many people who are technically neither artist nor scientist, there will be those who will partake more or less consciously of what is here more or less consciously partaken of. In the form of its presentation it is inevitably restricted to the objective symbol of the written word; nevertheless, in the subjective encompassment of each that is its common inclusion of both, it may equally reach and unite the basic personalities of poet and craftsman, of male and female, of artist and scientist.

In this sense and in this spirit of a common involvement in the unconscious of my fellows, I feel that to some, at least, my meaning will seem clear and my motive not untoward. For there are those who, like myself, are only " normal " under duress and who secretly revolt against the compromising yoke of the social as well as of the individual unconscious. It is for these that I have written. To speak fearlessly and with freedom to the few, who are fearless and free enough to understand, means far more to me and will, I believe, prove ultimately far more fruitful in making clear the real meaning of our human need than half-hearted statements muttered with bated breath and trimmed to suit the fear-ridden prepossessions of the

[1] " There are ages, when the rational and the intuitive man stand side by side, the one full of fear of the intuition, the other full of scorn for the abstraction; the latter just as irrational as the former is inartistic.' Nietzsche, *Early Greek Philosophy and Other Essays.*

collective mind as it tends in its blind autocracy to dominate the clearer vision of us all.

The more I consider the factor of one's personal hesitancy to entrust himself unreservedly to the societal aggregate through unbosoming his own unconscious wish to repress his share in its collective dissociation, the more it is clear to me that in this very symptom of one's own— for such it is—lies the strongest corroboration of the impersonal or societal interpretation of the neurosis. For, as I have said, it is the acceptance of the oneness of each of us individually within the encompassing societal organism as an aggregate that alone points the way to our release from the fear or separateness that is the neurosis of the societal organism.

To consider the instinct of the societal bond without mentioning its influence in the development of the formulations that have resulted from the conceptions of Freud, would be to waive acknowledgment of the very determinants which have made possible the present societal interpretation. Abstract truths are the personal relics of genius ; their vindication in the concrete text of experience is the heritage of our common consciousness. If the significance of personality lies in the organismic consciousness of man, the springs of all creative genius are to be traced to this common source. This organic consanguinity is the very essence of genius. Holding its incisive course against all obstacle, this societal urge makes of genius the socially solitary expression that it is. The source of genius is nuclear, original, essential.. Moving amid the surface crusts of " types " which in their restriction of outer contact may only absorb or reflect the impressions about them, genius eradiates from the common centre of our societal organism sustained by an impulse that is cosmic. For this reason, it is the unalterable sentence of genius that it break with every accustomed adherence. It is its law that it raise itself out of habitual inertias and see straight and clear, beyond all temporary immediacies, into the unfurbished truth of

RESOLUTION OF NEUROSIS—PERSONAL

things. In this wise, in face of the personal criticism and resentment of the very world whose progress it was the all-engrossing effort of his genius to further, Sigmund Freud saw and reported what he saw, fearless, determined and alone. There is no more isolated appointment than this to which genius is summoned. It is in this appointment and in the societal implication of it, that lies the real significance of Freud. Should we fail to realize this, we would ourselves be overlooking the societal urge that is phyletically inherent in Freud's psychology.

In the course of our development the period of men's substitutive image-production was first interrupted through the return to reality inaugurated by Darwin's theory of evolution. What still remained over in man's mental life has been further threatened by Freud's theory of the evolutionary processes of the unconscious. When the evolutionary theories of Darwin and Freud are carried to their ultimate social conclusion, the result will be the entire repudiation of man's image-production and a re-uniting of his organic and conscious life into a single constructive whole.

In an essentially psychological study of this kind in which the effort has been made to trace the mechanisms of unconscious processes in their social application, there is not place for discussing the practical outcome, political, economic and industrial, that must follow through the very altered position of man's conscious outlook as a result of a more inclusive interpretation of our societal background. It is impossible to conjecture the influence upon man's behaviour socially and nationally that would result from a complete dispelling from his mind of the images that now occupy the place of his organic reality. How much the reaction that is ostensibly the most disastrous in our social life—the reaction of war—is due to the obsession of the social mind with mere images having no reality, it would only be extravagant to attempt to surmise. But these are practical considerations that must occupy us in subsequent discussions if the basis here outlined in its fundamental biology shall be found of value amid the growing processes of man's thought.

There is a further statement I wish to make. In this statement I should like to be understood as speaking in the fullest sincerity of which I am capable, my feeling being uninfluenced either by sentimental modesty or by any deprecatory wish to refer to extraneous agencies the sponsorship for this record. This thesis in a very true sense is not my thesis—it represents no intellectual achievement of mine. On consideration it will readily be seen that of its very nature it could not be my thesis. The outgrowth of automatic conditions stoutly resisted by me, it is the product of environmental circumstances over which I had no control. It was exacted under pain of repudiating in actuality the theoretical interpretations for which my work has stood. It is the outcome of inevitable concession to the ordeal of facing in its grim detail the fabric of substitution and disparity composing the structure of my own daily living. Convictions have been wrung from me against my own personal will, against every tradition about me and in spite of every effort of subtlety on my part to escape their exactions. Through many months I have fought their acceptance over every step of the way. As, little by little, a more relative and societal conviction has been borne in upon me, it has proved that the realization I have so long and so resolutely resisted has been the actuality of my own separatism and unconsciousness, as contrasted with the undifferentiated, organic life of which my personal work has been but the theory. It is because this work in its actuality is the expression of an urge common to life, sweeping aside in the strength of its organic tide every claim to personal consideration, that there is due the acknowledgment that it has come to expression unbeholden to me, that its motive has been, as far as humanly possible, not personal but societal.

The organic theory here offered has been advanced by me hitherto on grounds of mere conceptual intuitions.

RESOLUTION OF NEUROSIS—PERSONAL

Its present form embodies in its spirit of an impersonal, affective participation, however imperfectly fulfilled, the subjective record of an organic experience. In its plea for a wider acceptance of the common fellowship of man's native consciousness, I well realize that it is only with the years that we may hope to yield it fuller accord.

I shall be glad if this embodiment of whatever societal acceptance may have found expression in these pages may bring a clearer meaning, a quieter understanding to any whose need has been deep and unfulfilled. For my own part, this expression is the response to what is the deepest demand of my own life—the need for the organic unification of personality that I feel resides alone in the common consciousness of man.

INDEX

Absolutism—
  in affects, 39, 227
  in present system of consciousness, 33, 43, 63, 104, 227
  in psychoanalysis, 67, 68, 73, 101
  in the Church, 66-68, 73
  see also Personal absolute
Adler, 113, 174
Affects, 115, 121, 130, 178, 205, 227
Affective life, 115, 125
  components, 57, 58, 62
Allocentric and autocentric—
  complementary, 203, 213
  definition, 188
  reactions, 191-196, 218
Allosexuality—
  and autosexuality, 207, 208, 211
  definition, 201, 202
  identical basis, 209
  see also Sex
Alternative—
  bidimensional, 80-85, 93, 96, 97, 226-228, 239
  in art and drama, 85-87, 96
  in psychoanalysis, psychology, and psychopathology, 97, 100-103, 229-233
  individual expressions of, 88-91
  occurrence in group analysis, 223, 224, 236
  social expressions of, 85, 92-95, 99, 102, 207
  see also " Good and bad "
Ambivalence, 86, 94, 196, 228
  see also Alternative
" Anal complex," 216
Analysis—
  aim of, 26, 137, 164, 165, 166
  see also Dream ; Group analysis ; Psychoanalysis
Aquinas, 158
Art, 87, 96, 183
Artist, 96, 218, 219
Autocentric—
  see Allocentric
Autosexuality, 206, 215, 244
  see also Allosexuality

Besant, Annie, 139
Belief, 47, 143

Bidimensional plane, 41, 42, 58, 60, 62, 104
  see also Alternative ; Relativity of consciousness
Bleuler, 94
Buddha, 218

Calvin, 158
Cerebro-spinal nervous system, 189-192, 194
Childhood—
  consciousness of, 22, 23, 145
  imposition of social images upon, 52-55, 58, 59, 92, 93, 116, 123, 132, 145, 213
Christ, 218
Christianity, 85, 193, 196
Church—
  as social systematization, 65-75
Claparède, 156
Collective unconscious—
  see Social unconscious
Complexes, 47, 72
Compulsion neurosis, 81
Consciousness—
  absolutism of present system, 43, 44
  as unconsciousness, 24, 110, 111, 114, 115, 119, 143
  definition, 119
  individualistic compared with societal, 51, 62, 109, 144
  ontogenesis, 119-121
  phylogenesis, 118, 160, 162
  relativity of, 32-40, 48
  unification of, 122, 126, 169, 173, 212, 218, 242
  see also Dissociation ; Self-consciousness ; Societal concept of consciousness

Darwin, 249
Dementia præcox, 124, 136, 137, 195, 203
Depression, 91, 94
Descartes, 124
Differentiation, 129, 169, 178, 242
  delusion of, 120-122, 125, 131

INDEX

Dissociation—
individual and social, 45-47, 76, 109, 110, 132, 144, 148-153, 155, 176, 185, 241
Division of personality, 81, 85, 95, 147, 222
genesis of, 116-119
physiological substrate, 189-191
see also Dissociation ; Neurosis ; Repression
Doubt—
attitude of Church toward, 65, 66, 68, 69, 71
compared with resistance, 71-74
Drama, 85-88, 182, 183
Dream, 178-183, 185, 195
analysis, 88, 176, 177, 184
and personal absolute, 90, 111-113
and wish, 89

Eddington, A. S., 32
Education, 92, 93, 214
see also Childhood
Ego-sexuality, 201-203, 206-208
see also Sex
Einstein, 32, 36, 37, 38, 186
Eliot, George, 218
Ellis, Havelock, 158
Extravert, 187, 201

Family, 204, 234, 235
Feeling—
as subjective experience, 20, 21, 115
Freud, 1, 4, 5, 9, 14, 38, 47, 101, 108, 109, 110, 111, 112, 113, 126, 154, 156, 157, 158, 159, 174, 199, 204, 236, 248, 249
Freudian analysis, 1-5, 38, 47, 138, 168, 172, 231
Freud's theory—
of the neuroses, 12, 14, 37, 94, 108, 109, 126, 156, 157, 196, 228, 229, 236, 237
of resistance, 61, 154

" Good and bad "—
as image of personal advantage, 55, 59, 62, 81, 85, 90, 192, 200
bidimensional alternative, 53, 58, 62, 65, 78, 81, 91, 102, 103, 201, 227, 239
pretence underlying, 54-56, 58, 92
see also Image
Group analysis, 131, 223-226, 234-238, 246

Heterosexuality—
see Allosexuality ; Homosexuality ; Sex
Homophyllic, 208, 210

Homosexuality, 94, 97, 199, 211
and heterosexuality, 198, 200-202, 210
and paranoia, 174, 175
see also Sex
Hysteria, 63, 97, 143, 189, 191
social, 16

Ideas of reference, 136, 223
Image, 40-42
as substitution, 16
basis of marriage, 207
basis of sexuality, 14, 15
bidimensional, 53, 57-59, 226-228
contrasted with reality, 41, 79
of male and female, 96, 216
of parent, 55, 103, 173, 235
see also " Good and bad " ; Mother-image ; Social images
Incest-Awe, 147, 148
Individual—
as systematization, 70, 76
as separative element, 126, 150, 152, 153, 160, 243
as societal element, 115, 117, 127, 130, 148, 156
Infantilism, 215, 244
Insanity, 23, 24, 91, 124, 137
see also Neurosis ; Social neurosis
Instinct, 60, 127
common societal, 200
organic instinct of sex, 202
Introvert, 187, 201

Jung, 113, 156, 204, 205

Kropotkin, P., 159

Libido, 156

Mania, 91, 94
Marriage, 93, 94, 204, 206-209
Masturbation, 211
Meyer, Adolf, xx
Mood-alternation, 91, 94
Mother-image, 141, 172, 234
Mysticism, 125, 134, 139-142

Napoleon, 218
Narcism, 157, 202
Nettleship, Richard Lewis, 106
Neurosis, 15, 76, 77, 83, 102, 117
and sexuality, 157, 173, 174, 209, 237
marital, 93, 94
source, 53, 125, 169, 173
see also Normality ; Social neurosis
Neurotic personality, 13-16, 24, 44, 168, 191, 214, 243, 244
and organic consciousness, 11, 12, 23, 153, 209

INDEX 255

Newton, 35, 36
 Newtonian system, 32, 33, 35, 37, 38
Nietzsche, 23, 139, 218, 247
Normality—
 and personal absolute, 47, 63
 and sexuality, 173, 203, 209, 244
 as criterion, 11, 27, 30
 as neurotic manifestation, 12-16, 175, 176, 191
 mysticism in, 125, 134, 139-141
 unconsciousness of, 26, 27, 147, 179, 181, 203

Objective observation, 18
 within subjective sphere, 19-21, 51, 121-124, 167, 176, 178
Organismic—
 definition, 3
 see also Societal concept of consciousness

Paranoia—
 and homosexuality, 174, 175
Paranoiac, 94, 97, 143, 199
Personal absolute, 102, 103
 and war, 83
 as resistance, 61, 62, 76, 82, 84
 as right, 82, 83, 90, 92, 98, 112
 in psychoanalysis, 73, 101, 102
 underlying social system, 45-48, 63, 70, 72-76, 80-84, 240
 see also Absolutism ; Resistance ; Will-to-self
Personal equation, 4
Plato, 218
Precoid, 63, 97, 195
Preconscious mode, 10, 119, 137, 189, 196
Primary identification, 115, 116
 principle of, 218
Psychasthenic, 94, 193, 195
Psychiatrist, 107, 124, 136, 223
Psychiatry, 123, 136, 137, 183, 187
Psychoanalysis—
 alternative in, 103, 196, 198, 229-233
 as social systematization, 65, 67-76, 101
 as theory, 17-19, 21, 25
 duration of treatment, 230-233
 impasse in, 109, 172, 223, 224
 misconceptions, 2, 197
 personal absolute in, 3, 73, 101, 102
 position of, 9, 10, 229
 unconscious element in, 3, 143, 167, 234
 see also Analysis ; Group analysis

Psychoanalyst—
 attitude toward patient, 24, 166-172, 181, 183, 195, 229, 230, 232-234
 involvement in social unconscious, 110, 111, 183, 184, 222, 223
 qualifications of, 28, 29
Psychology, 5, 33, 36, 38, 65, 97
Psychopathology, 63, 100, 101, 123, 124, 223
 of war, 130
Ptolemaic system, 38

Relativity of consciousness, 32-40, 43, 45, 48, 51, 57-62, 104, 246
Religion, 64, 96, 98, 99
Repression—
 and bipolarity, 216, 217
 and sexuality, 156-159, 162, 163, 174, 193, 215, 242
 and suggestion, 55, 142, 189, 192, 200, 201, 218
 individual and social, 7, 13, 15, 30, 76, 77, 131, 154, 162, 163
 physiological substrate, 189-193
Resistance—
 as personal absolute, 61, 62, 76, 82, 84, 230
 attitude of psychoanalysis toward, 69-76
 compared with doubt, 71-74
 individual and social, 43-45, 65, 75, 76, 152, 154, 155

Schreiner, Olive, 218
Self—
 and sexuality, 15, 173, 200, 201, 210, 211
 image of, 16, 58-61, 79, 82, 83, 141
 preservation and race-preservation, 127
Self-consciousness, 116, 118-120, 125, 132, 147, 161, 162, 205
Sex—
 and sexuality, 11, 156-159, 163, 193, 200-217, 237
 as organic unity, 11, 163, 199, 208-212, 220
 intermediate, 214, 215, 217
 oppositeness in, 211, 213, 214, 216
Sexuality, 15
 as replacement, 10, 163
 see also Repression ; Sex
Shields, Clarence, xix, 233
Social images, 96, 102, 135-138, 161, 229
 and childhood, 51-55, 58, 59, 92, 93
 as distortion of reality, 87-90
 see also Image ; Mother-image

Social neurosis, 101, 125, 130-133, 162, 245
and images, 229
individual implication, 84, 246
Social unconscious, 117, 133, 162, 222, 223, 228, 245
as basis of normality, 11-14, 26, 27, 44, 47, 176
see also Unconsciousness
Societal concept of consciousness, 31, 45, 46, 127-131, 148, 149, 160-163
see also Relativity of consciousness
Socrates, 218
Subjective sphere—
see Feeling ; Objective observation
Sublimation, 189

Suggestion—
see Repression
Sympathetic nervous system, 189-192, 194

Transference, 167, 172, 230

Unconsciousness, 5, 15, 111, 126, 135, 144, 173, 178, 183-185, 192, 193, 204, 234
as resistance, 34, 76
underlying normality, 47, 125
see also Consciousness ; Dissociation ; Social unconscious

War, 14, 16, 34, 35, 83, 129-132, 249
Wilde, Oscar, 78
Will-to-self, 13, 75, 90, 98, 129, 156
Wish, 89, 111-113, 173, 180, 195, 232

The
International Library

OF

PSYCHOLOGY, PHILOSOPHY AND SCIENTIFIC METHOD

Edited by
C. K. OGDEN, M.A.
Magdalene College, Cambridge

The International Library, of which nearly one hundred volumes will be ready before the end of 1931, is both in quality and quantity a unique achievement in this department of publishing. Its purpose is to give expression, in a convenient form and at a moderate price, to the remarkable developments which have recently occurred in Psychology and its allied sciences. The older philosophers were preoccupied by metaphysical interests which for the most part have ceased to attract the younger investigators, and their forbidding terminology too often acted as a deterrent for the general reader. The attempt to deal in clear language with current tendencies whether in England and America or on the Continent has met with a very encouraging reception, and not only have accepted authorities been invited to explain the newer theories, but it has been found possible to include a number of original contributions of high merit.

Published by
KEGAN PAUL, TRENCH, TRUBNER & Co., Ltd.
BROADWAY HOUSE: 68-74 CARTER LANE, LONDON, E.C.
1931

CLASSIFIED INDEX

A. PSYCHOLOGY

I. GENERAL AND DESCRIPTIVE

		Page
The Mind and its Place in Nature	C. D. Broad, Litt.D.	8
The Psychology of Reasoning	Professor E. Rignano	5
Thought and the Brain	Professor Henri Piéron	10
Principles of Experimental Psychology	Professor Henri Piéron	14
Integrative Psychology	William M. Marston	17
*The Mind and its Body	Charles Fox	18
The Nature of Intelligence	Professor L. L. Thurstone	6
The Nature of Laughter	J. C. Gregory	6
The Psychology of Time	Mary Sturt	7
Telepathy and Clairvoyance	Rudolf Tischner	6
The Psychology of Philosophers	Alexander Herzberg	13
*Invention and the Unconscious	J. M. Montmasson	18

II. EMOTION

Emotions of Normal People	William M. Marston	13
The Psychology of Emotion	J. T. MacCurdy, M.D.	8
Emotion and Insanity	S. Thalbitzer	9
The Measurement of Emotion	W. Whately Smith	4
Pleasure and Instinct	A. H. B. Allen	15
The Laws of Feeling	F. Paulhan	16
The Concentric Method	M Laignel-Lavastine	15

III. PERSONALITY

Personality	R. G. Gordon, M.D.	9
The Neurotic Personality	R. G. Gordon, M.D.	11
Physique and Character	E. Kretschmer	8
The Psychology of Men of Genius	E. Kretschmer	17
The Psychology of Character	A. A. Roback	10
Problems of Personality	(Edited by) A. A. Roback	8

IV. ANALYSIS

Conflict and Dream	W. H. R. Rivers, F.R.S.	4
Individual Psychology	Alfred Adler	6
Psychological Types	C. G. Jung	5
Contributions to Analytical Psychology	C. G. Jung	13
The Social Basis of Consciousness	Trigant Burrow, M.D.	10
The Trauma of Birth	Otto Rank	14
*The Development of the Sexual Impulses	R. E. Money Kyrle	18
Character and the Unconscious	J. H. van der Hoop	5
Problems in Psychopathology	T. W. Mitchell, M.D.	11

V. SOUND AND COLOUR

The Philosophy of Music	William Pole, F.R.S.	6
The Psychology of a Musical Prodigy	G. Revesz	7
The Effects of Music	(Edited by) Max Schoen	11
Colour Blindness	Mary Collins, Ph.D.	8
Colour and Colour Theories	Christine Ladd-Franklin	13

VI. LANGUAGE AND SYMBOLISM

Language and Thought of the Child	Professor Jean Piaget	9
The Symbolic Process	John F. Markey	12
The Meaning of Meaning	C. K. Ogden and I. A. Richards	5
Principles of Literary Criticism	I. A. Richards	7
Creative Imagination	Professor June E. Downey	13
Dialectic	Mortimer J. Adler	12
Human Speech	Sir Richard Paget	14

* Ready shortly.

CLASSIFIED INDEX—(continued)

VII. CHILD PSYCHOLOGY, EDUCATION, Etc.

		Page
The Growth of the Mind	Professor K. Koffka	7
Judgment and Reasoning in the Child	Professor Jean Piaget	11
The Child's Conception of the World	Professor Jean Piaget	13
The Child's Conception of Causality	Professor Jean Piaget	15
The Growth of Reason	F. Lorimer	14
Educational Psychology	Charles Fox	9
The Art of Interrogation	E. R. Hamilton	14
The Mental Development of the Child	Professor Karl Buhler	15
*The Psychology of Children's Drawings	Helga Eng	18
Eidetic Imagery	Professor E. R Jaensch	15
The Psychology of Intelligence and Will	H. G. Wyatt	17

VIII. ANIMAL PSYCHOLOGY, BIOLOGY, Etc.

The Mentality of Apes	Professor W. Köhler	7
*The Social Life of Apes and Monkeys	S. Zuckerman	18
Social Life in the Animal World	Professor F. Alverdes	10
The Social Insects	Professor W. Morton Wheeler	12
How Animals Find Their Way About	Professor E. Rabaud	12
Theoretical Biology	J. von Uexküll	10
Biological Principles	J. H. Woodger	14
Biological Memory	Professor E. Rignano	9

IX. ANTHROPOLOGY, SOCIOLOGY, RELIGION, Etc.

Psychology and Ethnology	W. H. R. Rivers, F.R.S.	10
Medicine, Magic and Religion	W. H. R. Rivers, F.R.S.	4
Psychology and Politics	W. H. R. Rivers, F.R.S.	4
*The Theory of Legislation	Jeremy Bentham	18
Political Pluralism	K. C. Hsiao	11
History of Chinese Political Thought	Liang Chi-Chao	15
Crime and Custom in Savage Society	Professor B. Malinowski	9
Sex and Repression in Savage Society	Professor B. Malinowski	10
The Primitive Mind	C. R. Aldrich	17
The Psychology of Religious Mysticism	Professor J. H. Leuba	7
Religious Conversion	Professor Sante de Sanctis	11

B. PHILOSOPHY

Philosophical Studies	Professor G. E. Moore	4
The Philosophy of 'As If'	Hans Vaihinger	6
The Misuse of Mind	Karin Stephen	4
Tractatus Logico-Philosophicus	Ludwig Wittgenstein	4
The Analysis of Matter	Bertrand Russell, F.R.S.	11
Five Types of Ethical Theory	C D Broad, Litt.D	15
Chance, Love and Logic	C. S. Peirce	5
Speculations	T. E. Hulme	6
Metaphysical Foundations of Modern Science	Professor E. A. Burtt	7
Possibility	Scott Buchanan	12
The Nature of Life	Professor E. Rignano	15
Foundations of Geometry and Induction	Jean Nicod	15
The Foundations of Mathematics	F. P. Ramsey	17

C. SCIENTIFIC METHOD

I. METHODOLOGY

Scientific Thought	C. D. Broad, Litt.D.	5
Scientific Method	A. D. Ritchie	5
The Technique of Controversy	Boris B. Bogoslovsky	12
The Statistical Method in Economics	Professor P. S. Florence	14

II. HISTORY, Etc.

Historical Introduction to Modern Psychology	Gardner Murphy	13
Comparative Philosophy	P. Masson-Oursel	9
The History of Materialism	F. A. Lange	8
The Philosophy of the Unconscious	E. von Hartmann	17
Psyche	Erwin Rohde	8
Plato's Theory of Ethics	Professor R. C. Lodge	12
*Outlines of the History of Greek Philosophy	E. Zeller	17

* Ready shortly

4 INTERNATIONAL LIBRARY OF PSYCHOLOGY

VOLUMES PUBLISHED.

Philosophical Studies. By *G. E. Moore, Litt.D.*, Professor of Philosophy in the University of Cambridge, author of 'Principia Ethica,' editor of 'Mind'. 15s. net.

'Students of philosophy will welcome the publication of this volume It is full of interest and stimulus, even to those whom it fails to convince.'— *Oxford Magazine* 'A valuable contribution to philosophy.'—*Spectator*

The Misuse of Mind: a Study of Bergson's Attack on Intellectualism. By *Karin Stephen*. Preface by *Henri Bergson*. 6s. 6d. net.

'This is a book about Bergson, but it is not one of the ordinary popular expositions It is very short; but it is one of those books the quality of which is in inverse ratio to its quantity, for it focusses our attention on one single problem and succeeds in bringing it out with masterly clearness '— *Times Literary Supplement*

Conflict and Dream. By *W. H. R. Rivers, M.D., Litt.D., F.R.S.* Preface by *Professor G. Elliot Smith*. 12s. 6d. net.

'Rivers had that kind of commanding vigour that is one of the marks of genius. Nothing could be more fascinating than to watch him separating the gold from the alloy in Freud's theory of dreams. His book is as different from the usual Freudian book on the same subject as is a book of astronomy from a book of astrology.'—*Daily News*.

Psychology and Politics, and Other Essays. By *W. H. R. Rivers, F.R.S.* Preface by *Professor G. Elliot Smith*. Appreciation by *C. S. Myers, F.R.S.* 12s. 6d. net.

'In all the essays in this volume one feels the scientific mind, the mind that puts truth first Each of the essays is interesting and valuable.'— *New Leader*. 'This volume is a fine memorial of a solid and cautious scientific worker '—Havelock Ellis, in *Nation*.

Medicine, Magic, and Religion. By *W. H. R. Rivers, F.R.S.* Preface by *Professor G. Elliot Smith*. Second edition, 10s. 6d. net.

'This volume is a document of first-rate importance, and it will remain as a worthy monument to its distinguished author.'—*Times Literary Supplement*. 'Always, as we read, we feel we are in close contact with a mind that is really thinking '—*Nation*.

Tractatus Logico-Philosophicus. By *Ludwig Wittgenstein*. Introduction by *Bertrand Russell, F.R.S.* 10s. 6d. net.

'This is a most important book containing original ideas on a large range of topics, forming a coherent system which is of extraordinary interest and deserves the attention of all philosophers.'—*Mind*. 'Quite as exciting as we had been led to suppose it to be.'—*New Statesman*.

The Measurement of Emotion. By *W. Whately Smith, M.A.* Foreword by *William Brown, M.D., D.Sc.* 10s. 6d. net.

'It should prove of great value to anyone interested in psychology and familiar with current theories; while the precision of the author's methods forms an object lesson in psychological research.'—*Discovery*.

Scientific Thought. By *C. D. Broad, Litt.D.*, Lecturer in Philosophy at Trinity College, Cambridge. Second edition, 16s. net.

' This closely-reasoned and particularly lucid book is certain to take a chief place in the discussions of the nature and import of the new concepts of the physical universe. The book is weighty with matter and marks an intellectual achievement of the highest order '—*Times Literary Supplement.*

Psychological Types. By *C. G. Jung*. Translated with a Foreword by *H. Godwin Baynes, M.B.* Third edition, 25s. net.

' Among the psychologists who have something of value to tell us Dr. Jung holds a very high place. He is both sensitive and acute ; and so, like a great writer, he convinces us that he is not inadequate to the immense complexity and subtlety of his material. We are conscious throughout of a sensitiveness, a wide range of understanding, a fair-mindedness, which give us a real respect for the author.'—*Times Literary Supplement*

Character and the Unconscious : a Critical Exposition of the Psychology of Freud and Jung. By *J. H. van der Hoop.* 10s. 6d. net.

' His book is an admirable attempt to reconcile the theories of Jung and Freud He shows that the positions taken up by these two psychologists are not as antagonistic as they appear at first sight The book contains a very adequate account of Freud's teaching in its salient features, and his treatment of both theories is clear and sympathetic '—*New Statesman.*

The Meaning of Meaning : a Study of the Influence of Language upon Thought. By *C. K. Ogden* and *I. A. Richards*. Supplementary Essays by *Professor B. Malinowski* and *F. G. Crookshank, M.D.*, Third edition, 12s. 6d. net.

' The authors attack the problem from a more fundamental point of view than that from which others have dealt with it The importance of their work is obvious. It is a book for educationists, ethnologists, grammarians, logicians, and, above all, psychologists. The book is written with admirable clarity and a strong sense of humour.'—*New Statesman*

Scientific Method. By *A. D. Ritchie*, Fellow of Trinity College, Cambridge. 10s. 6d. net.

' The fresh and bright style of Mr Ritchie's volume, not without a salt of humour, makes it an interesting and pleasant book for the general reader. Taken as a whole it is able, comprehensive, and right in its main argument '—*British Medical Journal.* ' His brilliant book '—*Daily News.*

The Psychology of Reasoning. By *Eugenio Rignano*, Professor of Philosophy in the University of Milan. 14s. net.

' The theory is that reasoning is simply imaginative experimenting. Such a theory offers an easy explanation of error, and Professor Rignano draws it out in a very convincing manner.'—*Times Literary Supplement.*

Chance, Love and Logic : Philosophical Essays. By *Charles S. Peirce*. Edited with an Introduction by *Morris R. Cohen*. Supplementary Essay by *John Dewey*. 12s. 6d. net.

' It is impossible to read Peirce without recognizing the presence of a superior mind. He was something of a genius.'—*F. C. S Schiller*, in *Spectator.* 'It is here that one sees what a brilliant mind he had and how independently he could think.'—*Nation.*

The Nature of Laughter. By *J. C. Gregory.* 10s. 6d. net.

'Mr. Gregory, in this fresh and stimulating study, joins issue with all his predecessors In our judgment he has made a distinct advance in the study of laughter ; and his remarks on wit, humour, and comedy, are most discriminating.'—*Journal of Education.*

The Philosophy of Music. By *William Pole, F.R.S., Mus. Doc.* Edited with an Introduction by *Professor E. J. Dent* and a Supplementary Essay by *Dr. Hamilton Hartridge.* 10s. 6d. net.

'This is an excellent book and its re-issue should be welcomed by all who take more than a superficial interest in music. Dr Pole possessed not only a wide knowledge of these matters, but also an attractive style, and this combination has enabled him to set forth clearly and sufficiently completely to give the general reader a fair all-round grasp of his subject.'—*Discovery.*

Individual Psychology. By *Alfred Adler.* Second edition, 18s. net.

'He makes a valuable contribution to psychology His thesis is extremely simple and comprehensive : mental phenomena when correctly understood may be regarded as leading up to an end which consists in establishing the subject's superiority '—*Discovery*

The Philosophy of 'As If'. By *Hans Vaihinger.* 25s. net.

'The most important contribution to philosophical literature in a quarter of a century Briefly, Vaihinger amasses evidence to prove that we can arrive at theories which work pretty well by " consciously false assumptions". We know that these fictions in no way reflect reality, but we treat them *as if* they did. Among such fictions are : the average man, freedom, God, empty space, matter, the atom, infinity.'—*Spectator.*

Speculations: Essays on Humanism and the Philosophy of Art. By *T. E. Hulme.* Edited by *Herbert Read.* Frontispiece and Foreword by *Jacob Epstein.* 10s. 6d. *net.*

'With its peculiar merits, this book is most unlikely to meet with the slightest comprehension from the usual reviewer. Hulme was known as a brilliant talker, a brilliant amateur of metaphysics, and the author of two or three of the most beautiful short poems in the language. In this volume he appears as the forerunner of a new attitude of mind.'—*Criterion.*

The Nature of Intelligence. By *L. L. Thurstone,* Professor of Psychology in the University of Chicago. 10s. 6d. net.

'Prof. Thurstone distinguishes three views of the nature of intelligence, the Academic, the Psycho-analytic, the Behaviourist. Against these views, he expounds his thesis that consciousness is unfinished action. His book is of the first importance. All who make use of mental tests will do well to come to terms with his theory.'—*Times Literary Supplement.*

Telepathy and Clairvoyance. By *Rudolf Tischner.* Preface by *E. J. Dingwall.* With 20 illustrations, 10s. 6d. net.

'Such investigations may now expect to receive the grave attention of modern readers. They will find the material here collected of great value and interest. The chief interest of the book lies in the experiments it records, and we think that these will persuade any reader free from violent prepossessions that the present state of the evidence necessitates at least an open mind regarding their possibility '—*Times Literary Supplement.*

INTERNATIONAL LIBRARY OF PSYCHOLOGY

The Growth of the Mind: an Introduction to Child Psychology. By *K. Koffka*, Professor in the University of Giessen. Fifth edition, revised and reset, 15s. net.

'His book is extremely interesting, and it is to be hoped that it will be widely read.'—*Times Literary Supplement*. Leonard Woolf, reviewing this book and the following one in the *Nation*, writes : " Every serious student of psychology ought to read it [*The Apes*], and he should supplement it by reading *The Growth of the Mind*, for Professor Koffka joins up the results of Köhler's observations with the results of the study of child-psychology.'

The Mentality of Apes. By *Professor W. Koehler*, of Berlin University. Second edition, with 28 illustrations, 10s. 6d. net.

' May fairly be said to mark a turning-point in the history of psychology. The book is both in substance and form an altogether admirable piece of work. It is of absorbing interest to the psychologist, and hardly less to the layman. His work will always be regarded as a classic in its kind and a model for future studies.'—*Times Literary Supplement.*

The Psychology of Religious Mysticism. By *Professor James H. Leuba*. Second edition, 15s. net.

' Based upon solid research.'—*Times Literary Supplement* ' The book is fascinating and stimulating even to those who do not agree with it, and it is scholarly as well as scientific.'—*Review of Reviews* ' The most successful attempt in the English language to penetrate to the heart of mysticism '—*New York Nation*.

The Psychology of a Musical Prodigy. By *G. Revesz*, Director of the Psychological Laboratory, Amsterdam. 10s. 6d. net.

' For the first time we have a scientific report on the development of a musical genius. Instead of being dependent on the vaguely marvellous report of adoring relatives, we enter the more satisfying atmosphere of precise tests. That Erwin is a musical genius, nobody who reads this book will doubt.'—*Times Literary Supplement*

Principles of Literary Criticism. By *I. A. Richards*, Fellow of Magdalene College, Cambridge, and Professor of English at Peking University. Fourth edition, 10s. 6d. net.

' An important contribution to the rehabilitation of English criticism—perhaps because of its sustained scientific nature, the most important contribution yet made. Mr. Richards begins with an account of the present chaos of critical theories and follows with an analysis of the fallacy in modern aesthetics '—*Criterion.*

The Metaphysical Foundations of Modern Science. By *Professor Edwin A. Burtt*. 14s. net.

' This book deals with a profoundly interesting subject. The critical portion is admirable.'—Bertrand Russell, in *Nation* ' A history of the origin and development of what was, until recently, the metaphysic generally associated with the scientific outlook . . . quite admirably done.'—*Times Literary Supplement.*

The Psychology of Time. By *Mary Sturt, M.A.* 7s. 6d. net.

' An interesting book, typical of the work of the younger psychologists of to-day. The clear, concise style of writing adds greatly to the pleasure of the reader.'—*Journal of Education.*

Physique and Character. By *E. Kretschmer.* With 31 plates, 15s. net.

'His contributions to psychiatry are practically unknown in this country, and we therefore welcome a translation of his notable work. The problem considered is the relation between human form and human nature. Such researches must be regarded as of fundamental importance We thoroughly recommend this volume.'—*British Medical Journal.*

The Psychology of Emotion : Morbid and Normal. By *John T. MacCurdy, M.D.* 25s. net.

'There are two reasons in particular for welcoming this book. First, it is by a psychiatrist who takes general psychology seriously. Secondly, the author presents his evidence as well as his conclusions. This is distinctly a book which should be read by all interested in psychology. Its subject is important and the treatment interesting '—*Manchester Guardian*

Problems of Personality : Essays in honour of *Morton Prince.* Edited by *A. A. Roback, Ph.D.* 18s. net.

'Here we have collected together samples of the work of a great many of the leading thinkers on the subjects which may be expected to throw light on the problem of Personality. Some such survey is always a tremendous help in the study of any subject Taken all together, the book is full of interest '—*New Statesman*

The Mind and its Place in Nature. By *C. D. Broad, Litt.D.*, Lecturer in Philosophy at Trinity College, Cambridge. Second impression. 16s. net.

'Quite the best book that Dr. Broad has yet given us, and one of the most important contributions to philosophy made in recent times.'—*Times Literary Supplement* 'Full of accurate thought and useful distinctions and on this ground it deserves to be read by all serious students '—Bertrand Russell, in *Nation.*

Colour-Blindness. By *Mary Collins, M.A., Ph.D.* Introduction by *Dr. James Drever.* With a coloured plate, 12s. 6d. net.

'Her book is worthy of high praise as a painstaking, honest, well-written endeavour, based upon extensive reading and close original investigation, to deal with colour-vision, mainly from the point of view of the psychologist. We believe that the book will commend itself to everyone interested in the subject '—*Times Literary Supplement.*

The History of Materialism. By *F. A. Lange.* New edition in one volume, with an Introduction by *Bertrand Russell,'F.R.S.* 15s. net.

'An immense and valuable work.'—*Spectator.* ' A monumental work of the highest value to all who wish to know what has been said by advocates of Materialism, and why philosophers have in the main remained unconvinced '—From the *Introduction.*

Psyche : the Cult of Souls and the Belief in Immortality among the Greeks. By *Erwin Rohde.* 25s. net.

' The production of an admirably exact and unusually readable translation of Rohde's great book is an event on which all concerned are to be congratulated. It is in the truest sense a classic, to which all future scholars must turn if they would learn how to see the inward significance of primitive cults.'—*Daily News.*

Educational Psychology. By *Charles Fox*, Lecturer on Education in the University of Cambridge. Third edition, 10s. 6d. net.
' A worthy addition to a series of outstanding merit.'—*Lancet*. ' Certainly one of the best books of its kind.'—*Observer*. ' An extremely able book, not only useful, but original '—*Journal of Education*.

Emotion and Insanity. By *S. Thalbitzer*, Chief of the Medical Staff, Copenhagen Asylum. Preface by *Professor H. Höffding*. 7s. 6d. net.
' Whatever the view taken of this fascinating explanation, there is one plea in this book which must be whole-heartedly endorsed, that psychiatric research should receive much more consideration in the effort to determine the nature of normal mental processes '—*Nature*.

Personality. By *R. G. Gordon, M.D., D.Sc.* Second impression. 10s. 6d. net.
' The book is, in short, a very useful critical discussion of the most important modern work bearing on the mind-body problem, the whole knit together by a philosophy at least as promising as any of those now current.'—*Times Literary Supplement*. ' A significant contribution to the study of personality '—*British Medical Journal*.

Biological Memory. By *Eugenio Rignano*, Professor of Philosophy in the University of Milan. 10s. 6d. net.
' Professor Rignano's book may prove to have an important bearing on the whole mechanist-vitalist controversy. He has endeavoured to give meaning to the special property of "livingness." The author works out his theory with great vigour and ingenuity, and the book deserves the earnest attention of students of biology.'—*Spectator*

Comparative Philosophy. By *Paul Masson-Oursel*. Introduction by *F. G. Crookshank, M.D., F.R.C.P.* 10s. 6d. net.
' He is an authority on Indian and Chinese philosophy, and in this book he develops the idea that philosophy should be studied as a series of natural events by means of a comparison of its development in various countries and environments.'—*Times Literary Supplement*

The Language and Thought of the Child. By *Jean Piaget*, Professor at the University of Geneva. Preface by *Professor E. Claparède*. 10s. 6d. net.
' A very interesting book. Everyone interested in psychology, education, or the art of thought should read it. The results are surprising, but perhaps the most surprising thing is how extraordinarily little was previously known of the way in which children think.'—*Nation*.

Crime and Custom in Savage Society. By *B. Malinowski*, Professor of Anthropology in the University of London. With 6 plates, 5s. net.
' A book of great interest to any intelligent reader.'—*Sunday Times*.
' This stimulating essay on primitive jurisprudence.'—*Nature*. ' In bringing out the fact that tact, adaptability, and intelligent self-interest are not confined to the civilized races, the author of this interesting study has rendered a useful service to the humanizing of the science of man '—*New Statesman*.

Psychology and Ethnology. By *W. H. R. Rivers, M.D., Litt.D., F.R.S.* Preface by *G. Elliot Smith, F.R.S.* 15s. net.

' This notice in no way exhausts the treasures that are to be found in this volume, which really requires long and detailed study. We congratulate the editor on producing it. It is a worthy monument to a great man.'— *Saturday Review.* ' Everything he has written concerning anthropology is of interest to serious students.'—*Times Literary Supplement*

Theoretical Biology. By *J. von Uexküll.* 18s. net.

' It is not easy to give a critical account of this important book. Partly because of its ambitious scope, that of re-setting biological formulations in a new synthesis, partly because there is an abundant use of new terms. Thirdly, the author's arguments are so radically important that they cannot justly be dealt with in brief compass. No one can read the book without feeling the thrill of an unusually acute mind.'—J Arthur Thomson, in *Journal of Philosophical Studies*

Thought and the Brain. By *Henri Piéron*, Professor at the Collège de France. 12s. 6d. net.

' A very valuable summary of recent investigations into the structure and working of the nervous system. He is prodigal of facts, but sparing of theories His book can be warmly recommended as giving the reader a vivid idea of the intricacy and subtlety of the mechanism by which the human animal co-ordinates its impressions of the outside world '—*Times Literary Supplement*

Sex and Repression in Savage Society. By *B. Malinowski*, Professor of Anthropology in the University of London. 10s. 6d. net.

' This work is a most important contribution to anthropology and psychology, and it will be long before our text-books are brought up to the standard which is henceforth indispensable.'—*Saturday Review.*

Social Life in the Animal World. By *F. Alverdes*, Professor-extraord. of Zoology in the University of Halle. 10s. 6d. net.

' Most interesting and useful. He has collected a wealth of evidence on group psychology '—*Manchester Guardian.* ' Can legitimately be compared with Köhler's *Mentality of Apes.*'—*Nation.* ' We have learnt a great deal from his lucid analysis of the springs of animal behaviour.'—*Saturday Review.*

The Psychology of Character. By. *A. A. Roback, Ph.D.* Second edition, 21s. net.

' He gives a most complete and admirable historical survey of the study of character, with an account of all the methods of approach and schools of thought. Its comprehensiveness is little short of a miracle ; but Dr Roback writes clearly and well ; his book is as interesting as it is erudite.'— *New Statesman.*

The Social Basis of Consciousness. By *Trigant Burrow*, M.D., Ph.D. 12s. 6d. net.

' A most important book. He is not merely revolting against the schematism of Freud and his pupils. He brings something of very great hope for the solution of human incompatibilities. Psycho-analysis already attacks problems of culture, religion, politics. But Dr. Burrow's book seems to promise a wider outlook upon our common life.'—*New Statesman.*

INTERNATIONAL LIBRARY OF PSYCHOLOGY 11

The Effects of Music. Edited by *Max Schoen*. 15s. net.
' The results of such studies as this confirm the observations of experience, and enable us to hold with much greater confidence views about such things as the durability of good music compared with bad.'—*Times Literary Supplement.* ' The facts marshalled are of interest to all music-lovers, and particularly so to musicians.'—*Musical Mirror.*

The Analysis of Matter. By *Bertrand Russell, F.R.S.* 21s. net.
' Of the first importance not only for philosophers and physicists but for the general reader too. The first of its three parts supplies a statement and interpretation of the doctrine of relativity and of the quantum theory, done with his habitual uncanny lucidity (and humour), as is indeed the rest of the book.'—*Manchester Guardian.* ' His present brilliant book is candid and stimulating and, for both its subject and its treatment, one of the best that Mr. Russell has given us.'—*Times Literary Supplement.*

Political Pluralism : a Study in Modern Political Theory. By *K. C. Hsiao.* 10s. 6d. net.
' He deals with the whole of the literature, considers Gierke, Duguit, Krabbe, Cole, the Webbs, and Laski, and reviews the relation of pluralistic thought to representative government, philosophy, law, and international relations. There is no doubt that he has a grasp of his subject and breadth of view.'—*Yorkshire Post.* ' This is a very interesting book.'—*Mind.*

The Neurotic Personality. By *R. G. Gordon, M.D., D.Sc., F.R.C.P.Ed.* 10s. 6d. net.
' Such knowledge as we have on the subject, coupled with well-founded speculation and presented with clarity and judgment, is offered to the reader in this interesting book.'—*Times Literary Supplement* ' A most excellent book, in which he pleads strongly for a rational viewpoint towards the psychoneuroses.'—*Nature.*

Problems in Psychopathology. By *T. W. Mitchell, M.D.* 9s. net.
' A masterly and reasoned summary of Freud's contribution to psychology. He writes temperately on a controversial subject.'—*Birmingham Post.* ' When Dr. Mitchell writes anything we expect a brilliant effort, and we are not disappointed in this series of lectures '—*Nature.*

Religious Conversion. By *Sante de Sanctis*, Professor of Psychology in the University of Rome. 12s. 6d. net.
' He writes purely as a psychologist, excluding all religious and metaphysical assumptions. This being clearly understood, his astonishingly well-documented book will be found of great value alike by those who do, and those who do not, share his view of the psychic factors at work in conversion.' *Daily News.*

Judgment and Reasoning in the Child. By *Jean Piaget*, Professor at the University of Geneva. 10s. 6d. net.
' His new book is further evidence of his cautious and interesting work. We recommend it to every student of child mentality.'—*Spectator.* ' A minute investigation of the mental processes of early childhood. Dr. Piaget seems to us to underrate the importance of his investigations. He makes some original contributions to logic.'—*Times Literary Supplement.*

Dialectic. By *Mortimer J. Adler*, Lecturer in Psychology, Columbia University. 10s. 6d. net.

'It concerns itself with an analysis of the logical process involved in ordinary conversation when a conflict of opinion arises. This enquiry into the essential implications of everyday discussion is of keen interest.'—*Birmingham Post.*

Possibility. By *Scott Buchanan.* 10s. 6d. net.

'This is an essay in philosophy, remarkably well written and attractive. Various sorts of possibility, scientific, imaginative, and "absolute" are distinguished. In the course of arriving at his conclusion the author makes many challenging statements which produce a book that many will find well worth reading.'—*British Journal of Psychology.*

The Technique of Controversy. By *Boris B. Bogoslovsky.* 12s. 6d. net.

'We can only say that, in comparison with the orthodox treatise on logic, this book makes really profitable and even fascinating reading It is fresh and stimulating, and is in every respect worthy of a place in the important series to which it belongs.'—*Journal of Education.*

The Symbolic Process, and its Integration in Children. By *John F. Markey, Ph.D.* 10s. 6d. net.

'He has collected an interesting series of statistics on such points as the composition of the childish vocabulary at various ages, the prevalence of personal pronouns, and so on. His merit is that he insists throughout on the social character of the "symbolic process".'—*Times Literary Supplement.*

The Social Insects: their Origin and Evolution. By *William Morton Wheeler*, Professor of Entomology at Harvard University. With 48 plates, 21s. net.

'We have read no book [on the subject] which is up to the standard of excellence achieved here.'—*Field* 'The whole book is so crowded with biological facts, satisfying deductions, and philosophic comparisons that it commands attention, and an excellent index renders it a valuable book of reference.'—*Manchester Guardian.*

How Animals Find Their Way About. By *E. Rabaud*, Professor of Experimental Biology in the University of Paris. With diagrams, 7s. 6d. net.

'A charming essay on one of the most interesting problems in animal psychology.'—*Journal of Philosophical Studies.* 'No biologist or psychologist can afford to ignore the critically examined experiments which he describes in this book. It is an honest attempt to explain mysteries, and as such has great value.'—*Manchester Guardian.*

Plato's Theory of Ethics: a Study of the Moral Criterion and the Highest Good. By *Professor R. C. Lodge.* 21s. net.

'A long and systematic treatise covering practically the whole range of Plato's philosophical thought, which yet owes little to linguistic exegesis, constitutes a remarkable achievement. It would be difficult to conceive of a work which, within the same compass, would demonstrate more clearly that there is an organic whole justly known as Platonism which is internally coherent and eternally valuable.'—*Times Literary Supplement.*

Contributions to Analytical Psychology. By *C. G. Jung. Dr. Med.*, Zurich, author of 'Psychological Types'. Translated by *H. G.* and *Cary F. Baynes.* 18s. net.

'Taken as a whole, the book is extremely important and will further consolidate his reputation as the most purely brilliant investigator that the psycho-analytical movement has produced.'—*Times Literary Supplement*

An Historical Introduction to Modern Psychology. By *Gardner Murphy, Ph.D.* Third Edition, 21s. net.

'That Dr. Murphy should have been able to handle this mass of material in an easy and attractive way is a considerable achievement. He has read widely and accurately, but his erudition is no burden to him. His summaries are always lively and acute '—*Times Literary Supplement*

Emotions of Normal People. By *William Moulton Marston,* Lecturer in Psychology in Columbia University. 18s. net.

'He is an American psychologist and neurologist whose work is quite unknown in this country. He has written an important and daring book, a very stimulating book He has thrown down challenges which many may consider outrageous.'—*Saturday Review*

The Child's Conception of the World. By *Jean Piaget,* Professor at the University at Geneva. 12s. 6d. net.

'The child-mind has been largely an untapped region. Professor Piaget has made a serious and effective drive into this area, and has succeeded in marking in a considerable outline of the actual facts They are of interest to all who want to understand children We know of no other source from which the same insight can be obtained '—*Manchester Guardian.*

Colour and Colour Theories. By *Christine Ladd-Franklin.* With 9 coloured plates, 12s. 6d. net.

'This is a collection of the various papers in which Mrs Ladd-Franklin has set out her theory of colour-vision—one of the best-known attempts to make a consistent story out of this tangle of mysterious phenomena. Her theory is one of the most ingenious and comprehensive that has been put forward '—*Times Literary Supplement*

The Psychology of Philosophers. By *Alexander Herzberg, Ph.D.* 10s. 6d. net.

'It has been left for him to expound the points in which the psychology [of philosophers] appears to differ both from that of *l'homme moyen sensuel* and from that of men of genius in other walks of life It may be admitted freely that he puts his case with engaging candour '—*Times Literary Supplement*

Creative Imagination : Studies in the Psychology of Literature. By *June E. Downey,* Professor of Psychology in the University of Wyoming. 10s. 6d. net.

'This is an altogether delightful book Her psychology is not of the dissecting-room type that destroys what it analyses. The author's own prose has a high literary quality, while she brings to her subject originality and breadth of view.'—*Birmingham Post.*

The Art of Interrogation. By *E. R. Hamilton, M.A., B.Sc.*, Lecturer in Education, University College of North Wales. Introduction by *Professor C. Spearman, F.R.S.* 7s. 6d. net.

'His practical advice is of the utmost possible value, and his book is to be recommended not only to teachers but to all parents who take any interest in the education of their children. It sets out first principles with lucidity and fairness, and is stimulating.'—*Saturday Review.*

The Growth of Reason: a Study of Verbal Activity. By *Frank Lorimer*, Lecturer in Social Theory, Wellesley College. 10s. 6d. net.

'A valuable book in which the relation of social to organic factors in thought development is traced, the argument being that while animals may live well by instinct, and primitive communities by culture patterns, civilization can live well only by symbols and logic.'—*Lancet.*

The Trauma of Birth. By *Otto Rank*. 10s. 6d. net.

'His thesis asserts that the neurotic patient is still shrinking from the pain of his own birth. This motive of the birth trauma Dr. Rank follows in many aspects, psychological, medical, and cultural He sees it as the root of religion, art, and philosophy There can be no doubt of the illumination which Dr. Rank's thesis can cast on the neurotic psyche.'—*Times Literary Supplement.*

Biological Principles. By *J. H. Woodger, B.Sc.*, Reader in Biology in the University of London. 21s. net.

'The task Mr. Woodger has undertaken must have been very difficult and laborious, but he may be congratulated on the result.'—*Manchester Guardian.*
'No biologist who really wishes to face fundamental problems should omit to read it.'—*Nature.*

Principles of Experimental Psychology. By *H. Piéron*, Professor at the Collège de France. 10s. 6d. net.

'Treating psychology as the science of reactions, Professor Piéron ranges over the whole field in a masterly résumé. We do not know of any general work on the subject which is so completely modern in its outlook. As an introduction to the whole subject his book appears to us very valuable.' *Times Literary Supplement.*

The Statistical Method in Economics and Political Science. By *P. Sargant Florence, M.A., Ph.D.*, Professor of Commerce in the University of Birmingham. 25s. net.

'It sums up the work of all the best authorities, but most of it is the author's own, is fresh, original, stimulating, and written in that lucid style that one has been led to expect from him Its breadth and thoroughness are remarkable, for it is very much more than a mere text-book on statistical method.'—*Nature.*

Human Speech. By *Sir Richard Paget, Bt., F.Inst.P.* With numerous illustrations. 25s. net.

'There is a unique fascination about a really original piece of research The process of detecting one of Nature's secrets constitutes an adventure of the mind almost as thrilling to read as to experience. It is such an adventure that Sir Richard Paget describes. The gist of the theory is that speech is a gesture of the mouth, and more especially of the tongue. We feel that we can hardly praise it too highly '—*Times Literary Supplement.*

The Foundations of Geometry and Induction. By *Jean Nicod*. Introduction by *Bertrand Russell, F.R.S.* 16s. net.

'Anyone on first reading these two essays might be tempted to underrate them, but further study would show him his mistake, and convince him that the death of their author at the age of thirty has been a most serious loss to modern philosophy.'—*Journal of Philosophical Studies.*

Pleasure and Instinct : a Study in the Psychology of Human Action. By *A. H. B. Allen*. 12s. 6d. net.

'An eminently clear and readable monograph on the much-discussed problem of the nature of pleasure and unpleasure. Since this work amplifies some of the most important aspects of general psychology, the student will find it useful to read in conjunction with his text-book.'— *British Medical Journal*

History of Chinese Political Thought, during the early Tsin Period. By *Liang Chi-Chao*. With 2 portraits, 10s. 6d. net.

'For all his wide knowledge of non-Chinese political systems and the breadth of his own opinions, he remained at heart a Confucianist Amidst the drums and trumpets of the professional politicians, this great scholar's exposition of the political foundations of the oldest civilization in the world comes like the deep note of some ancient temple bell.'—*Times Literary Supplement.*

Five Types of Ethical Theory. By *C. D. Broad, Litt.D.*, Lecturer at Trinity College, Cambridge. 16s. net.

' A book on ethics by Dr. Broad is bound to be welcome to all lovers of clear thought. There is no branch of philosophical study which stands more in need of the special gifts which mark all his writings, great analytical acumen, eminent lucidity of thought and statement, serene detachment from irrelevant prejudices '—*Mind.*

The Nature of Life. By *Eugenio Rignano*, Professor of Philosophy in the University of Milan. 7s. 6d. net.

' In this learned and arresting study he has elaborated the arguments of those biologists who have seen in the activities of the simplest organisms purposive movements inspired by trial and error and foreshadowing the reasoning powers of the higher animals and man It is this purposiveness of life which distinguishes it from all the inorganic processes.'—*New Statesman.*

The Mental Development of the Child. By *Karl Bühler*, Professor in the University of Vienna. 8s. 6d. net.

'He summarizes in a masterly way all that we have really learned so far about the mental development of the child. Few psychologists show a judgment so cool and so free from the bias of preconceived theories. He takes us with penetrating comments through the silly age, the chimpanzee age, the age of the grabber, the toddler, the babbler.'—*Times Literary Supplement.*

The Child's Conception of Physical Causality. By *Jean Piaget*, Professor at the University of Geneva. 12s. 6d. net.

' Develops further his valuable work. Here he endeavours to arrive at some idea of the child's notions of the reasons behind movement, and hence to consider its primitive system of physics. His results are likely to prove useful in the study of the psychological history of the human race, and in the understanding of primitive peoples, as well as that of the child. His method is admirable.'—*Saturday Review.*

Eidetic Imagery, and the Typological Method. By *E. R. Jaensch*, Professor in the University of Marburg. 7s. 6d. net.

' While the work of Professor Jaensch is well-known to psychologists and educationalists, it is too little known to physicians. An excellent translation recently published leaves no excuse for ignorance of a subject as important, as it is interesting. . . . The author epitomizes much of the recent work on these fascinating topics and gives us a glimpse of a subject which promises a fruitful field of research in the realm between general medicine and psychopathology.'—*Lancet*

The Laws of Feeling. By *F. Paulhan.* Translated by *C. K. Ogden.* 10s. 6d. net.

It is strange that so important a contribution to our knowledge of feeling and emotion should have suffered neglect. The main thesis that the author advances is that all feeling, even pleasure and pain, and all emotion are due to the arrest of tendencies. He goes far beyond elementary affective phenomena, and the laws he formulates are such that they take into their ken the most complicated tendencies'—*Saturday Review*

The Psychology of Intelligence and Will. By *H. G. Wyatt.* 12s. 6d. net.

' Its value lies, not merely in the analysis of volitional consciousness and the definite relation of will-process in its highest form of free initiative to the capacity for relational thinking in its most creative aspect, but in the reasoned challenge which it makes to all forms of mechanistic psychology.'
— *Journal of Philosophical Studies*

The Concentric Method, in the Diagnosis of the Psychoneurotic. By *M. Laignel-Lavastine,* Associate-Professor of the Paris Medical Faculty. With 8 illustrations. 10s. 6d. net.

The author enjoys an international reputation for his work on the sympathetic nervous system, which he here relates to general diagnosis. Organic defects, Ascetic and Mystical Experience, and the Devil, receive special attention

Integrative Psychology: a Study of Unit Response. By *William M. Marston, C. Daly King,* and *Elizabeth H. Marston.* 21s. net.

This book offers a new and wholly objective basis for systematic treatment of psychology as a physical science It attempts to show, on scientific grounds, that human beings possess the ability to free themselves from environmental control and use environment for selective self-development.

The Foundations of Mathematics and other logical Essays. By *F. P. Ramsey.* Edited by *R. B. Braithwaite,* Fellow of King's College, Cambridge. Preface by *G. E. Moore, Litt. D.,* Professor of Mental Philosophy and Logic in the University of Cambridge. 15s. net.

Collected papers on mathematics, logic, and economics, by a scholar whose recent death deprived Cambridge of one of its profoundest thinkers

The Philosophy of the Unconscious. By *E. von Hartmann.* Introduction by *C. K. Ogden.* 15s. net.

A new edition of this standard work, with an historical introduction.

The Primitive Mind and Modern Civilization. By
C. R. *Aldrich.* Introduction by B. *Malinowski,* Professor of
Anthropology in the University of London. Foreword by
C. G. Jung. 12s. 6d. net.

Develops the theory that the gregarious instinct is the most potent formative force in the development of society.

The Psychology of Men of Genius. By *Professor E. Kretschmer.*
With 72 portraits, 15s. net.

A study, based on wide psychiatric experience, of the nature of genius and its relation to insanity. A vast amount of biographical material has been examined and is incorporated in the text.

Outlines of the History of Greek Philosophy. By
E. *Zeller.* Thirteenth Edition completely revised by *Dr.*
W. *Nestle.* About 12s. 6d. net.

A new and up-to-date edition of this standard work. Contents include The Pre-Socratic Philosophy (Pythagoreans, Eleatics, Sophists, etc.) ; Attic Philosophy (Socrates, Plato, and Aristotle) ; Hellenistic Philosophy (Stoics, Epicureans, Sceptics, Eclectics) ; Philosophy of the Roman Empire (Revival of Old Schools, Neo-Platonism).

NEARLY READY

The Psychology of Children's Drawings, from the First Stroke to the Coloured Drawing. By *Helga Eng.* With 8 coloured plates and numerous line illustrations, about 10s. 6d. net.

The bearing of a normal child's drawings upon some of the chief problems of human development has only recently been appreciated. Dr. Eng's collection of material bears upon some of the keenest controversies in ethnology, art-criticism, and psychology.

The Social Life of Apes and Monkeys. By *S. Zuckerman, M.A., M.R.C.S., L.R.C.P.,* Anatomist to the Zoological Society of London. Illustrated, about 15s. net.

A study of the individual and social behaviour of apes and monkeys, based on first-hand observation. An indispensable companion volume to Kohler's now standard work in this series, *The Mentality of Apes.*

Invention and the Unconscious. By *J. M. Montmasson.* Translated, with an Introduction, by *H. Stafford Hatfield.* About 12s. 6d. net.

Discusses the problem of the generation of inventions, using the word to include religious and philosophical disciplines as well as patentable technical improvements. He shows how large a part the Unconscious plays in such inventions.

The Theory of Legislation. By *Jeremy Bentham.* Introduction by *C. K. Ogden.* About 7s. 6d. net.

A new edition of this famous work, with an Introduction showing its significance at the present time, a collection of important notes, and some new and hitherto unpublished material of Bentham.

The Mind and its Body : the Foundation of Psychology. By *Charles Fox,* Lecturer on Education in the University of Cambridge. About 10s. 6d. net.

A critical consideration of the mass of new material dealing with the relationship of mind and body leads to a clearing away of many misconceptions and to a number of positive conclusions.

The Development of the Sexual Impulses. By *R. E. Money Kyrle.* About 10s. 6d. net.

An attempt to present the psychoanalytic theories of libido and the sexual impulse in terms of experimental and behaviourist psychology

VOLUMES IN PREPARATION

(Not included in the Classified Index)

Ethical Relativity	Edward Westermarck
The Spirit of Language in Civilization	K. Vossler
The Gestalt Theory	Bruno Petermann
Mencius on the Mind	I. A. Richards
On Fictions	Jeremy Bentham
The Dynamics of Education	Hilda Taba
The Child's Conception of Morality	Jean Piaget
Psychological Optics	D. Mc. L. Purdy
The Nature of Mathematics	Max Black
The Theory of Hearing	H. Hartridge, D.Sc.
Learning and the Living System	George Humphrey
Emotional Expression in Birds	F. B. Kirkman
The Mind as an Organism	E. Miller
Animal Behaviour	H. Munro Fox
The Psychology of Insects	J. G. Myers
Colour-Harmony	C. K. Ogden and James Wood
Gestalt	K. Koffka
Theory of Medical Diagnosis	F. G. Crookshank, M.D., F.R.C.P.
Language as Symbol and as Expression	E. Sapir
Psychology of Kinship	B. Malinowski, D.Sc.
Social Biology	M. Ginsberg, D.Lit.
The Philosophy of Law	A. L. Goodhart
The Psychology of Mathematics	E. R. Hamilton
Mathematics for Philosophers	G. H. Hardy, F.R.S.
The Psychology of Myths	G. Elliot Smith, F.R.S.
The Psychology of Music	Edward J. Dent
Psychology of Primitive Peoples	B. Malinowski, D.Sc.
Development of Chinese Thought	Hu Shih

CPSIA information can be obtained at www.ICGtesting.com
Printed in the USA
LVOW11s0914110115

422303LV00001B/142/P